EMOTIONAL CLEARING...

"This work is both thoroughly conceived and personal. A very helpful approach to self-therapy emerges from processing the emotional dialogue between mind and body. Rarely is Eastern wisdom presented in terms that can be so easily understood by the Western mind."
Terry Hunt, Ed.D.
Psychotherapist
co-author of *EMOTIONAL HEALING*

"This book presents a step-by-step text for those sincere individuals tired of coping or making do, who are willing to 'go for it now!' It reveals the patterns for actualizing and realizing one's Highest Self, and would be well worth review by every student and practitioner of psychology interested in the concept and attainment of Selfhood."
Hazel Stanley
Bioenergetic Analyst/Psychotherapist

"An excellent approach to self-therapy – it successfully shows you how to combine your own psychotherapy with meditation and the spiritual quest, to break through your blocks, and to truly reach to the love inside. I recommend it!"
Brad Ryan, Ph.D.
Psychotherapist

"I have been meditating and have been involved in therapy for years, but was never able to see the common ground until reading this book. In spite of my therapy, I now see how I have been rejecting my feelings, and preventing my inner healing. Integrative Processing has given me a clear method to work on myself – something I have long been looking for – and I am overjoyed at the changes I am seeing in myself."
Sarah Jennings

"*EMOTIONAL CLEARING* is a journey into the emotive realms of the accepted Self ... a vision quest that takes us into the very nucleus of the human experience which is ... our feeling essence."
Sharry Rose
Transpersonal Therapist/Artist

"This book has done more to change my approach to addiction recovery work than any other single book I have read. For years, I have always thought that it was not O.K. to be where I was emotionally. I understand now the crucial importance of emotional self-acceptance that Ruskan eloquently explains. I am recommending this book to anyone connected to recovery work."
Jim Brenner

"An extraordinarily clear discussion of the principles of psychotherapy and the spiritual arts, put together in a unique and exciting way. A highly effective approach to self-transformation."
Claude Roberts
Therapist

EMOTIONAL CLEARING

The Handbook of Integrative Processing

JOHN RUSKAN

published by
R. WYLER & CO.
NEW YORK

EMOTIONAL CLEARING
by JOHN RUSKAN

ISBN: 0-9629295-0-6
First printing 1993

Published by:
R. Wyler & Co.
220 West 19th St., Suite 2A
New York, N.Y. 10011

Printed in the United States of America

Library of Congress Cataloging-in-Publication Data:

Ruskan, John.
    Emotional clearing : releasing negative feelings and awakening unconditional happiness / John Ruskan.

    p. cm.

    Includes bibliographical references and index.
    ISBN 0-9629295-0-6 (pbk.)

    1. Psychology. 2. Emotions.
    3. Meditation. 4. East/West Psychology.

CIP 93 - 221606

TABLE OF CONTENTS

Foreword

The wound in the human psyche that produces fear, anger, greed, mistrust and violence is the most difficult to heal. Yet that wound is the one responsible for the many thousands of ways we all suffer.

Our failure to free ourselves from the sickness that infects the whole human race is evident everywhere in our world. We destroy our environment with our greed and carelessness. We spend more energy producing weapons of mass destruction than we do helping each other to improve the quality of life. We fear intimate contact with each other. Mistrust is our first reaction to the approach of our own kind. We kill our children in terrible wars. We oppress and brutalize those among us who are in any way different from ourselves. We quickly become addicted to *anything* that allows us brief consolation from the terrible pain of our condition.

"Who wants to hear about this?" you may ask. "It's described everywhere in the media. We don't need more gloom and doom!" That may be so, but we *do* need to understand more about ourselves and our condition if there is ever to be the possibility of a healthy society. It is entirely possible to have a healing of the heart. It is within the power of each of us to unite in wholeness the divided parts of our own body-minds. We are at war only with ourselves. The painful wound of separation of one part from another, the fear and hatred that result from that division, occurs only within each one of us. Real healing takes place when we experience the truth of that wound and face it. We must feel our own sickness deeply. Willingness to feel one's own pain and fear is a kind of surrender to this life, as this body, at this moment. Healing into love and wholeness has never been anything more than surrender to oneself, surrender into the "feeling body." That is the way of self-acceptance. It is very simple, but it certainly is not easy.

Healing will only happen with our participation. In the practice of medicine, we have discovered that the patient must want to get well. The longing for wholeness must be strong enough and conscious enough in us to endure the *ordeal* of healing.

Our spiritual geniuses and the major religious movements that have grown from their inspiration have taught us the same message for thousands of years. More recently, our psychology has been arriving at the same truths. Our journey is the awakening to acceptance of our very own selves. In order to do that, we must be willing to feel what is true of ourselves without limitation: all of it, the joy as well as the suffering. We live so little of our potential intelligence, because of our refusal to be entirely here in feeling and body.

John Ruskan has accomplished a great work in these pages. He has written a book that integrates the wisdom of ancient spiritual practices with our modern psychological understanding, and he has done it skillfully. Even more important to us at this time of world crisis, he has described, in practical detail, the healing process that can lead to mental, emotional, and physical health. Step by step he has clarified a method of self-work that can truly open the way to well-being, Wisdom, and the recovery of love for oneself and the world.

The concepts described in this book are so simple they are

often difficult to grasp. They are even more difficult to communicate. I appreciate John Ruskan for his successful accomplishment of both. As you enter these pages, do so slowly and with openness of mind. Savor the wisdom you find here, and then with curiosity and interest, discover the experience of truth they point toward.

Robert K. Hall, M.D.
Lomi School Foundation
Tomales, California

Preface

Throughout my years of involvement in the spiritual and healing communities, I have noticed something that has prompted the writing of this book: Many people who are earnest seekers after spiritual growth tend to be unfamiliar with the methods or the importance of working with the emotional component of the psyche. They – as well as myself for a long while in the past – approach inner growth only by concentrating on the "higher" idealistic aspects that they hope to develop, such as love, and ignore the more unpleasant emotional aspects of the self. Indeed, there is often a tremendous gap in awareness about the emotional self, and even the assumption that the emotions are not really important. At the same time, those involved in psychological therapy, where emotional healing is the main concern, often cannot see how to combine spiritual arts with their inner work.

The premise of this book is that no real growth into higher consciousness can occur unless working with the emotions becomes a central part of inner work. Moreover, I hope to show that working with emotion as well as feeling in general can become a most vital and even primary path to self-realization, enabling us to release the inner forces that keep us blocked and from our full potential.

This book is the product of the merging of two cultural, intellectual, and spiritual traditions. As I have worked, I have felt these two lines of tradition meeting in my thoughts and then converging into the writing, like a prism in reverse. Like female and male, mother and father, Yin and Yang, each element has been necessary to fully actualize the other.

In the broadest terms, the East has represented the mother – the nurturing connection to the inner source of spiritual replenishment, healing, and growth. The West has represented the father – the intellect, the organizing, pragmatic principle that gives form and structure to the healing force.

What has resulted is not a comparison or analysis of these two ways, but a synthesis. It has been my intention to show how both paths may be unified into a single approach that will provide a system of self-work that can be intellectually followed and will lead to an opening of the Heart. I feel that this approach can be vital for us of the West in our quest for spiritual wholeness and resolution of the ever-present pain of existence.

If this book, my gift to you, can be of any value to you, you have in turn helped me as well as all of us, because the pain you feel is not only your pain, but the pain of the world. Separateness is an illusion. When you heal yourself, you heal the world.

I wish you continual fulfillment in every aspect of your life. I wish you the wisdom to make the most of the limitless possibilities that life offers. Most importantly, I wish you the power to activate the love and healing that lie so close within.

John Ruskan
New York, 1993

I understand that my love for myself is the greatest possession I will ever have. Love for myself comes into being only when I accept and experience my feelings as they are, at this very moment, both pleasant and unpleasant. As I welcome my painful self, it heals. Loving myself provides the power for transformation.

Introduction

The Art of
Loving Yourself

People sometimes envy the artist's life. They feel the artist's life is an exciting one, expressing the instinct to break free. The artist is seen as struggling with the essential problems of human existence, facing those issues within, and bringing them into concrete expression. The courage to engage in the inner confrontation is admired. I know I felt like this before deciding to devote much of my time to the understanding and practice of art. It is one reason I became an artist.

The real artist – one who is truly exploring issues of self-expression and not just exploiting a technique – is operating on a high level of consciousness. Artistic expression comes from the Creative center of consciousness, which, in Eastern psychology, is even higher than the Heart, accounting for the unusually intense experience of the artist.

Artists can run into problems with their work, however. This often begins when the artist tries to establish a sense of social identity and acceptance through the art. The motivation shifts from pure self-expression to concern with what is being gained from the work. The shift of motivation can be subtle, but can still result in hampered creativity and eventual self-defeat.

Even though I was strongly drawn to art and the quest for inner growth at about the same time – just after college in the sixties – the spiritual principles that I was learning did not prevent me from falling into the cycle I am about to describe. I had been taught that happiness did not come from the results of one's work, or from the approval of others, but from the joy of the doing. I agreed, and in my own work as an artist, I felt that I was coming from the heart, not looking for approval. Art for me meant going inside and bringing forth. Creative expression was exhilarating and ecstatic. I felt I was developing the capacity to mobilize the incredible energies I perceived.

Because for me, the essence of the creative act was *perception*. I could find ecstasy in just looking at painting, dance, architecture, or listening to music. I later realized that the power is in the perceiver. The work of art is simply the framework onto which we project our artistic experience, much like life in general.

From the act of perception it was natural for me to go to actual creation. Yet, it wasn't really me who created. I just doodled while some other creative power came forth. My role as the artist was to perceive, to be moved by what manifested. My skill as the artist was in getting my conscious mind out of the way so the process could occur. If something happened in this process that moved me, then I had produced a piece of "art," something interesting enough to share with others. And sharing was something I wanted to do.

For while I was aware of the pitfalls of using art as a means of bringing attention to myself, it seemed natural to want to share what I had created with others. I allowed that I was not perfect, and there was bound to be a certain amount of ego attachment to my work. If I needed to have a minimum of recognition, I felt I should accept the need, along with whatever limitations it might bring.

The incident that helped me become aware of the destructive cycle in which I was enmeshed occurred during a week-long workshop on Body Wisdom I was attending. By the third day, there had not yet been much catharsis in the group. Our leader guided us into an extended holding of a Yoga posture, the Mountain. Holding this posture puts a great strain on the body, and many people started trembling and shaking. Energy was starting to move in our bodies. We finally released the pose, and were instructed to move around the room in any manner we chose.

As I moved, I suddenly began to sense the energy in my body. The energy was taking the form of classical ballet positions I could not name. Although I have not had any ballet training, I have always had a natural aptitude for dancing, and many of my friends have been dancers. I had always assumed that somewhere in the past, if there really were past lives, I had been a dancer. Still, I had never gone beyond the intellectual assumption.

This experience was not intellectual. The energy in my body was assuming perfect classical positions, drawing my imperfect physical pose into as close a correspondence as possible. The inner seeing and feeling of the energy taking the archetypal ballet positions, the realization that the positions were indeed archetypal, and the ecstasy from the inner perception were all overwhelming. I was taken through a beautiful and moving artistic experience.

Nevertheless, linked with the beauty that I was witnessing inside myself was the sense of pain – the pain of isolation. I realized that I was reliving my pain from the past life as a dancer. I went into a major catharsis of emotion. I knew that whenever catharsis is linked to what might be a past life recall, there is a good possibility that the recall is real and not imagined. I knew I was tying into my suppressed pain from the previous life and that it was being released.

I saw that a large part of my present life had been the same as the previous life, except now I was involved mostly with music. I was again consumed with the ecstasy of creation and the pain of isolation, without understanding that the two – at

least for me – are inseparable, that they are dualistic complements. The suppressed pain from the previous life was the
source of the present pattern.

The incredible experience of creation that artists have focused on does not come without its complement. The act of
creation brings with it the sense of isolation and inner emptiness
from having exhausted energies. The ecstasy is balanced by the
pain.

After understanding the dualistic nature of my creative
experience, my life came into focus. I had spent much of my life
taking in the ecstasy, and then not understanding what the pain
was all about. The pain of isolation, from both the present and
previous life, was the motive behind sharing my work and the
strong, partly unconscious, motivation for establishing a social
identity as an artist. I felt if I could reach out with my work,
the terrible pain of isolation would be relieved. That it never
was relieved added to my confusion because even when my
work received acceptance – when I got the recognition – the
pain was still there. I became confused and hurt. Recognition
became pointless. I questioned the value of what I was doing
and became self-destructive, probably in more ways than I even
now realize.

The problem came into being when I allowed myself to be
motivated by the pain of isolation; when I tried to seek its relief
through recognition – what I thought was my desire to share.
In similar ways, we all try to avoid our pain, without understanding that when we are motivated by the desire to avoid
negativity, there is no escape from it.

I had spent much of my life unconsciously locked into a
cycle of addiction to creative work. From the ecstasy of the
creation, I would fall into its complement, the isolation of the
creator. Seeking to avoid the negative aspect, I would either
turn to sharing my work as the antidote for the isolation, or not
finding relief there, would again go back to the creative experience to escape the pain. I became compulsive about creating as
a means to escape the isolation that came with creating. Not
being released, the isolation was only suppressed. It built to the

point where I became compulsive in other areas of my life as well, such as relationships. Eventually, the suppressed pain became so great that I had to stop work, reaching the point of burn-out. The catharsis I had in the workshop helped me understand that it was the build-up of suppressed pain, from both the present and previous life, which had contributed to blocking me and holding me back.

How do we get rid of the isolation that may come with the act of creating, as well as other emotional problems we may have? That is what this book is about. The first step is to *integrate,* to reclaim and accept, the feelings we are concerned with. When something has been integrated, it has not gone away, but is no longer perceived as disturbing. Most of the pain is there because the feelings are unintegrated. Integration starts the process of healing and clearing. All aspects of life, not just the creative, have both positive and negative complements. We must learn how to integrate, not avoid, the negative. In doing so, something may be learned from the artist.

Artists are concerned with the unwholesome side of life as well as the beautiful. Artists often portray ugliness, disharmony, strife; indeed, many artists today live in the ghettos of our cities. They appear to have some connection to the sordid side of life that goes beyond the low rent. This is because the artist accepts, celebrates, and expresses the negative aspect of existence, both in the outer world and the inner feelings. The artist does this primarily to achieve his or her integration of it, but also to show us that we cannot escape the responsibility of integrating our own personal experience. When we try to escape, we only suppress, and whatever we try to escape from or fight keeps building.

The inclination to escape is a problem inherent to the New Age. When first attracted to New Age activity, we may approach it with the intent of enjoying peace and harmony. This may be an important first step, especially if we are stressed out, but we miss the point if we continually try to avoid the negative in favor of the positive. We must learn how to integrate what we seek to avoid, with the courage of the artist.

We can all become artists, for art does not depend upon technique, but upon the sensitivity of the perceiver. You can change your mode of perceiving so that life is not seen as something outside yourself that you must battle and control. Life becomes a reflection of yourself, which you may either accept or reject, in turn accepting or rejecting yourself.

When you perceive with acceptance, you allow the creative process to begin. Just as when an artist produces a painting by stepping aside and letting another power come through in the creation, you can use the same approach in ordinary life. You become the artist, with life as your canvas. You become the witness to creative transformation. You experience the exhilaration of the creative act, and find beauty in the most miserable parts of existence.

When you perceive with acceptance, something else is accomplished. You learn that acceptance is love, and that in accepting yourself and your feelings as they are, you build the experience of love for yourself in a way that could never be done through any other means. Loving yourself becomes the healing power that transforms your inner world. Loving yourself is the highest art.

PART I
EMOTIONAL CLEARING

When I accept myself and my feelings as they
are, I become whole. I am no longer split –
fighting or condemning part of myself.
The power of self-acceptance and self-love
builds within me. I acquire the ability
to heal myself and the conditions of my life.
I awaken the power for transformation.

1

The Acceptance of Feeling

We all want to be whole. We would like to have an approach that can help us in this quest. We are too familiar with the sensation of being split, working against ourselves in spite of our best intentions. A path to inner growth that invites us to accept ourselves as a means to becoming whole would appear to be reasonable. Yet, when we learn exactly what is to be accepted, confusion and doubt may arise.

The acceptance of joy seems natural, but it may not be clear why we should accept anger or fear. Negative feelings like these are exactly what we want to avoid. We normally think of negative feelings as preventing or interfering with happiness.

We all have some concept of ourselves as we would like to be – without certain faults, limitations, or emotional "problems." We fight these conditions, expecting to be happier if we could only get rid of the negative aspects of ourselves, if we could only improve ourselves. We fight unhappiness itself.

Nevertheless, contemporary psychology teaches that there is a place for acceptance of negative feelings and conditions. In fact, by *not* accepting, we perpetuate negativity instead of re-

15

leasing it. Acceptance is a difficult concept to grasp, because we have been trained to resist and fight what we don't like. Indeed, the understanding of acceptance is subtle, and the basic questions remain: How? How do I accept my anger? What does it mean to accept my fear? How can I resolve my problem if I accept it?

Feelings are painful and become problems only because they are not accepted, or *integrated*. We create pain through resistance and non-acceptance. To go beyond pain, and to enjoy wholeness, we must learn to integrate those parts of life we find painful and would like to avoid. Once integrated, they are no longer painful. Instead, they add new dimensions to our existence.

These new dimensions cannot be foreseen. Life becomes richer, resulting in real, not pseudo, spiritual and material prosperity consciousness. The creative is allowed to manifest. Happiness becomes unconditional. We become artists of life, and realize that what we were resisting was really inside ourselves, not in the outside world.

Integrative Processing is a method of inner work that will enable you to simply and effectively transform your emotions and your life. You will learn exactly *why* acceptance is important, and *how* to accept in a way that does not mean you must try to like something you don't. The essence of processing is to accept your feelings, whatever they are, even your feelings of dislike. The problem is that you usually resist and reject the feelings, thus creating the pain.

We will explore concepts that may be new and challenging to you, but that are of immense value. You will learn a definite and clear method of resolving any psychological or material problem. Moreover, you will learn a highly practical approach to life that enables you to use all your experiences, both negative and positive, in the most productive way possible. You will awaken your latent potential for love and creativity, and initiate personal growth.

THE THERAPEUTIC ENCOUNTER

For the past 50 years or so, psychological therapy has been the most common means for people in the West to receive help in dealing with stressful emotional conditions, or to simply become more sensitive to themselves. Before therapy became available, the church was the place where such help was provided. Today, the psychological has largely become separated from the spiritual. Spirituality is often overlooked, or not desired, by persons who turn to psychology for assistance.

The therapeutic effort is devoted, first, to uncovering or making conscious the feelings and patterns that are unconsciously influencing the client in undesirable ways. Second, therapy is directed toward releasing stored negativity through various approaches, depending on the school.

The therapist accepts the client

Regardless of the approach, therapists who are effective share a common quality: they accept the client without conditions. Unconditional acceptance can be startling and transformative, because the problem is not what the client usually thinks it is. The real problem is that the client is not self-accepting, often not even having any concept of self-acceptance. Through the therapist, the client learns how to accept him- or herself, outgrowing negative patterns.

During therapy, blocks are uncovered and loosened up, and the client becomes aware of self-limiting tendencies. This happens primarily because of the attitude of acceptance by the therapist, and not because of incredible insights or wonderfully effective techniques. The therapeutic use of acceptance can be understood and applied only by one who has mastered self-acceptance on a deep level; it is fallacious to assume that one who is not whole within could ever provide this kind of healing for another.

A successful outcome to therapy is achieved when the client

no longer needs the supportive energy of the therapist, but can provide support through self-acceptance. The client has not become a perfect human being, but is now self-sustaining, able to provide nurturing and healing from within.

The role of therapist in the West closely corresponds to the traditional role of guru in the East. The guru provides the same kind of nurturing relationship that the therapist does, for the same reasons. The guru accepts the disciple unconditionally, knowing that acceptance from another is what the disciple needs to learn self-acceptance and to grow as a human being. In the East, however, the role of guru is more comprehensive, including not only psychology, but philosophy, religion, and physical culture, all addressing the question of spiritual growth.

This broadness of perspective does not in the least render the psychological aspect shallow or unstudied. The Eastern understanding of the mind has a history and tradition thousands of years old. The ancients of the East were, indeed, master psychologists. Western psychological thought is, for the most part, a few hundred years old and is still being formulated; Eastern thought has been formulated, and offers much to be learned.

Psychology's connection
to spirituality is critical

Psychology in the East has a built-in connection to spirituality. In contrast, Western psychology becomes limited exactly because it usually has no such link. Many psychologists are now coming to this realization and are trying to establish a spiritual connection. For some, this may mean turning to organized Western religion, which to me is like going one step forward and two steps back. Certain religious institutions of the East may also be considered dogmatic and outdated but, when we come to Yoga or Buddhism, we find a flexible and intelligent approach to both psychology and spirituality.

We are not going to directly discuss spirituality in this book. The principles of psychology that we will discuss, however, are related to developing the capacity for spiritual experience. The overwhelming contribution of Eastern thought is that as we go within, we discover the Infinite. Nothing more need be said about spirituality. Some Western thinkers have come to a similar conclusion, notably Jung, but he was deeply influenced by Eastern thought. Please note, then, that when I refer to "spirituality," I am referring to the inner meeting with the self, not to the trappings of any organized religion, East or West.

We have discussed briefly the function of the therapist or guru in awakening the power of self-acceptance in the client or disciple. It is noteworthy that in the East, this guidance is traditionally considered to be a normal requirement of education; in the West, it is usually reserved for those in a stressful or unstable condition. Lest we romanticize the East, it should be recognized that in modern times only a small percentage of people there are exposed to traditional teachings, just as in the West, only a small percentage are exposed to psychotherapy. Still, we should reconsider the conservative view that therapy is primarily for the mentally ill. Therapy of some sort is the choice of the sensitive and intelligent individual concerned with personal growth.

The student of the East learns, in this basic training for life, a vast and refined system of knowledge, including disciplines for strengthening and purifying mind and body. "Purifying" has exactly the same purpose as in Western psychology, that of surfacing and dissolving unconscious blocks that interfere with the productive enjoyment of life.

Nevertheless, there is an understanding that techniques for personal growth are most effective when the disciple has direct contact with a guru. This is not because only the guru can give correct instructions in technique, but because it is through this personal interaction that the disciple learns self-acceptance. The concept of acceptance is at the core of both Eastern and Western psychology.

ACCEPTANCE

Why is acceptance so powerful and transformative? We will explore this question at length throughout the book. No short explanation can hope to convey a real understanding. Still, I may say a few things here, to introduce you to the topic.

Acceptance means
opening to your feelings

Acceptance does *not* mean automatic approval of any event, whether an inner feeling or the interaction with another person or happening in the outside world. Acceptance means rather that we are open to the experience of the event. We may retain our intellectual discrimination, preferring that something be different from the way it is now manifesting; however, we do not allow our preference to interfere with the experience. This is possible because experience takes place on a *feeling* level, not an intellectual level. As we open ourselves to the full experience of something, on the feeling level, we accept it.

The capacity for feeling is of utmost importance. Feelings are our connection to life; without them, we are stale, hollow, and cut off from true fulfillment. Self-blocking occurs on the feeling level, not the mental or intellectual level. The feeling level is where we are most unconscious. People who have achieved self-acceptance have developed the capacity for feeling deeply, without resistance, whatever is happening in their inner life. Most of us do not do this, but block feelings from entering consciousness, resulting in emotional imbalance and confusion.

When we interact with a person who is self-accepting, we sense that this relationship differs from most. A self-accepting person has the ability to accept others, to be open to others, and to receive their energy without resistance. A person who is not self-accepting cannot accept or be open to others. Because we seldom encounter self-accepting people, we have no real sense of what a relationship based upon acceptance is like.

When we meet a self-accepting person who accepts us, who does not unconsciously resist us, we experience a revelation. We can *feel* that we are being accepted on a deep energy level. We are disarmed. There is no reason to resist back. We sense love. Love is nothing more than acceptance. Unconditional love is unconditional acceptance, whether of yourself or another person.

When unconditional acceptance is part of the therapeutic encounter, it supplies the power for transformation. Healing occurs because of the power of love. Psychological blocks dissolve; there is no need to fight them. The relationship with the therapist intensifies, and there is always the potential problem of dependency.

AWAKENING SELF-ACCEPTANCE

As we have discussed, the real purpose of the therapeutic relationship is the ultimate awakening of self-acceptance in the client. This happens magically in the interaction, through a kind of resonance. The result is what has been called self-actualization in the West, and self-realization in the East. In either case, what has been awakened is the ability to love oneself. One gains the ability to evoke healing power from within, through self-love.

There is no longer any craving or searching for love outside oneself; one is complete as one is, feeling love from within. Relationships are approached as a vehicle through which the love within is expressed, rather than as a context in which one seeks to be loved. Life has become essentially, miraculously changed.

Must you find a therapist or guru before you can effectively learn to love yourself? This is a controversial question; authorities in the field advocate both sides. There is no doubt that the kind of relationship I have described can be instrumental in awakening self-love. Yet, finding such a relationship can be difficult, and is customarily thought of as "happening," rather than being found through active search.

I have seen through my own experience and that of others that it is possible to make substantial, if not completely adequate, progress on our own. For that reason, I have formalized the system of Integrative Processing, a self-therapy devoted to awakening the power of self-acceptance and self-love, as well as the higher centers of consciousness and realization. You will learn how to activate yourself through the intellectual approach, rather than through the personal influence of a teacher.

If you have a personal healer, therapist, or guru with whom you are working, however, feel free to stay with them if you so desire. Processing is non-dogmatic and compatible with any humanistic psychology with which you may be involved. As you learn processing, you will gain a technical knowledge, both theoretical and practical, of powerful psychological principles. If you have no personal teacher, assume that you don't need one at this point. You will surely draw someone into your life at the right time, if you need such a relationship.

WORKING ON YOURSELF

Many people have never been exposed to either a therapist or guru. Yet, virtually all of us need to learn how to awaken the qualities of self-acceptance and self-love. I feel this is the tremendous spiritual challenge of our time.

Life is evolutionary, and we are all "works in progress." The purpose of life is to awaken and expand our dormant capacities for love, creativity, and intelligence, but a program is needed to support us in the awakening. When you get in sync with this natural evolutionary urge, you will immediately feel more at peace with yourself – you are no longer purposeless. The joy that comes from growth itself is enough to keep you interested in life.

To seek personal evolution means you must work on yourself. Most people understand that effort is required and apply themselves with enthusiasm. No one, not even your therapist, can do the work for you. You must be at the point where you understand that working on yourself is a priority – that you are tired of functioning (or not functioning) as you are.

Even so, many people tend to make a mistake when beginning to work on themselves. It is normal to question one's life, and perhaps decide that changes are required, but questioning can carry over into a non-productive habit – the habit of excessive thinking.

Working on yourself is not
constantly thinking about yourself

The issue of excessive thinking is crucial. Working on yourself is *not* primarily analyzing yourself and your motives, or being thoughtfully introspective, or trying to control yourself and do better, or trying to be something you are not. Using the mind in this manner is self-defeating. You must learn to substitute feeling for thinking. **You must learn to sense "what is" through the feeling center, rather than project "what I expect" through the thinking center.**

Many people who think they are working on themselves are deceiving themselves, because they do not have an accurate understanding of what is required. They spend their time in constant self-evaluation, which merely makes them absorbed in themselves. After you have read this book, you will have a definite understanding of how to work on yourself.

INTEGRATIVE PROCESSING

To integrate means to form into a whole; to reclaim, accept, and include what was previously apart from. "Processing" is a psychological term that refers to the concept of accepting and staying with experience as it manifests, allowing it to unfold by itself in the here and now.

Integrative Processing is the name I have given to the system of self-therapy that has evolved from my own work on myself. It incorporates the above principles and is derived from the traditional wisdom of the East as well as the contemporary psychological knowledge of the West, both of which I have been a student for more than 20 years. I have tried to combine the strongest and most compatible elements from each tradition.

Integration means accepting yourself and your feelings as you are

Integration is the condition of accepting and including, of not resisting, parts of yourself or your experience. When something is not integrated, it forms the basis of conflict. We resist something – a feeling, for example – because we believe the feeling is bad for us. It makes us uncomfortable. In fighting the feeling, we further the split between ourselves and the feeling, and increase the sense of conflict.

Resistance creates pain

The conflict that is created through resistance causes pain. This is a key concept. **What causes most of our pain is our resistance to a feeling, not the actual feeling itself, even a "negative" feeling.** Negative feelings may have a certain amount of pain inherent in them, but we amplify, exaggerate, and prolong that pain through resistance. Learning how to *accept* experience is the means to minimizing pain.

Experiencing takes place in the moment

After we have learned to accept, however, experience is not yet completely integrated. It must be digested in a certain way, called *direct experience,* in which it is absorbed or dissolved completely. In learning how to enter direct experience, we gain an understanding of what is known as "being in the moment."

Being in the moment is a mystical perspective. Witness consciousness is activated, and we function on a new and higher plane that results in a sense of well-being and euphoria as well as calling into play transpersonal powers that have been blocked by the personal ego. These powers operate on a very practical level, effecting *transformation* in situations that we previously resisted. By accepting, we go beyond. We reach the spiritual through the mundane. We discover the spiritual *in* the mundane.

It is essential to learn *how* to open up on the feeling level. You may think you are feeling your pain right now. The problem, however, is that you continue to resist the pain with unconscious self-rejection. Self-rejection is an act of the mind that creates the pain and then prevents it from dissolving. Developing the capacity to accept leads to unobstructed feeling, catharsis, and the release of pain. It is possible to feel only when the mind is self-accepting.

Processing consists of four steps, each step corresponding to a function of our individuality. The steps are taken to achieve integration of any event. The event can be an inner feeling or emotion, or a happening in the external world. Processing can be used especially in stressful circumstances, but also as an approach to all life's happenings, "positive" as well as "negative." Once integrated, we no longer fail to experience the event completely. The energy of the event is dissolved, having run its natural course, instead of being trapped and continuing to affect us. We become "clear."

The Steps of Integrative Processing

STEP	FUNCTION
1. AWARENESS	Intellectual: Knowing
2. ACCEPTANCE	Mental: Thinking
3. DIRECT EXPERIENCE	Body: Feeling
4. TRANSFORMATION	Spiritual: Transcending

1. **AWARENESS.** Intellectual function: Basic awareness of the event, whether a feeling or an external happening. Awareness includes the recognition that the event corresponds to a projection of suppressed energy held in the subconscious; in other words, the "owning" of the event. Awareness also includes understanding the basic principles of how to work on yourself and consciously deciding to apply them.

2. **ACCEPTANCE.** Mental function: Ceasing resistance to the event. Normally, experience is unconsciously blocked through various self-rejecting maneuvers of the mind. In accepting ourselves, these mechanisms become conscious and are dropped. In doing so, self-love is awakened, and the gate to direct experience of feeling is opened.

3. **DIRECT EXPERIENCE.** Body function: Being in the feeling center, or "in the moment" with the event. Feelings are entered completely, without resistance, analysis, or blame. The event is experienced on a body level until the energy is dissolved.

4. **TRANSFORMATION.** Spiritual function: Witness consciousness is activated, and the higher transpersonal intelligence guides the energies, resulting in unexpected creative external change and internal catharsis. The flow of life is not obstructed. Adjustment occurs spontaneously and without conscious control.

Thus, we sequence through the various levels of experience in logical order, culminating in the spiritual. What may be surprising to many is that the spiritual is reached through the body, or the feeling center, not the mind or intellect. Of course, I am not referring to the sensual nature of the body, but to the higher centers of consciousness that are approached only through feeling.

Our common misconception is that fulfillment, peace, and happiness can be reached through knowing, accomplishment, or possession. As we survey the Twentieth Century, the fallacy of this position should be most evident. True happiness is unconditional; it is achieved when we use the intellect to understand that knowledge is important, but not ultimately fulfilling; when we go beyond the self-orientation and possessiveness of the mind; when we enter the direct experience of ourselves and the Universe; when we have the perception that we *are* the Universe.

I understand that when I don't accept myself or my feelings, I create a debt to myself. The feelings don't go away, but become hidden in my subconscious, only to come out later. When I accept my feelings as they are, I no longer create a debt. I experience life fully and allow growth to occur.

2

Creating the Subconscious

RESISTING OUR EXPERIENCE

It is human nature to strive for a sense of well-being. We have basic legitimate needs for sustenance, shelter, companionship, love, and self-expression. We work to arrange circumstances to satisfy these needs. In acting with goals in mind, we become selective about how we expend our energy, and about the results of our work. We find it natural to accept certain happenings and to resist others.

Our selective orientation toward experience becomes associated with pleasure or pain. We develop a natural predisposition to choose conditions that are either pleasurable in themselves or lead to pleasurable outcomes, and to resist conditions that are painful or lead to painful outcomes. What could be wrong with this? It seems to be a basic description of what life is all about.

Philosophers through the centuries, however, have had to address the implications of a life based on seeking pleasure and avoiding pain, because experience has demonstrated that such a life does not lead to happiness. These philosophers have then conceived of other systems of values or *beliefs* that might be more helpful in leading to the sense of fulfillment we seek.

Of course, our level of maturity has much to do with what we consider worth pursuing. As we grow, we outgrow certain needs and adopt – hopefully – broader, less self-centered ones. Still, the basic needs of security, sensation, power, and relationship are what most of us revolve around, even though some of us may have refined the interpretation of our needs to a more sophisticated level.

Many of our "needs" are the result of social conditioning. They are artificial – created by our aggressive, goal-oriented society. However, we react to these needs as if they were essential to our well-being. We feel the same anxiety about the attainment of artificial needs as we would in genuinely life-threatening situations. This mistake is the result of our level of consciousness, our lack of vision. However, there is no point in my trying to describe what these false needs might be. My opinions would not do the slightest to change anyone else's opinions, nor should they. We are all at our own individual and proper level of growth.

BELIEFS

Needs result from beliefs. Beliefs are the filters through which we perceive reality. Aside from instinctual beliefs, such as the belief in basic survival, we have acquired false beliefs from our social conditioning. We also have developed beliefs based on our personal patterns. Many beliefs are irrational, limiting, and destructive. Once we become aware of their counterproductive nature, we may want to change them – but deliberate change is difficult.

Beliefs are maintained by
suppressed energy patterns

Beliefs are conditioned states of mind, occurring mostly on the unconscious level. What may be a limiting belief is difficult to reprogram directly, even with the use of techniques such as affirmations, because it is held in place by suppressed energy patterns. In our work, we do not attempt to directly change beliefs. In accepting ourselves, we accept our beliefs as they are. Processing of feelings will release the energy that is behind the belief and maintains it. The limiting or destructive belief is outgrown naturally, instead of in a forced manner.

Much of what we consider to be important is important only because we consider it to be so. Our outlook will change as time goes by, and as growth occurs, but for now we assign an emotional value to the attainment of circumstances which our beliefs call for, and to the avoidance of whatever threatens the circumstances.

Thus, the teenager buying his first car agonizes over what model to get; the scientist agonizes over the results of his work. They are at different levels of growth concerning their goals. Still, both may undergo unnecessary anxiety because of a mis-placed, compulsive attachment to the outcome of their respective endeavors, unconsciously believing that their self-worth depends on the approval of their peers. In this respect, they are at psychologically similar levels of growth.

It may be assumed, therefore, that the individual has an extensive, intensive, self-projected belief system which he or she considers primary in attaining happiness. The belief system creates needs. Through subjective pain when these needs are not realized, the individual learns to strive for conditions to satisfy the needs. The habitual orientation of evaluating which elements of experience will be allowed or resisted carries over into the inner life: the feelings, emotions, and attitudes. A strong judgmentalism develops toward inner experience, as toward outer experience.

We have fallen into a trap. We must resist certain conditions to survive, but we unwittingly extend this logic to areas where resistance is inappropriate, leading to unresolved energies, entanglement, and sickness. Resistance of experience occurs on a subtle, yet powerful level, and is the beginning of what is called *suppression*.

SUPPRESSION

Suppression is a psychological mechanism that leads to the emotional and spiritual dysfunction called neurosis. Suppression is something that everyone does. People who reach the point of not being able to function or relate to others have merely gone further in suppressing than the average person; people who are considered well-balanced suppress less than average.

Thus, the standard of emotional health in our society is far below the potential possible for humankind, but this just has to do with our current evolutionary level of growth. The function of all growth therapy is to clear suppressed material that is affecting us adversely, or making us neurotic. It is important to have a clear understanding of how suppression works.

Suppression begins
with resistance

When something is resisted, a condition is set up within ourselves that affects us deeply. The electromagnetic field surrounding the individual, known as the aura, actually becomes steeled against letting in any outer experience which is resisted. In effect, resistance builds a shield to the exchange of energy on the psychic level, where experience primarily takes place. This shield is quite tangible on the psychic level, and may be felt and seen by a psychic. A person with ordinary but sensitive perceptions can sometimes sense the shield, or "wall," around people who are particularly suppressed.

With inner feelings, resistance has a similar effect. An energy shield is built around the feeling centers, so feelings will not be allowed into consciousness. As experiences occur and are resisted, the energy of the feeling encounters the shield. The energy is unable to be released because it has been blocked, rather than absorbed; it cannot discharge into consciousness. What we don't realize is that when the energy of a feeling is not released, it does not go away, but stays with us, in latent form, attached to the psychic energy body. Over time, the habit of resistance results in chronic blocking of the centers.

The motive behind resistance to an unpleasant event is that we would rather not feel the pain involved. Avoidance of feelings also implies avoidance of responsibility for them – not always done out of choice, but because we lack the knowledge to confront life directly. We don't know how to experience fully, so there are no loose ends, no lingering, unresolved energies.

After blocking the energy of a feeling through resistance, we withdraw awareness from the blocked energy, completing the suppression. Thus, we do not succeed in avoiding the feeling, as we would prefer, but merely prevent the energy from entering our field of awareness. The energy of the feeling stays with us in latent form.

Suppression operates both inwardly and outwardly

Suppression is the act of rejecting experience from the field of awareness. Outwardly, we suppress awareness of other people, happenings, and conditions that are displeasing. We close ourselves off to many aspects of life, becoming judgmental and self-centered. Something appears evil when it merely conflicts with our "need."

Inwardly, we suppress awareness of painful feelings, including anything about ourselves that we dislike – what we perceive as faults, weaknesses, or negative patterns. External suppression can make us limited and even bigoted, but the consequences of internal suppression can be more severe.

We think that it is possible to simply close the door on pain and regain tranquility. We forcefully try to exclude pain from our awareness, by any number of evasive maneuvers. What we are doing, however, is rejecting ourselves, because the pain *is* part of ourselves.

The problem with suppression of feelings is that the feelings are not resolved, but merely hidden. When something is suppressed, it is made temporarily unconscious, only to build up and break forth at some later time. Anger, for example, does not dissolve when suppressed, but remains as forceful as when originally felt, except that it is no longer within the field of awareness. When we suppress an unpleasant feeling, we interrupt the natural flow of energies. We do not allow the feeling to clear itself, to resolve itself, to regain its natural equilibrium. The energy becomes trapped, held in storage in a static condition. Where does the energy get stored? It is held in what has come to be called "the subconscious."

Suppression creates
subconscious Karma

The mechanism of suppression, therefore, creates much – if not all – of the mysterious subconscious that has been puzzled over and glamorized since Freud. The subconscious is nothing more than a build-up of energies, potential forces which lie dormant because they were never adequately resolved when they originally occurred. In rejecting our experience, we have created the reservoir of the subconscious. In Eastern terms, the build-up of subconscious forces is called *Karma*.

THE SUBCONSCIOUS

The subconscious is not a distinct and separate entity that necessarily has an independent existence of its own. It is just a part of ourselves from which we have turned away – where we no longer look. The capacity of the mind to achieve withdrawal of awareness and subconscious containment of energies is remarkable, and although it appears to be mostly unbeneficial, the habit of suppression and the influence it has on us has been a major factor in shaping our life and history.

We have chosen to turn away, but can easily turn back to the feelings in the subconscious if we so desire. The inner wall that has grown to divide ourselves is not that solid, but is more like a gray area, where tips of the iceberg are always coming into view. We have only hypnotized ourselves not to fully see and feel those hidden things.

The problem with suppressed feelings is that they don't go away, but influence us continually. They contribute to and create events in unsuspected ways, leaving us much in the position of being ruled by hidden forces – forces which at times can seem uncontrollable, with an intelligence of their own.

We become guided by neurotic, unconscious urges that lead to irrational, usually self-destructive behavior. We are attracted to the wrong people, reject the right people, and become compulsive, addictive, and unreliable, all in spite of our best intentions. Our urges are strong and difficult to oppose. Indeed, opposition is impossible because the suppressed energy eventually has to come out. Holding it back will only bring a more destructive release later. We go through life leaving more or less a shambles behind us, accumulating more unresolved energies and adding to our Karma.

Energy is what
becomes suppressed

Unpleasant feelings as well as unresolved situations are the kinds of things that are suppressed, but when we suppress, it is *energy* that is being put into storage. Emotions can run high, and emotions are nothing but energy moving through the centers of consciousness. When people interact, there is an energy exchange between them. Energy is what enables us to have experiences. Experiences are kinds of energy that the psychic body assimilates. Of course, I am referring to psychic energy, which is not yet generally recognized by science. Nevertheless, subconscious energy can build to a considerable strength. It becomes part of our personality, affecting us as well as others.

Since we suppress in consistent, yet individual ways, we build a reservoir of negative energy of a specific type. Some people suppress mainly fear; some, anger or sexual impulses, for example. The suppressed energy then creates patterns: unconscious, individualistic ways in which we meet life. Patterns would not be a problem, except that they are often negative, keeping us from creative participation in life. Because patterns are usually unconscious, we don't know why we are limiting ourselves, or even that we are doing it at all.

*Suppression leads
to addiction*

To suppress requires psychic energy. It takes energy to suppress energy; it takes energy to block. The demand for energy becomes a drain on our resources, creating conditions that encourage the addictive cycle. Because addiction provides energy, taken either from outside sources or inner reserves, it facilitates suppression. When this additional energy is not available, it is not as easy to suppress, and we come face to face with our pain. Thus, when we suppress, energy is diverted from its positive and constructive expression; we become split, working against ourselves, unaware of what is happening.

Repression

The suppression syndrome becomes unconscious when it reaches the point of *repression*. Repression is the same as suppression, except that there is no awareness of the feeling or the avoidance of it. For example, if you are angry, but do not consciously recognize your anger, it becomes repressed. Proper release is not possible, and the anger is stored subconsciously.

Repression, unfortunately, is common in the modern world. Freud, in *Civilization and Its Discontents,* stated that he thought it was unavoidable. His statement is even more appropriate today. Repression comes about because of all the desensitizing that we undergo. Life is so busy, so anxiety ridden, with our attention constantly enticed outward, that we do not realize what our real feelings are. We have lost touch with ourselves.

Continual repression results in neurosis and extensive blocking of the human organism. The result on the emotional level is anxiety, addiction, rage, and unconscious destructive patterns; and on the physical level, disease. Blocked energy can easily reach the level where it affects the physical, and what is disease but blockage? Looking at prevalent Twentieth Century diseases such as heart disease and cancer, I can't help but feel that their main cause must be the buildup of subconscious negative forces that the modern way of life encourages.

However, it should not be forgotten that humans have been creating their subconscious all throughout history, so modern life should not be condemned outright. The average person, now and in previous times, has always had personal blocking and patterns to contend with. That we all have our Karma is the rationale behind presenting any system of self-work to begin with.

We are all so similar when looked at from a distance. We all have unconscious, yet individualistic tendencies that keep us from reaching our maximum potential. Rarely do we fully realize the higher side of our nature, the love and creative centers. Rarely do we relate to others or ourselves directly, without distorting grossly through our own particular filters of suppressed energy. We must recognize the truth without becoming pessimistic. We are as we are because life and consciousness is evolutionary. We are growing, and in progress. Our capacities only reflect our current levels of growth.

Let's look specifically at what kinds of feelings are commonly suppressed or repressed, becoming buried in the subconscious. Our feelings usually relate to the following areas:

1. **SURVIVAL:** Fear, anxiety, insecurity about health, money, possessions, death.

2. **SENSATION:** Sexual feelings, cravings for food, alcohol, smoking, drugs.

3. **POWER:** Anger, hostility, aggressiveness, helplessness, insignificance.

4. **RELATIONSHIP:** Loneliness, jealousy.

Limiting patterns of behavior arise from the chronic suppression of feelings. Different feelings may be linked, forming complex systems of suppression and blocking. Thus, sexual issues may be associated disharmoniously in one person with security issues, and in another with power issues. The accumulation of these negative energies results in stress. If we knew how to dissolve and avoid the build-up of negative energies, we could avoid stress.

The buildup of suppressed energy can vary over short or long intervals. Short-term emotional suppression can happen with fears, sexual impulses, or any feeling that cannot be immediately dissolved. For example, one may experience anger in the work environment and not know how to release it, and then come home and take it out on the family. The attempt to release the energy by venting it on a neutral party is known as *displacement*. Displacement is common, resulting in hurt feelings, miscommunication, and damaged relationships.

Long-term avoidance of feelings builds a structure of a quite different and unsuspected magnitude. It can build to the extent that one's whole life is shaped by internal forces of which one has no conscious knowledge. Conditions that were unresolved in the past have a way of recurring with new faces or circumstances, and we have the choice of taking responsibility and experiencing, or avoiding and suppressing once again.

The subconscious is carried
over from previous existences

It may seem remarkable that such complex systems of avoidance, suppression, and blocking could be formed in one short lifetime. My feeling is that they aren't, but that our patterns have formed over extensive periods in prior existences. Whether you choose to believe in reincarnation or not is a personal choice. For me, it seems obvious that there is some sort of pre-existence prior to physical birth. Just looking at how quickly and definitely children form their individualities is enough to convince me of a previous life.

I believe that Karma, the subconscious, is carried over from previous existences. Life's events are then formed and played out by subconscious forces. It is not necessary to agree with the doctrine of reincarnation to have success with processing, but the notion of a previous existence may help clarify a few things for you.

For one, you will find it easier to take responsibility for yourself and where you are at, rather than blaming your childhood and your parents. You will realize that early incidents with family, no matter how painful, were merely catalysts to make you conscious of what was already latent within you. In fact, you chose those very circumstances for just that opportunity.

Because there is usually no conscious memory of previous existences, and because the causes of most emotional patterns are in those existences, it is difficult to pinpoint the source of any current condition. However, understanding the cause is not necessary. In our work, we focus on present feelings, not causes. Contemporary psychology agrees for the most part with the futility of depth analysis.

Accepting the possibility of a previous existence also implies the continuity of life after "death." This idea helps me – intellectually at least – in working with the fear of death, which is really the only primal fear. Psychics have brought back much documentation of life on the "other side." I personally find their reports, taken as a whole, to be adequate evidence of something beyond the earthly shell.

PROJECTION

Projection results from the accumulation of energy generated by suppression. It is an automatic, unconscious mechanism, which assigns subjective value and identity to persons or events in the "outside" world. Feelings that are suppressed are then experienced indirectly through other persons or events. In projection, suppressed qualities are attributed to others, or those qualities are experienced as being caused by or coming from others. Others are usually criticized for the very qualities that have been projected onto them.

In projection, we try to avoid
responsibility for certain feelings

When we project, we unconsciously assign responsibility for our feelings to other persons or situations, thinking that they "caused" our experience. We generally choose persons or situations skillfully, to appear justified to others and to ourselves. We fail to see that the other is only "bringing up" suppressed material from inside ourselves. They are not the cause of our feelings, although they may be considered to be the stimulus.

If that feeling or reaction was not already latent within us, we would not have responded in that particular way. Think of how differently various people react to the same situation. In projecting, we see through the distorting filters of our own suppressed energies. We do not see reality as it is, and we always react inappropriately.

For example, if you have suppressed your anger, you will see others as responsible for "making" you angry because of what they do. You will blame them. You will also perceive others as being angry and directing their anger toward you when you are not angry. You will be likely to condemn them for their anger. If you have suppressed your sexual feelings, you will perceive others as making uncalled-for sexual approaches toward you, and you may judge them harshly. If you have suppressed your feelings of rejection toward others, you will think others are rejecting you, and you will blame them.

Similarly, after you have blocked your power through suppression of your own energies, you will assign that role to outside agencies, thinking they are responsible for blocking you. You will appear to be entirely justified in your blame. Even an impartial observer might agree that you are contending with an outside force.

The truth is that there is no outside force. Miraculously, we project our subconscious energies onto what appears to be the outside world, creating our entire experience. We are literally responsible for our perceptions as well as whatever happens to us. Accidents that happen "to us" are, unfortunately, only extreme cases of the negative forces that are hidden and stored within building to the point where they can affect us physically. Remember, *energy* is what gets stored in the subconscious, and energy can build to powerful levels if not released.

We never see *"what is."* We only see what we have projected. Because of the hidden magnitude of the built-up subconscious, the extent and significance of the suppression-projection mechanism cannot be clearly perceived. To succeed in processing, you must intellectually accept the condition of suppression-projection as a working axiom, even if you have to do so on faith. As you begin to integrate material that was previously suppressed, the truth will gradually become evident, and you will be astounded as well as fascinated.

Up to now, we have discussed the suppression of negative feelings and interactions. However, positive events are also suppressed and then projected onto the "outside" world. The shield that was created to avoid negative feelings also blocks positive feelings, and projection becomes the sole means to connect to the feelings. Your most cherished times, someone you thought really loved you, was just the love already within you. Someone who helped you was you helping yourself.

To succeed at self-transformation, you must make the leap from perceiving the universe as a collection of separate individuals and objects acting on you, to perceiving it as a field for your energies, which you project and then perceive as if there was an objective outside world. Incredibly, other individuals also have the exact same capability of creating their own universes, simultaneously with you. Try this right now to develop your feeling capability:

EXERCISE

Feel your energies as they go out into the world. Assume that you assign the value and identity to everything you perceive. Your impression of the external world comes to you through your filters of suppressed energy, and your suppressed energy draws corresponding events to you. Assume that when something happens, it has not happened by itself, but that you unconsciously created it through projection or attracted it to you. If a person seems to behave in a certain way, it is your perception. Focus your awareness on your energy field, and feel the connection you have with your perceptions and reactions. I am not referring to intellectual understanding, but to feeling. Simply feel your connection to what you perceive as the qualities of the other.

While you should cultivate a sense of responsibility for your feelings and experiences, you should by no means assume guilt or be self-condemning. Guilt is another form of self-rejection. Remember that others are also ultimately responsible for what happens to them, even though this does not excuse us from not helping them.

We have taken the concept of suppression-projection further than psychology usually goes with it. We have entered the mystical realm where reasoning and thinking do not apply. This is necessary to reach our goal of inner integration. Fulfillment can never be found through the analytic faculties of the mind; fulfillment comes through the feeling center.

When we project, the world becomes a mirror, reflecting our own qualities back to us. Of course, a great deal of independent activity does go on outside of ourselves, and other identities do have a basis of independent character. When we project, we carefully select the appropriate "screen" – a person or situation with some element of what we are projecting, and we load our perception of them with our own energy.

If we try to analyze how much of our perception is projected, and how much is "real," we become distracted from our work on ourselves. No objective evaluation is possible anyway, because we are not clear within ourselves. Therefore, we assume that we are projecting the entire contents of our perception when we use processing techniques. It is very likely that after the issue has been integrated, we will spontaneously see exactly what the other is bringing and what we are bringing to the situation.

The client projects onto the therapist

In light of our discussion of projection, we may more completely understand the value of the relationship with the enlightened therapist. In contrast to an interaction with an average person, where both people normally project onto each other, the therapist ideally does not project subconscious energies onto the client, or at least remains nonreactive to these projections. This includes having no demands or expectations. In addition, the therapist does not react to or reject, but accepts the projections of the client. This is the essence of therapy and the catalyst for the healing transformation. The client is able to become aware of his or her projections more clearly than in relationship with other people, because the mirror is now exceptionally clear. Nonetheless, you should not become discouraged from processing interactions with people in general.

Whenever you react strongly to the stimulus that another

person provides, it is safe to assume that suppressed energies within you are surfacing. If you were clear within yourself, you would not be so affected by the negativity of others. Your reactions would not be as pronounced or as judgmental. You might then experience a "normal" amount of negative emotion in response to certain circumstances, but processing techniques are still an excellent approach for clearing these feelings.

CLEARING

On the psychic level, the purpose of projection is clearing. The psychic body, which stores the suppressed emotional energy, naturally wants to clear, or cleanse, itself of this negativity. Projection automatically occurs to bring the energy to a conscious level. If this clearing procedure is not recognized, it is all in vain. The projected experiences are resisted and resuppressed, and the amount of negative energy in the subconscious grows. The opportunity to learn through projection is lost.

Feelings must be experienced
in order to clear

Clearing of suppressed material takes place only when you finally allow yourself the experience that you have been avoiding. The energy, the feeling, must be allowed into consciousness without resistance, in order to be integrated. With painful events, the pain must be accepted and experienced, but you will learn how to minimize and neutralize pain by observing it from the Witness vantage point. The Witness capacity brings about a *nonidentification* with painful feelings, making them more easily integrated and released.

Suppressed energy is released through conscious experience of it. As you allow yourself to have the feeling, the feeling will change. Pain will dissolve, becoming neutralized. Facing feelings is all that is necessary to clear suppressed negativity, and once something is faced, it can be cleared in a surprisingly short interval. The problem is that our unconscious self-rejection prevents us from really facing our feelings, even when we want to.

Life becomes your therapist

As you go through life, you will have various encounters that bring up your subconscious energies into conscious awareness. These energies surface when conditions are appropriate for them to be released. If you can learn to integrate these energies as they come up, you will be meeting life most creatively. You will be *using* your circumstances, instead of being abused by them. It is for this opportunity that we incarnate on the Earth plane.

Amazingly, each individual's life is designed to provide just the right circumstances for the clearing of hidden negative forces within. By correctly utilizing these circumstances, you can very effectively work on yourself without a therapist. Life becomes the therapist, and indeed, life is the best and ultimately the only therapist. Your circumstances at this very moment are the ones you need. They are bringing up negative energies from your subconscious that need to be cleared. When you integrate them, that is, when you accept and experience them without resistance, clearing takes place.

Projection may lessen if you practice contacting your feelings directly, as in meditation. However, you should not expect to stop projecting, because projecting is a natural way of clearing. You must learn to become aware. Realizing what is happening, you will smile to yourself. You will not "buy into" thinking that the other is responsible for your experience; you will "own" your experience, meaning that you take responsibility for what is before you. In doing so, you achieve the control over your life that you seek.

I recognize that the nature of life is balance – that I will always experience the "up" as well as the "down." If I fight and try to avoid the "down," I fight life itself. If I accept both in an understanding way, I will be at harmony with life, and with myself.

3

The Play of Opposites

Projection can be taken one step further by relating it to the concept of duality. Duality is a theory; there is no way of conclusively proving it. For me, duality is something to refer to as I observe and learn from life. It is a concept to use when taking a long look at your ups and downs; it is not a dogma or rule to adopt blindly, to which you try to fit your life. Still, if you feel sympathetic toward the idea, it can give you a new perspective. You can gain a more balanced insight into the nature of existence.

DUALITY

The theory of duality states that the manifest world is composed of opposites. However, these are not really opposite as they might appear, but are in fact complementary. Each of any pair of complementary qualities depends for its existence upon the other; neither could exist by itself. Examples of these pairs are day and night, hot and cold, up and down, solid and soft. If something were to exist without its complement, there would be no way of perceiving it, because the experience of both qualities is needed to know either one separately. It is impossible to imagine day without knowing night.

Certain things are not obvious because their complements are hidden. Thus, we are not usually conscious of the atmosphere, but would be if we were transported into space. We have never been without the atmosphere, so we are hardly aware of it, and it normally has no emotional content.

Duality is most easily understood and agreed with in terms of physical examples. Controversy begins when feelings are considered, because the exact same principles apply to our inner life: the day and night of emotions, the hot and cold of relationships, the up and down of what is usually called "happiness," the ceaseless entanglement of pleasure and pain.

We would not recognize pleasure if our experience did not also include pain of equal degree at around the same point in time. The hungrier we are, the more we enjoy eating. The lonelier we are, the more meaningful the closeness with another. The obstacle in our path makes possible the joy of overcoming. The pain of relationship is proportionate to the love. Our ecstatic highs are balanced by our depressive lows.

The mind creates Duality

Why does it have to be this way? Duality is simply the nature of perception and feeling; it is not a form of punishment. The mind perceives by sensing a pair of complements. When anything affects the mind, it must also have an experience of similar intensity with the complement – not simultaneously, but near in time – in order to even be aware of it.

Moreover, it is *we* who unconsciously assign the positive and negative value to each side of the experience, in almost an arbitrary manner at times. The mind *creates both* the pleasure and the pain. Dualistic experience, therefore, will vary between individuals.

Take any experience, and the mind will divide it into parts: one part pleasure, and one part pain. We are not normally aware of how extensively the mind categorizes our experience. It appears as if the event is genuinely composed of both "positive" and "negative" elements. We don't realize that we make something painful, or rather, we assign pain to some aspect of the event, only to achieve the required balance of experience. Thus, pain has no real existence but, of course, we perceive it as real.

Duality also means that the emotional value of any experience will change as it is repeated. You may like something, but as you repeat it, trying to recapture the original feeling, it changes. You go through unexpected painful stages, balancing positive and negative, without being aware that you are the one who is making the experience change, and assigning the emotional value to it.

Duality affects whatever
is most important to you

I would not ask you to accept the theory of duality without question, but try to look at your experiences from this viewpoint, and judge for yourself if it has any credibility. You will probably agree that there is at least something to it, especially when you examine the issues you expect will give your life meaning, like relationship or career. Important issues are the very ones in which the dualistic experience is most strongly evoked.

Romantic relationships are notorious for their love-hate aspects. Relationships start with the best of feelings and intentions, but before long, the negative side becomes apparent. There will always be a negative side, because we can't feel love *on a dependent level* without resentment.

Actually, we have projected both our love and our hate. We assign both qualities to aspects of the other person that best accept the projections. If there is nothing really objectionable to attach the resentment to, we will exaggerate something out of proportion, or invent something.

Success in career, or attainment of ego needs in general – security, sensation, or power – is always experienced dualistically. Perceived success is followed, or even accompanied, by perceived failure. The failure may happen in the same field as the success, or in an apparently unrelated department of life. If nothing happens that might be taken as failure, we either project failure or become blatantly self-destructive, causing real loss. Either way, the sense of failure balances success.

Please note that I am not describing the mechanism of duality to encourage you to be more careful in avoiding negativity. Negativity cannot be avoided; it can only be suppressed. There is a deep and inextinguishable need in us to live through the negative; we do not rest until this need is filled. We go out of our way to create negative, complementary conditions.

Realizing how duality affects us, it is possible to fall back into an overriding pessimism, which may seem justified because any move toward security, pleasure, or success is bound to include its opposite. People become cynical without ever hearing of the theory of duality, because they have known success to be accompanied by failure. They decide to avoid failure by avoiding success, and end up missing life. This non-confrontational attitude is fairly common, and usually unconscious.

A more positive reaction to the understanding of duality would be to recognize that we unnecessarily make life difficult by compulsively focusing on "success," as is common in our goal-oriented society. Of course, we must still provide for essential needs, but what we consider to be essential makes all the difference. Again, it is important to distinguish between real and perceived or addictive needs.

Addiction exaggerates Duality

This is what must be understood about duality: We are subject to the law most strongly when addicted to the satisfaction of any desire. Addicted, we are compulsive, we must have the object in question. Addicted, fulfillment is dualistic, alternating between pleasure and pain.

Our need systems are artificial, compulsive, and addictive, setting us up for strong dualistic experiences. When not addicted to outcomes, we do not go through the same intensity of dualistic swings, if only because we do not look for intense satisfaction to come from the activity. We are more relaxed, and don't need as much to be happy.

Growth is a gradual process; we learn we don't need this, and then that. The elimination of compulsive needs, or what we think we just have to have, is an important part of personal liberation. But exactly how is growth achieved? You cannot free yourself from compulsive needs by an act of will. Processing of perceived needs results in a gentle, natural, outgrowing of them. Do not force yourself to be something you are not; do not want to be something other than what you are. In accepting yourself as you are, you allow growth to occur.

DUALISTIC PROJECTION

Let's get back to how duality relates to projection. We have discussed how the mind projects in order to clear the subconscious. But as it projects, the mind must create a balance of positive and negative to be able to perceive at all. One of the poles of the dualistic projection will bring up suppressed energy; the other will not, but will be created solely to balance. The "primary projection" brings up the suppressed energy. The "secondary projection" is created spontaneously to balance the energy experience, and does not represent clearing of the subconscious. Secondary projection may be internalized. Let's go over a few examples that detail how dualistic projection works.

Anger / Celebration

A man has a run-in with someone during the day. He projects his anger and perceives someone as being angry with him for no good reason, or becomes angry himself, and believes that the other person "caused" it. Then, he goes to his favorite bar and talks to his buddies, telling them of the episode. Feelings of camaraderie ensue, wherein they all denounce the other person together, balancing the whole episode. The initial argument was the primary projection, based on the suppressed energy trying to release, and the good time in the bar was the secondary projection, constructed to balance. Of course, before he went to the bar, he could have gone home and kicked the dog in an attempt to displace the still unreleased anger.

Love / Rejection

Let's take another example. Suppose a woman has repressed her feelings of rejection for other people. Traditional psychologists might say she wants to reject others because of the rejection and lack of love she received as a child. However, if we acknowledged the influence of previous life Karma, we would say she came into the present life with these subconscious tendencies intact, and that her childhood merely served as the catalyst for her problem. She represses (unconsciously) the feelings of rejection for others because the feelings do not fit in with her self-image. She projects, therefore, and perceives others as being cold and rejecting to her. This is the primary projection, and is experienced painfully. The secondary projection assumes the form of her "love" for one person. She idealizes the image of her lover, searching for the proper person, or screen, on which to project. If she finds the person, her love affair will be ecstatic to the degree that her perceived rejection by others has been painful.

She will not see her lover as a real person, or will only give token attention to the real person, because she is in love with her projection. Her "love," being dependent and unreal to begin with, will change as well, according to duality, becoming fear and resentment, affording new opportunities for suppression.

She also could have internalized the secondary projection,

seeing herself, for example, as a martyr, someone who loves and sacrifices for humanity, but who is misunderstood and rejected. She receives support and pleasure from the internalized self-image to the extent that she feels pain from the primary projection.

Hostility toward authority /
Rebellious self-determination

Let's take one more example. A child grows up in a military environment, and "reacts" badly. Traditional psychology might say he developed a suppressed hostility toward authority because of his childhood. Our viewpoint would be that he came into the present life with an authority issue, choosing an early environment that would serve as a catalyst to his problem. He grows up becoming a rock singer, intent on demolishing authority with his message. His perception of authority as evil is a projection of suppressed energy. If he had originally been able to release the hostility instead of suppressing it, there would have been no latent energy available to form the projection.

The original cause of the suppressed energy is not known, but possibly because of previous-life difficulty in a similar environment, suppression on a large scale occurred. He may have been in a situation where his personal power was severely limited by an authority figure, and he was unable to release the resulting resentment; but this in itself would have been the result of Karma from yet another previous life. Possibly, there never was any outside authority, but he limited himself with his own blocking, projecting the responsibility onto outside authority. Trying to trace back to the original cause is difficult if not futile, as well as irrelevant.

His primary projection assumes the form of irrational hostility toward authority per se, in his thinking that he is being controlled. His secondary projection is internalized. He styles his self-image as that of a free agent; unbound, spontaneous, defiant, rebellious – a rock star. His enjoyment of the secondary projection is dependent on and balanced by the pain of the primary projection. He suffers real pain in the primary projection. He finds real pleasure in the self-image, the secondary projection. They are balanced.

His audience consists mostly of people who share a similar authority conflict. They identify with both sides of the projection, seeing themselves as victims of authority, and also unconsciously identifying with authority because they assign their self-blocking functions to it. In the performance, they gain a heightened sense of participation through the dramatic presentation of both poles of the energy-projection.

In much the same way we go though life projecting and balancing our experience. This is not something only "neurotics" do, but something we all do, all the time. Some events balance out immediately; some dictate the course of our entire lives. The great novelists concern themselves with circumstances and themes such as these; that is why there is always a mixture of fulfillment and frustration in the lives of their characters. Indeed, the inevitability of duality is a large part of their message.

What significance does duality have for us? Obviously, that we cannot blindly pursue what is normally considered to be pleasure, happiness, or fulfillment, and hope to achieve the positive without the negative. We think we will find meaning through a worthwhile activity, career, or relationship, but we encounter as much heartbreak as satisfaction.

Should we stop striving after happiness? As human beings, it is our nature to pursue happiness, in whatever form we individually conceive. Nevertheless, duality is heightened to the extent that we are addicted to the positive and compulsively avoid the negative.

If you can accept that your highs will always be balanced by lows – that you would not even recognize the highs without the lows – you will be able to relax when things become uncomfortable, instead of reacting in panic. By accepting unhappiness, you transcend it. You paradoxically achieve a higher, more unconditional form of happiness.

INTEGRATION OF DUALITIES

The key to resolving the problem of duality is integration. By trying to avoid the negative, it becomes suppressed and part of our subconscious Karma. If the theory of duality is at all valid, the futility of continual avoidance of the negative becomes plain. We are trying to avoid the unavoidable, and creating a debt that must eventually be paid. By choosing to avoid the negative now, it will affect us even more subversively in the future, keeping us bound to the irrational and destructive urges of the subconscious that suppression creates.

Integration means accepting
and including the negative

Instead of trying to separate one part of life from another, we acknowledge that the negative is an integral part of life; that experience could not be without it; indeed, that we ourselves have unconsciously assigned the negative value to balance the forces. We accept and surrender to the experience of the negative.

As we stop running from the negative, there is bound to be suppressed pain to be faced. Pain avoided in the past has become suppressed in the subconscious. There is no other way to get rid of the pain except to bring it to the surface and experience it. This is what is done in therapy. It is a necessary part of the integration process. However, meeting pain becomes easier when done from the Witness, which we will examine.

Integration brings
freedom from pain

Our goal is not merely to endure pain, but to go beyond pain. Integration does not mean endless confrontation with pain. Once suppressed pain is cleared, it is gone forever. Integrated dualities are not painful, because both poles are balanced.

When dualism is integrated, life becomes whole, or "holistic." Integration of both poles of experience brings freedom from duality, the trap of pleasure and pain. We transcend, no longer frantically clinging to the positive and fearfully trying to avoid the negative. We find ourselves with a new awareness and freedom; we have grown; happiness is more unconditional.

Integration does not mean that the negative side of any dualistic experience is eliminated, but that our perception of the negative changes so it is no longer disturbing. Life is still encountered in terms of dualities, but in a non-compulsive manner – a natural ebb and flow. Just as day and night, hot and cold are not regarded as problems, the poles of feeling are experienced as non-problematical.

When a duality is not integrated, we fear and suppress one side, which makes us compulsively addicted to the other side. When the duality becomes integrated, non-compulsive expression of both sides takes place. We use the "negative" productively. This is the goal of processing and other growth therapies.

A good example of one of the basic dualities that applies to everyone is relationships. Unintegrated, we experience the poles of isolation/dependency. Integrated, we enjoy autonomy/relatedness.

Unintegrated, we fear being alone. Lonely and anxious, we seek to escape from the sense of isolation through relationship. Being driven by the fear of being alone, we depend on the other to eliminate our loneliness. We become addicted to the other. If the other is lost, we experience and exhibit symptoms that would be present in any addiction withdrawal.

Integrated, we enjoy our aloneness. We become creative when alone, recharging our energies, and even look forward to being alone. We then enjoy being with others in a non-dependent manner, which makes our company even more pleasant. Our expression of this duality becomes balanced.

Each aspect of life may be broken down and understood in terms of its dualistic complements. The integration of dualistic experience becomes an art in itself.

My body is the most important friend
I have. It is always with me, to support
and serve me. It is the center of my
feelings. If I love my body, I will
love myself. If I am aware of and accept
my body, I will be aware of and be
able to accept my feelings. I will
grow, and become whole.

4

Feeling Through the Body

Our discussion so far has been concerned with what might be called the workings of the mind. I would now like to direct your attention to another aspect of our individuality, the body. In our culture, the body is usually viewed either as a servant of the mind or as an instrument of pleasure or vanity, but it is not given the status it deserves. If we are to develop sensitivity to ourselves, we must do so through both approaches, that of the body as well as the mind.

The study of both body and mind leads to the conclusion that they are not unrelated but that there is, after all, a deep connection between them. Each influences the other, each may be observed and understood through the other, and each blends into the other, almost eliminating the distinction between them.

Therefore, learning to approach ourselves through the body is an important aspect of our self-work. If this emphasis were omitted, we would be at a disadvantage in our effort to integrate ourselves. The same serious disadvantage, I feel, is incurred in any therapy or inner growth practice that does not include work with the body. The importance of the body in psychological therapy comes about in the following ways.

STORING NEGATIVITY

We learned, in earlier chapters, how suppression stores unreleased negative energy. Storage takes place on the psychic level when energy attaches to the emotional body; but energy is also stored in the physical body.

Storage in the physical body comes about because there is no distinct dividing line between physical and psychic. Physical and psychic only appear to be distinct because our physical senses can perceive vibrations within a certain limited range – we then label unperceived vibrations as "psychic," not sensing the continuity. The physical body can be seen as an accurate representation of suppressed psychic energy. The body is, for practical purposes, where such negativity may be considered to be stored.

Moreover, working with the physical body can release energy stored in the physical-psychic continuum. As a result, various types of "bodywork" have emerged, each effecting the release of negative psychic energy through work with the physical.

The interfacing of the physical and psychic has become known as the body/mind correlation. Even though the concept of body/mind has been a fundamental part of Eastern psychological theory for thousands of years, it is relatively new in the West. Wilhelm Reich is generally credited with being the first to bring this concept into contemporary psychological practice. Two of Reich's followers, Alexander Lowen and John Pierrakos, founded Bioenergetics, a therapy based upon working with the body in order to release suppressed and "held" emotions. I have personally taken part in a workshop led by John Pierrakos, who has gone on to form Core Energetics, and was impressed by his brilliance in bringing suppressed material to the surface, mainly through working with the body, using verbal, manipulative, and intuitive techniques.

Our attitudes toward the body affect us more than we realize. We have learned to think of the body as a servant, as the means to achieve goals. We become "mind-oriented," because goals are of the mind, instead of "feeling-oriented." We don't pay attention to feelings because they don't help us accomplish goals. In turning away from feelings, we turn away from body awareness, because feeling is a body function. We become unconscious in our bodies, and allow the build-up of negative energies. Let's examine exactly why feeling is considered to be related to the body.

THINKING AND FEELING

People working in the psychological field usually state that the body reflects the mind, but this is not quite accurate. The body really corresponds to the psychic feeling capacity, which includes the emotions. Emotions are felt in the body. Blocks in the emotions "set up" in the body.

The mind, on the other hand, has somewhat of an antithetical function to feeling. The mind is composed of thoughts. Thoughts have no emotional value in themselves, except as they act on feelings. Thoughts are cold: they are composed of judgments, comparisons, evaluations, reasoning, plans, etc. The common quality of all thoughts is that they deal in the past, in learned and remembered values. Then, based on the past, thoughts extend into the future, creating goals. The mind acts like an impersonal computer, essentially learning to associate pleasure or pain with memory.

The mind, however, does not have the capacity to experience. Experiencing is the function of the feeling center. We run into trouble when we attempt to experience through the mind. Instead of experiencing, we end up comparing what is happening to some remembered event in the past or anticipated event in the future, and we never fully perceive the actual event taking place before us.

The feeling center is the proper function to use in experiencing

In direct experience, there is no thought present, no comparison or evaluation, just the awareness of what is happening. What is happening could be an inner event, or the interaction with someone or something in the outer world. In either case, the experience is allowed to occur as a feeling, without resisting or blocking. We allow ourselves simply "to be" with the experience.

The feeling centers correspond to the chakras. The chakras are psychic centers located in the body. They are centers of energy, consciousness, and feeling. When we block ourselves from experiencing – which happens when we try to experience through the mind – we block ourselves from these centers of consciousness, and therefore, from the body. Feelings of alienation from the body result. This tendency can be reversed, and sensitivity to our feelings developed, by getting in rapport with the body.

Thus, if you are too much in the mind and not enough in the body you will feel alienated, or out of touch with yourself. You will have the sense of being an identity with a body, instead of the sense that you *are* the body. Being out of touch with yourself is also why you feel out of touch with others. As you increase your connection to the body, you increase the capacity for feeling, self-acceptance, self-love, and the ability to love others.

The body is always in the moment

While the mind is always in either the past or the future, the body is always in the moment because of its feeling nature – feeling is inherently in the moment. Being in the moment is a condition that you should strive to develop, because life is taking place in the moment. When locked in the mind, in expectations of the future based on the past, you do not confront and experience life.

Not being in the moment contributes to the sensation of being an isolated "I," an ego. If asked to physically locate the "I," we typically feel that it is somewhere above the neck, out of touch with the body, which is considered to be merely the dumb beast that carries the "I" around. This is characterized by our modern dress code for men of a tight collar and tie around the neck, and also the belt around the waist. It is notable that women's fashion allows freer flowing, non-constrictive designs, suggesting that women are generally more in touch with their bodies and feelings than men. Men tend to drive their bodies from the mind, while women tend to feel through situations.

One who feels a connection to the body will not feel like an isolated "I," a separate ego, but will feel a deep connection within, both to the self and to others. The connection to the body is felt on a deep and satisfying level; energies are contacted that are unknown to the isolated person.

The sense of isolation, the "I" or the ego, is of central concern in Eastern psychology. One of its goals is to expand the ego to the point where the oneness of creation is perceived. However, we should not attempt to be something we are not, but should accept and celebrate ourselves as we are. As we develop our consciousness, which can be effectively thought of as developing contact with the feeling centers of the body, we will naturally increase our sense of perspective.

Western psychology uses the term "ego" differently. The ego is thought of more as the core of the individuality, not as something to be outgrown. Western psychology traditionally is dedicated to strengthening and making the ego function more smoothly. This approach may have to do with the lack of contact with spiritual values that I mentioned earlier, but is more likely due to the urgency of the cases with which it must contend, as well as reflecting our culture.

Eastern psychology recognizes that a strong ego is a

requirement before higher work can be undertaken, but it is concerned more with developing our evolutionary potential than with just making us functional. The developing of higher qualities necessarily involves the loosening of the ego. However, there is no need to become fixated on ego/non-ego disputes or aspirations. We only have to allow ourselves to grow naturally.

RELEASING NEGATIVITY

Negativity stored in the body becomes trapped in the muscles, chakras, and organs. Working with these areas is the primary concern in all types of bodywork. Bodywork is usually done in either of two ways – manipulation or stretching.

Manipulation

Manipulation consists of therapeutic massage. The actual massage stimulates the release of trapped energy, and emotional releases are common on the massage table. There are many different bodywork techniques and schools, and I feel they all have something to offer. The only drawback is that a practitioner is required, involving a certain inconvenience and expense, but getting bodywork treatments when possible will prove to be beneficial. Other non-manipulative bodywork techniques, such as Acupuncture and Polarity, involve balancing of the body's functional energy system, and can also result in release of suppressed energy.

Stretching

Stretching of muscles has been found to be effective in releasing blocked energy, and bodyworkers will use stretching as well as manipulation. However, the technique of releasing stored negativity through stretching has been worked out most systematically and beautifully in the age-old system of Yoga postures, which we might look at from a fresh perspective.

Yoga has a marked advantage in that it can be practiced alone, making it inexpensive and convenient, as well as effective in achieving its intent. Tension from daily living as well as long-term suppression is held in the muscles, and the practice of Yoga can go a long way toward helping us release negativity and stress.

In addition to stretching muscles, Yoga postures work directly on the chakra system, releasing blocks that have built up. The spine is kept flexible. The condition of the spine is important for good health; keeping it flexible maintains the energy flow in the body. The arteries are stimulated, counteracting hardening and congestion. Joints are kept loose. For our purposes, the most important aspect of Yoga postures is their suppression-releasing capabilities. When combined with breathing techniques, the result is a physical approach that is unsurpassed for stimulating the release of suppressed negativity stored in the body. A regular practice of Yoga will help to keep you relaxed, as well as gently uncovering the layers of the subconscious.

The release of suppressed material will be sensed as negative feelings coming into consciousness either with or without external stimulus. When feelings come up, you should not be alarmed, but should welcome the opportunity to cleanse, and process the material with the techniques you will learn.

Bodywork clears
negativity directly

The advantage of using any bodywork technique to implement clearing, including Yoga, is that imbalances are approached deeply and directly on the energy level. Clearing is stimulated by working with the blocks in the psychic body, through the physical body. The need for clearing through projection onto other people or onto events is reduced. We become more balanced when interacting with others, because clearing takes place through our own private practice. We also develop a sense of connectedness with the body and feeling centers.

Even so, bodywork is not all that is needed to facilitate personal growth. As you work on yourself, you must approach from other directions as well. Other approaches include processing, psychotherapy, meditation, spirituality, group work, or any growth technique that develops sensitivity to feelings, bringing suppressed material into awareness. Remember, psychotherapy should not be primarily of an analytical, thinking nature. The feeling side must be developed. Use your intellectual and thinking functions to understand the principles involved, and then leave thinking behind as you train yourself to feel.

Exercise in general does not have the same effect as Yoga or other kinds of bodywork. Strenuous exercise can keep you in shape, and perhaps help blow off some nervous energy, but muscle-held tensions will not be released. Actually, exercise such as weightlifting and bodybuilding do exactly the opposite, tightening the muscles and driving muscle-held suppressed energy deeper, increasing insensitivity to the feeling nature of the body.

Indeed, Yoga postures are not exercise, and should not be thought of as a replacement for exercise. Both forms of muscle releasing – manipulation and stretching – are passive, not active. Getting a massage is obviously passive, but Yoga has to be approached similarly. You should think of the poses as "postures of relaxation" – not as a performance, or as something in which you have to excel.

Yoga involves getting the energy "unstuck" in the body. You must cultivate the ability to allow the loosened energy to flow as it would prefer, not as your conscious mind would dictate. You must surrender to the innate intelligence of the body, the "wisdom of the body."

THE WISDOM OF THE BODY

If you decide to use Yoga as an approach to the bodywork aspect of your self-work, you should do so with a proper understanding of what is required in terms of attitude. Again, as in other areas of life, attitude is the most influential component.

The postures must be performed passively. They are entered deliberately, but with a sense that the body is assuming the posture by itself, not being directed by the mind. Do not push with the mind. What you do with the mind is simply to watch. Observe and feel what is happening in the body as you go through the sequence of poses, without trying to interfere or change it.

Choiceless awareness is essential
for higher consciousness

Choiceless Awareness is the capacity for feeling directly what is happening with no thought of wanting anything to be different. We accept, we don't block, experience. We become the Witness, refraining from choosing or controlling.

As choiceless awareness is maintained during bodywork, we begin to get more in touch with the body, and the feeling nature. Going further, we sense the presence of an intelligence previously unrecognized. This intelligence is non-verbal, non-mental, and non-dualistic; it may be compared to instinct, but is higher on the scale of evolution than conscious intelligence, while instinct is lower. This intelligence, which is activated through feeling, not thinking, is referred to as the wisdom of the body.

We become aware of the working of the wisdom of the body through sensation. Sensations are feelings; they may not always be pleasant, but their occurrence indicates that the body is balancing itself. If you do not understand that unpleasant sensations may be beneficial, you may become alarmed, and attempt to suppress them in an effort to feel better. However, if you know that unpleasant sensations can be signs that your body is healing itself, you will be able to relax, letting the body's process occur as it will. If you accept the feelings with love, you allow self-healing to occur. If you fight the feelings, you actually fight your own healing energies.

Allowing the wisdom of the body to work is basic to holistic healing on the physical level, and also relevant to healing on the psychological level. Strong emotional feelings are the psychic body's attempts to purge suppressed negativity. If you accept the feelings, you begin psychic healing.

You allow the wisdom of the body to heal you when you accept and experience feelings. The wisdom of the body is identical to the power that is invoked in the last step of processing, when the Higher Self guides the transformation which is taking place.

LOVING YOUR BODY

In contemporary society, there exists an enormous focus on body culturing. We normally approach body culturing with an idea of how the body should be – or more accurately, should appear – since most of our concern about the body is from a cosmetic viewpoint. We think our bodies are too fat, too thin, need to be in better shape, need more muscle. Esthetic considerations do have a legitimate place in the concern for health, but we are generally much too superficial in our goals.

Behind the concern with the appearance of the body is a sense of dislike, which can grow to the point of hatred. Hatred of the body is common. It is what motivates us to work so strenuously to change the body. Plan after plan – exercise, dieting, etc. – is entered upon to force the body into becoming the ideal that we hold in the mind. This forcing becomes a kind of violence we do to ourselves.

When we try to force the body to change, we are coming from the mind center, not the feeling center. We are in the mind because we have a goal, an ideal, a picture of what we want to be, what we think will bring us happiness. We relate to the body as an object that should be a certain way to please us. We therefore experience the body from a dualistic standpoint, never going beyond the ambivalence of like-dislike; it becomes impossible to be finally pleased with the body.

We are alienated
from the body

The reason we dislike the body is not because of what it looks like, or how it is, but because *we are not connected to it*, not in touch with it. We are not in the feeling center; therefore, we are alienated from the body. Being alienated from and disliking the body, we think the fault is in the body, and we strive to change the body. We are looking in the wrong direction. The fault is in our attitude toward the body, and if this basic attitude is not corrected, we will never be happy with the body, no matter what it looks like.

When viewed from the feeling center, the body is no longer an object, owned like any other possession. In contrast, the body is experienced as the self. Even though the body corresponds to the lower and not the Higher Self, the realization that the body is the self is powerful and meaningful. We transcend the tendency to think of the body as an object. We go beyond dualistic perception, and experience the body as energy.

Again the importance of attitude arises. We hardly ever understand how completely our lives are shaped by attitudes. Attitudes set up energy potentials in the aura, attracting corresponding conditions. When we dislike and try to change the body because of the dislike, the body essentially registers being rejected. It responds as anything or anyone will respond to rejection – by getting worse, instead of better. The effect of diet and exercise is very much secondary to the emotional message we give the body.

Of course, it is possible to bludgeon the body into shape to a certain extent, but it is an uphill fight, with impermanent results. Worse yet, we are left with the basic neurotic condition of being split against ourselves, of having to fight ourselves, because the body is the self.

Alienation and the resulting dislike of the body come from a deep and unconscious place. We have been rejecting the body for long periods of time, and have built strong, unconscious energy patterns that influence us. It is not possible to uncover and purge all this negativity overnight. Indeed, learning to love ourselves is the work of a lifetime.

We have fallen into a vicious circle. We dislike the body, and because we handle the dislike improperly, we reject ourselves. The rejection registers in the subconscious, creating more negative conditions such as being overweight or being in poor health, and we reject ourselves further. The pattern builds, furthermore, over many lifetimes.

Hatred of the body
is often projected

We hate ourselves, but suppress and project the hatred onto others. We hate them for no real reason except ones that we invent to justify our feelings. Or, we feel that others hate us. Since this may be true to a certain extent if our bodies are in bad shape, the projection is reinforced. We buy into the rejection, perceiving ourselves to be worse than we are.

In contrast, if we genuinely love the body as it is, imagine how different our experience would be. The healing power of love can bring about miraculous spontaneous changes. The body wants to balance itself, and has the intelligence to do so. It is prevented from doing so because it is crippled by messages of rejection.

But even if you want to love yourself and your body, the question remains of how to do this. You cannot intellectually love yourself. You cannot simply think what you consider to be loving thoughts about yourself, or pamper yourself, and assume that you are loving yourself, although actions like these may result from loving yourself.

Self-love is not a quality of the mind. Self-love comes about by developing the *feeling* capacity. You must learn how to accept and experience your feelings about your body, *even your hateful feelings*. This is what acceptance means. This is how you love yourself. This is what brings the catharsis.

When you learn how to accept and experience whatever hateful feelings you may have about yourself, you allow catharsis and real transformation to begin – you learn the art of loving yourself. Resisting, denying, trying to change, or being motivated by negative feelings only results in suppression.

Learning to love yourself first involves understanding what love is. For now, turn to your body with a readiness and openness to *listen,* rather than demanding. Listening with the Heart, or feeling, will start you in the direction of self-love.

BREATH

In our work, we use breath techniques to help integrate and release suppressed material.

In addition to supplying oxygen for respiration, the breath simultaneously draws in another quality, known as *prana*. Prana is the universal life force, the basic energy that sustains all living things. With proper techniques, the amount of prana that is taken in can be increased and directed to perform certain specific functions. Prana has an electrical quality, and interacts with the energy body and the aura; the conscious direction of prana is effective in clearing energy blocks in the body.

The connection between breathing and the psychological condition is recognized by scientists. Fritz Perls, the founder of Gestalt Therapy, stated, "Anxiety is the experience of breathing difficulty during any blocked excitement." We become unable to maintain proper breathing during the increased need for oxygen because of involuntary muscle clenching. Gestalt psychology, by the way, has a strong focus on the body.

Inhibition of breath can be observed in ourselves. We

encounter a challenging situation and respond by holding the breath, which is exactly what should not be done. You can learn to overcome the unconscious tendency to hold the breath by simply watching yourself, and reminding yourself to breathe fully whenever you feel stressed.

Breathe into stress

"Breathing into" means the conscious and deliberate focusing of prana, the life energy, into whatever stressful condition is present. The type of condition could be "negative," such as an unpleasant event or emotion, as well as "positive," such as being close to a loved one, because both negative and positive can be stressful and in need of integration.

Stress may be defined as the inability to be in the feeling center with whatever is happening, regardless of the nature of the event; the feeling center is blocked. Thrown out of the feeling center, we fall into the mind, becoming separated from what is before us. Breathing into the blocked center activates it, allowing the energy to rebalance.

You breathe into the blocked center by breathing deeply as you hold the feelings or event in your consciousness. The prana that is taken in with the breath has an intelligence of its own, much like the cells of the body do, and will find and stabilize the energy imbalance. The stressful condition may be physical or emotional pain, confrontation with another person, essentially anything that you encounter and must contend with, including joy. When you don't breathe into an event – or worse, if you hold your breath – anxiety is created, and you inhibit the ability to respond creatively.

The unblocking of energy is essentially a suppression-releasing function. Breath can be effective in performing this function, yet, as with bodywork, breath techniques by themselves cannot do the whole job. When the breath is incorporated with bodywork and a conscious psychological method for working on ourselves, satisfying progress with self-integration can be achieved.

During bodywork, you will cleanse suppressed energy. Various feelings will jump into your consciousness in the form of strong emotions, reliving past events, and so on. A major aid to the integration of this material is to breathe into it.

Specific breath techniques will be covered later.

In my body are my centers of consciousness. As I learn to feel in these centers, I come into contact with my real self. If I avoid feeling in these centers, I block myself. My love for myself grows as I joyously enter these centers, and lovingly behold what I find.

5

The Centers of Consciousness and Addiction

THE CHAKRAS

Before we begin discussing Integrative Processing itself, you should be familiar with the Eastern psycho-physiological system of the chakras. The chakra system fills a gap in contemporary psychology, giving us a matrix that can be used to classify energy needs that have been programmed into us as human beings. Using the chakra system is helpful because it supplies essential vocabulary and reference points, enabling us to more easily recognize the blocks within ourselves. Awareness, the first step in processing, is facilitated.

The chakras are energy centers, but may also be thought of as centers of consciousness, feeling, need, or experience. They are the "drives" to which psychology broadly refers. Each chakra, or center, as they are also known, provides a particular frame of reference through which our personal perception of the world comes to us. As we grow, we change our main focus from "lower" centers to "higher" ones. Our view of the world changes, our consciousness changes, we have a different experience. We develop the higher capacities of human potential.

There are many energy centers in the body, but usually only seven are considered to be of major importance. We all have at least a minimum of activity in each of these centers, but certain ones will be strongly developed while others will not, depending on the person. The individual balance of development through the centers determines our level of consciousness. Understanding the chakra system will give us insight into how blocks in the energy system come about, helping us recognize and deal with them more effectively in ourselves.

*The chakras are where
our blocks are located*

Because of our personal history of suppression, we have conditioned ourselves to block energy from flowing harmoniously through the centers. Reconditioning ourselves to allow energy to flow easily through centers is the goal of any psychological therapy.

Being centers of energy, the chakras are located in the energy body. The energy body, also called the astral, emotional, or psychic body, is actually identical in form to the physical body and exists coincident with it, although they may be separated under certain conditions, such as sleep.

In normal waking consciousness, we do not usually sense the difference between the energy and physical bodies. Feelings and emotions that actually occur in the chakras of the energy body are felt as if in the physical body. For practical purposes, then, we combine the two bodies in our work, referring to them as the body function, the home of the feeling capacity; hence, the emphasis on getting in touch with the physical body as the route to feeling.

"Chakra" is the Sanskrit word for "wheel." This name is appropriate because the chakras are actually in constant spinning motion. They are literally composed of energy, and, to the psychic vision, have a definite shape and color. Because they are energy, the chakras should be thought of as being tangible in nature; more subtle than the physical, yet substantial enough to be considered not just "mental."

It is because of this tangibleness that the chakras are referred to as "psycho-physiological." They represent states of consciousness, something that is often mistakenly considered to be only mental; but, having an energy-physical basis, they can be worked with through the body, as in any of the bodywork techniques, yielding substantial results in stimulating and aligning consciousness. You should realize that these centers are of basic importance in influencing your everyday state of being: how you feel, what you feel, what you are preoccupied with, etc.

The actual health of a center corresponds to its ability to receive and express universal energy into consciousness, through the function of feeling. Healthy chakras are vibrant. Unhealthy chakras are blocked and stagnant; the energy does not flow easily, leading to negative conditions such as depression, addiction, or poor health.

When the centers are stimulated and balanced with breath or bodywork, blocked energy is released. The resulting emotional cleansing can become an intense catharsis – it then becomes apparent how deeply the energy body influences our psychological condition. Energy balancing may also be aided with quartz and other healing crystals. The atomic vibrational structure of crystals enables them to interact with the aura, energy body, and chakras, clearing blocks and stimulating energy flow.

The chakras are located in
precise places in the body

The chakras are spaced from the base of the spine to the top of the head, in ascending order of consciousness. Although not normally sensed directly, as you increase your sensitivity to your body you will begin to feel the centers, as if they were located in the physical body. This ability is helpful for getting in touch with and stimulating the blocked energy. Yoga postures, in particular, develop sensitivity to the chakras, as well as to the movement of prana in the body.

There are seven main chakras, spaced from the bottom to the top of the body:

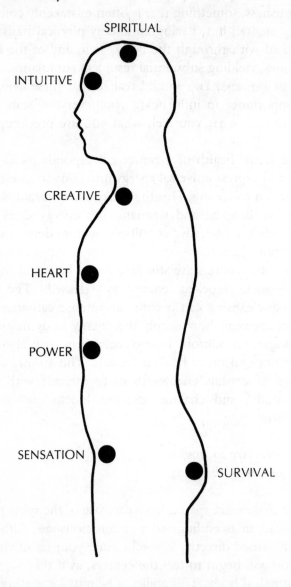

SPIRITUAL

INTUITIVE

CREATIVE

HEART

POWER

SENSATION

SURVIVAL

THE CHAKRAS

CHAKRA	LOCATION
7. Spiritual (Crown)	Top of Head
6. Intuitive	Forehead
5. Creative	Throat
4. Heart	Chest
3. Power	Solar Plexus/Navel
2. Sensation	Lower Abdomen/Perineum
1. Survival (Root)	Base of Spine

The first three centers, Survival, Sensation, and Power, are active, but unintegrated in most people today. Although these centers provide the raw force necessary to function in the material world, they are primarily selfish modes of consciousness, which manifest much negativity because they are usually suppressed and unintegrated.

The fourth center, the Heart, has the potential to be unselfish, but is usually aligned with the lower three centers. Love then has a possessive component.

The last three centers, the Creative, Intuitive, and Spiritual, more clearly mark the beginning of selfless orientation and higher consciousness. These three centers are not active in most of the world today. Love, when aligned with these higher centers, becomes unselfish.

Why is it better to be unselfish than selfish? For a selfish reason: to be happy. But what is the cause of our selfishness? The problem begins with the lack of ability to feel, to be closed off to our own energies, to be self-rejecting.

THE SENSE OF SEPARATION

Lack of contact with ourselves leads to the experience of *separation* from the world around us as well. The sense of separation is the basic cause of selfishness, anxiety, and unhappiness. We continually strive to overcome separation with unconscious, self-defeating behavior, such as substance abuse, conformity, consumerism, mass entertainment, dependent love, selfless sacrifice, striving for recognition, and addiction in general, but such efforts only provide temporary relief. The sense of separation and isolation is what is meant by the Eastern concept of the ego.

When selfishness is spoken about in a spiritual or psychological context, what is really being referred to is the sense of separation from others. Sometimes we become confused about selfishness, equating it with a lack of generosity. It should be understood that going beyond selfishness means more than just cultivating a generous attitude toward others. Generosity, of course, will be a result of higher consciousness, but it is also possible to be generous for entirely selfish reasons, and a spiritual seeker may choose to be giving only because it fits in with their spiritual self-image.

What is really meant by unselfishness is the altering of the basic perception that we are separate, isolated beings – a complete reversal of what is considered to be the normal perception today. Until this change of consciousness occurs, there is no point in trying to fake unselfishness. We only become hypocritical, although perhaps some good may come from a simple, more considerate attitude.

The lower centers
lead to isolation

You can never go beyond selfishness and isolation while immersed in the lower three centers of Survival, Sensation, and Power – that is simply their nature. The viewpoint from the lower centers is self-centered, isolated, and unhappy, even when success is attained on these levels. The lower centers reinforce the isolation that is experienced from a lack of feeling in general. You can grow into selflessness and non-isolation by activating your higher centers, through intelligent work on yourself.

Moreover, in the lower three centers, the law of Duality is strongly invoked. No lasting satisfaction in any accomplishment or possession can be found because of the alternating perception of pleasure/pain. Pleasure becomes a transparent facade, never quite covering the barren, inner isolation; pain is perceived as the reality from which we cannot escape. When we realize that most of the world, while attempting to operate from the lower three centers, is also suppressed and blocked on these same levels, we begin to get a picture of the real state of affairs.

THE FUNCTIONS OF INDIVIDUALITY

The chakras should not be confused with the functions of individuality. Aside from the Body function, there are the Mental, Intellectual, and Spiritual functions. Each function corresponds to a step of processing.

A chakra forms the link between all the functions. It is possible to be in a lower chakra and still bring full mental and intellectual capacities to the service of that center. Our abilities may be brilliant, and it may appear as if we are accomplishing with superb skill, but if we are focused on a lower center, we are functioning on a self-centered, and ultimately self-defeating level.

This is an important concept to appreciate. Our level of mental and intellectual ability has no correlation to the level of consciousness on which we operate.

In our culture, there is a misplaced emphasis on mental skills and personality. If we are smart, it is assumed that nothing else is needed. All of our education and training is intellectual. There is hardly any comprehension of emotional growth, which occurs through the development of the feeling centers. Why does this matter? Because if we are focused on lower centers, with no awareness of the higher, we will never find happiness and fulfillment.

DEVELOPMENT

The spacing of the centers vertically in the body is symbolic of the relative levels of consciousness, as well as the sequence of their development. Theoretically, the awakening of each center is preceded by the balanced functioning of the previous one. Centers do not always awaken in order, however, contributing to the energy imbalance, and therefore the psychological imbalance that is experienced.

The awakening of the chakras is evolutionary. We, as individuals, are growing and maturing as time goes by. The evolutionary scheme becomes clearer when the concept of reincarnation is included. It then makes better sense why growth takes so long, why individuals are at such different levels, why it is never too late to start working on yourself and foolish not to. We grow slowly, from life to life. Moreover, life is individually designed to provide just the right conditions to stimulate that growth, although they may seem harsh at the time.

*Be careful about awakening
the Heart prematurely*

The chakras awaken step by step. Our race as a whole is now at the point of developing the Heart center. It is not possible to move forward into the Heart, however, by concentrating on the Heart alone and ignoring the suppression and chaos in the first three centers. The Survival, Sensation, and Power centers must be integrated before the Heart can truly function. Spiritual seekers often make the mistake of trying to integrate the Heart ahead of the lower centers. Efforts to awaken the Heart prematurely lead to unstable experience in the Heart, mixed with the still unreleased negativity of the lower centers.

As integration and clearing of the lower centers proceeds, which can be accomplished effectively through the techniques you are learning, the character of these centers will change. This change cannot be willed or manipulated, but happens automatically. When integrated, a center will start to behave differently, in a more grown-up manner. It will come under control; it will be less self-oriented. There will be less of a problem with dualistic manifestation, and the center will supply the power for the center above.

If a lower center is integrated, the next center above will spontaneously begin to function, gradually and naturally. The reason we don't gently progress into the Heart center is because the lower three centers are not integrated, even though they are active. When integrated, the three lower centers become a dynamo of power, supporting the spontaneous awakening of the Heart. If we attempt to awaken the Heart without this support, it is likely we will not have the energy required.

INTEGRATION AND ADDICTION

A center is considered *integrated* when there is a balanced experience of the dualistic qualities of that center. This means we have learned to recognize and accept both the "positive" and "negative" poles of the duality, incorporating them into a basically positive experience. There is no large amount of avoidance and suppression occurring, and previously suppressed energies have been cleared. If we cannot realistically say that we have learned to experience the negative pole in a harmonious way, we at least have learned how to accept it and work with it constructively – for example, through processing.

Unintegrated, we become *addicted* at various levels of experience. We become addicted to the "positive" side of any one dualistic experience because we are not willing to face the "negative" side of its duality. We seek to escape to the positive side, often not even realizing that both sides are dependent upon one another for their existence.

However, because of the nature of dualism, the more we try to experience the positive, the more we also generate the negative. We become frustrated. We attempt to suppress the negative with more experiences of the positive, and the addiction cycle builds. Addiction occurs not only at the Sensation level, where it is normally recognized, but at all five lower centers. We develop a deep hunger for a particular need, but no matter what we do to try to satisfy the hunger, it remains, or even becomes worse. Addictive behavior is also known as "compulsive."

Addiction requires psychic energy

Each addiction can be related to a certain center of consciousness. Addiction is the result of an energy imbalance in that particular center. The center is blocked, and does not experience the normal energy flow of a healthy center. The center is blocked because of our suppression. Through the avoidance of feelings in the center, *we* create the block. To maintain the block requires energy, and this energy is supplied by the addiction.

The cravings that come up for a particular object of addiction are learned. Through experience, we learn that energy can be obtained from a certain source, and used to maintain the block. When the block begins to weaken, because the suppressing energy is getting low, we begin to get glimpses of what is being suppressed, and we experience discomfort, anxiety, depression, and so on. We then seek the addictive experience once more, to gain the energy required to maintain the block to our feelings. The feelings are re-suppressed, over and over.

Because the suppressed feelings will continue to build, the suppressing energy must also keep increasing, resulting in the extraordinary means that must be used to provide the energy. We enter the expanding cycle of addiction. All addiction provides an extra supply of energy, taken either from external sources or from the body's internal reserves.

Usually, we are addicted to a center's complement to the negative experience. However, we can also escape to another, usually higher center, and draw energy from there. The higher center will suppress the pain of the lower center. Thus, if we experience anxiety from an unintegrated first center, we could attempt to suppress it by becoming compulsively addicted to wealth and security, but we could also suppress it by compulsive seeking in any higher center, such as sex, power, love, even creativity.

The first step in breaking addiction is understanding how it works. When you know why you act compulsively, you weaken the power of the addiction. You must stop yielding to the addictive experience. Process the addictive urge as well as the feeling that you are suppressing with the addiction. Processing can be the main approach, but other approaches are helpful as well, such as therapy, group support, or medical support in cases of chemical dependency.

When you confront feelings related to addiction, you meet your demon head-on. You must realize that you are clearing accumulated negativity: proceed patiently and gently as well as sensibly. You must not demand too much of yourself, nor should you yield too easily. The delicate balance, the sense of making steady progress, must be established. As you learn how to work on yourself, you will acquire new tools that will help you tremendously. You will be able to cleanse negativity that previously compelled you to act in addictive ways.

THE CENTERS OF CONSCIOUSNESS

1. Survival

The Survival center is the most basic to human beings, as well as to other life forms. This energy center is located just below the base of the spine. It is concerned with physical survival, security, health, money, and is the home of the most primal fears, including the fear of death. Indeed, all concerns for matters in the Survival center are really backed by the fear of death. We are not usually conscious of this, thinking that we are concerned about more immediate and superficial circumstances.

Being focused but not integrated in the Survival center means the world is perceived as a jungle, where one must fight for survival. We become concerned with our own needs, and are primarily selfish. Addiction to anything that represents security is likely.

Addiction means that no matter how much "security" is attained, feelings of insecurity and fear will continue, because of the strong dualistic nature of this center. When fear is the motivation for pursuing and attaining material goals, that fear is not eliminated by the attainment of those goals. On the contrary, when we acquire more, we think we need more, and the cycle never ends.

Of course, basic physical needs must be met, but what is important is our sense of discrimination. Lack of integration means we will be unrealistic in perceiving what our real needs are, and will never be satisfied and secure, no matter how much we have. We will be coming from fear, and fear will not be eliminated by the attainment or possession of whatever we think we need to be secure.

What we really do is just find new situations on which to project our fear. We take care of one "need," and the fear seems to go away, but then it surfaces somewhere else, and we think we now have to take care of another need. These needs appear to be real and justified. We don't see that it is our suppressed fear that brings them to us. The cycle continues because we never confront and integrate fear itself, which is behind all the addictive impulses of the Survival center. We confront fear directly in our work. The result is integration and clearing, not temporary suppression.

If we are unintegrated on the Survival level, it is because we resist and suppress the fear of loss, poverty, physical pain or disease, but mainly, the fear of death. As a result, the suppressed fear constantly emerges as anxiety. We become anxiety-ridden, trapped and preoccupied with Survival consciousness.

We arbitrarily project anxiety onto situations, becoming

suspicious, distrustful, and paranoid. We experience isolation, because the first center is the most self-centered of all. We imagine that we would be happy and secure with one more possession, a better job, more money, or whatever. Such are the fantasies that result from being focused but unintegrated in the first center. As you may have noticed, this is where most of the world is immersed today.

The feelings related to this center that will respond to processing include: Fear in general, but more specifically, fear resulting from the threat of material loss, lack, bodily injury and disease, death; general anxiety, possessiveness, selfishness, insecurity, paranoia; the sense of limitation or delay; having your physical or psychological boundaries invaded; the desire for protection, safety, and basic survival.

If you have integrated this center, you are also functioning in higher centers. You will experience the Survival center in a more positive way. You will understand that change is unavoidable in life, and that clinging to any possession out of fear keeps you locked into a cycle of dependence. If you accept that uncertainty is an inherent part of existence, you will not feel as if you must compulsively guard against lack. Placing your trust in the flow of life, you find yourself provided for. Acceptance of insecurity and uncertainty will paradoxically bring about feelings of stability, security, and groundedness. The Survival center then serves as the foundation for a more HUMANISTIC outlook.

2. Sensation

The Sensation center, located in the lower abdomen, is the next major center activated in our evolution. This is the center of sensuality and sexuality. The world becomes the source of *pleasure gratification* when viewed from the Sensation center, and people are viewed as objects to be used.

Although sex is the primary manifestation of sensation needs, they can also take the form of cravings for touch, eating, drinking, drugs, smoking, entertainment, T.V., music, luxury, or any other sensual pleasure. All these activities stimulate the second center, and all can serve as the focus of addiction if the center is unintegrated. Cravings on the Sensation level are therefore somewhat interchangeable, and that is why if you are sexually frustrated, you can work off the energy with food or entertainment.

Because Sensation is the next center up from Survival, it can serve as relief for that center. If you are unintegrated in the first, you can escape to the second. In functioning on the higher level, you can forget your insecurities and feel as if you are in control for the time being. In our society, entertainment and sex are very important to keep survival anxiety suppressed.

Lack of integration here is usually concerned with sexual issues. There is a basic and unconscious rejection of the sexual impulse, resulting in sexual repression. This leads to sexual addiction, and as a result, satisfaction is impossible to achieve. Sexual addiction can take either of two forms.

The first is that no matter how much sex we have, we do not find the release that we seek, and we continue to want more. Sexual needs become compulsive. We may even think that we have no sexual problem because of our capacity to engage in it. The second form of sexual addiction results in inability to actually engage in sexual relationship because of self-blocking. If the Sensation center is integrated, sex is approached in a balanced and reasonable manner.

The feelings that can be processed in this center include the feeling of sexual desire, frustration, compulsiveness, violation, inhibition, revulsion; cravings and frustrated desires for touch, food, alcohol, drugs, smoking, entertainment, TV, and the physical sensations that such frustration may bring up.

The second center is also the social center, and we all need to play, as well as participate in communal festivity and art, which can also function on this level. Successful integration leads to a CULTURED society.

3. Power

The third major chakra is Power, located at the solar plexus/navel. This center is the psychological home of the ego, having to do with needs for aggressiveness, competitiveness, recognition, self-image, status, and in general, *significance*. We attempt to satisfy these needs by identifying with possessions, acquaintances, talents, accomplishments, or anything that appears to enhance our importance. It is possible to escape from the fear of the first center or sexual dysfunction of the second center into Power, only to become trapped here.

If we are particularly unintegrated on the Power level, we can be unaware of how much we crave recognition from others, and the extent to which we push ourselves to get it. We become addicted to success or accomplishment in the hunger for recognition. However, no amount of recognition can actually satisfy us. We always feel the need for more, and continue to compulsively pursue the non-attainable. This is the center where we must learn "we are enough," simply as we are.

We can become successful on the material level, hardly sensing the emptiness behind. Emptiness is a dualistic aspect of the Power center. The emptiness tells us that we have no significance. We cannot accept this, and we become driven. Instead of being unconsciously motivated by and suppressing emptiness, we must learn to work with and integrate this feeling.

The distorted need for significance can surface at any level of activity. Intellectuals, scientists, artists, even – and possibly especially – spiritual seekers, can be unconsciously driven by hunger for significance: to be "more."

In working with the Power center, it must be understood that I am not condemning accomplishment, success, possessions, or recognition when they happen as a result of real contribution. I am just trying to point out the importance of bringing under control the compulsive and destructive impulse for recognition that results from the unintegrated Power center.

Most of us are driven by this more than we realize.

Distorted significance needs can take the form of compulsive Power trips. We sense our importance and influence over others because of our position, which in turn depends on possessions, knowledge, skills, etc. Power trips can be completely engulfing, especially to one who is not used to them.

In Power trips, we actually feed on the energy of others. The *attention* they are forced or persuaded to give constitutes the actual transference of energy. This is experienced vividly by any performer, or anyone who is up in front of an audience, happening less dramatically in one-to-one encounters. The transference of energy becomes addictive – possibly the most addictive of any of the lower centers.

The problem with Power addiction is that it must be experienced dualistically. The incredible highs are balanced by equally depressive lows. The amplitude of the swings, especially for persons in front of an audience, becomes overwhelming. The addicted person does not usually understand what is happening, and often develops other second-center addictions to try to get through the lows, furthering the downward spiral.

The Power center corresponds to the traditional male role. Men are driven intensely when there is a lack of integration here, because their male identity is threatened. If they can relate to a more androgynous sense of self, they can handle unintegrated Power feelings more easily. Women need to develop this center to balance the inner male/female polarity. This does not mean that they should merely condition themselves to be more aggressive, but should integrate the feelings in the center, allowing a genuine, non-dominating strength to emerge.

When we identify with projected Power needs and then experience frustration, we experience the emotion we call anger. Anger is thought of as originating in the Power center, but it is felt and fed by all three lower centers.

Integration of this center starts with the awareness of the futility of trying to satisfy unintegrated Power needs, and the refusal to be driven by them any longer. By processing Power impulses instead of being motivated by them, an integrated balance of self-affirmation with social purpose is achieved.

The feelings related to this center that will respond to processing include: Anger, aggressiveness, hostility, frustration; the sense of worthlessness, inadequacy, helplessness, weakness, emptiness; feelings of being blocked by others or by circumstances, being used, manipulated, or cheated, being blamed or mistreated; not getting the credit you deserve; the desire for significance or importance, the desire for approval, recognition, and attention, the desire for influence over others, the desire to control; feelings related to the father and male side of the character in general; the pain of not having gotten the fathering you needed.

Becoming more integrated in the Power center, we see that there is a human need for accomplishment, but it is such that we don't have to attach our name to the work to feel the sense of fulfillment. We are not looking primarily for recognition, but for significant contribution. However, there will always be the human side that seeks and needs the recognition of others. We should not resist feeling this aspect of ourselves, although we should not be motivated by it. In processing, attempt to change nothing. Accept yourself as you are, with whatever ego attachments you have, but don't act on them. Integration of the Power center will lead to a more balanced expression of STRENGTH.

4. Heart

The Heart chakra is located in the center of the chest. The first of the higher centers, the Heart is where the potential for real humanity starts to develop. We become aware of our connection to others.

The Heart is the center of unconditional love. Most of us would agree that unconditional love is highly desirable, but then we criticize ourselves for not being able to live up to such an ideal. The problem is not that we can't live up to the ideal, but that our concept of the ideal is incorrect. We must expand our understanding of what is meant by unconditional love.

We assume that loving someone means liking them very much. Liking someone usually implies that we would not like them if certain conditions were not met. In relationships, we have a list of conditions that must be fulfilled, or we will no longer be "in love." This is called "dependent" love, because it is dependent on conditions, but also because we become psychologically dependent on the other.

Dependent love is tied to the lower centers, and is self-oriented. It is experienced dualistically, which is why it never lasts. In reality, we probably never outgrow having a certain amount of dependent love in our closest relationships, but as we grow, the dependency becomes less, and our dualistic swings also become less. We become conscious of ourselves, and how we approach the relationship.

What, then, is real love? Love is acceptance, and unconditional love is unconditional acceptance. To love someone unconditionally means that you are able to accept them even though you might not like the way you are *presently perceiving them.*

To love yourself unconditionally means that you are able to accept your own feelings at any time, pleasant or unpleasant. Self-acceptance of feelings as they are leads to self-love, and naturally extends to accepting and loving others. Self-acceptance is an ability that takes understanding and developing. It comes about as a result of higher consciousness, but can also be developed, and will lead to higher consciousness.

It may not even be apparent to you why you would want such a consciousness. All that can be said is that you must have the intuition that higher consciousness is possible, and that it can provide the answer to the problems that you face. Higher consciousness can lead to a form of happiness that cannot really be imagined before you have arrived, but it does in reality exist. This is what poets and prophets have always been trying to communicate.

The Heart is the feminine center. Women more easily feel and express the caring and nurturing aspects of the higher

Heart than men. At the same time, they are perhaps more vulnerable to the lower aspects of the Heart, the dependency and emotionalism. Men must learn to activate and integrate this center as a most primary part of their work on themselves.

The Heart center is where we feel lonely. We must understand that loneliness is only the dualistic complement to the pleasant feeling we get from dependent love. If you can integrate loneliness, you will transcend the duality of dependent love/loneliness, and be able to begin experiencing real love. If you cannot integrate loneliness, you remain attached to the addictive cycle of dependent love.

The feelings related to the Heart that can be processed include: Loneliness, isolation, sadness, shame, heartbreak, jealousy; grief over the loss of others; being abandoned, not being taken care of, not receiving the love you deserve, not being accepted; being hated or hating others; the desire for love, acceptance, belonging; feelings related to the mother and the feminine side of the character in general; feelings of not having gotten the mother love you needed.

As you integrate the Heart, you experience unconditional self-acceptance. You are no longer dependent on others for their acceptance, you are whole within yourself. As love without dependency or external cause grows within, you realize the higher aspects of the Heart. Your love grows until you naturally feel the desire to help others. You give without attachment; you are not emotionally dependent on the results of giving. You develop the capacity to nurture. Others will sense that you do not give with conditions in mind. You experience UNCONDITIONAL LOVE.

5. Creative

The Creative center is the fifth chakra, located in the throat. It is the center of self-expression. The fact that the Creative comes after the Heart center implies that genuine self-expression is possible only after the Heart has been integrated. Yet there are many people, in public life, for example, who have the skills of expression, but who are not coming from the Heart.

This is possible because the *lower* aspects of the Creative center can still be powerful. Unintegrated, the Creative will serve the lower three centers, particularly the Power center. The result is expressive powers that are self-oriented.

When the Heart is active and integrated, the Creative center begins functioning in its higher capacity. When motivated by love, we act in a *selfless manner*. We are not doing for ourselves, not even for the subtle gain that can be felt from many "unselfish" acts. Being motivated by love transports us into a new relationship with the universe, and just because we are not doing for ourselves, what we do comes back to us, multiplied. We gain, without expecting to. We activate the Law of Prosperity, the higher function of the Creative center. The Law of Prosperity is an aspect of the expressive powers of the Creative center – the law that what you put out returns to you, increased.

To have true experience of Prosperity consciousness, you must first be integrated in the Heart. People hear about Prosperity, and try to awaken it in themselves. The problem is that they are coming from fear and are only trying to satisfy their addictions. They are not coming from the love of the integrated Heart, and Prosperity is not activated by fear, but by love. Being a higher function of the Creative center, Prosperity cannot be used for personal gain, as many of the lower qualities can.

This limitation is really for our own good. If we were able to use the principle behind Prosperity at our present level of growth, we would bring all kinds of misfortune to ourselves. We would be putting out mostly fear and other negativities, which is what would return to us, magnified. To activate Prosperity, we must first work on the lower centers, because the Heart cannot be integrated without the three lower centers first coming into line.

The feelings of this center that can be processed include: not being able to express yourself or communicate; inner emptiness resulting from intense creative work, being creatively blocked; the desire to create or express.

Artists and creative people are largely working from the Creative center. However, in order for work to be inspired, it must be supported by the integrated Heart center. Art must be done for the love of doing it. If the motivation is mixed with lower-center survival or recognition needs, true artistic experience is thwarted. There may be a mixture of what one's motivation consists of, and the creative experience will alternate accordingly.

When you come from the Heart, you evoke the pure joy of the real creative act. When you come from Power, for example, you fall back into the dualistic experience of pleasure when you perceive that you are getting approval for your work, and pain when your hunger for recognition is unsatisfied. You limit your capacity for true EXPRESSION.

6. Intuitive

The sixth center is known as the Intuitive, or Witness center. It is located on the forehead, just above the eyebrows – the classical "Third Eye" point. Here, the capacity for intuitive knowledge and feeling in general is activated.

The Third Eye point represents the harmonious joining of left and right-brain functions. The left-brain capacity is the logical, reasoning, rational mind that we normally use. The right brain is our intuitive, creative, feeling side, which is often dormant in our culture. When activated by the functioning Third Eye, we gain access to and awaken the right brain. Reasoning continues to have a place in our lives, but we now can use a *balanced* amount of thinking and feeling in confronting life. We don't try to reason where we should be intuitive.

The feelings of this center that can be processed include intuitive feelings in general.

The Witness capacity of the sixth center is a special quality which is the beginning of what might be called the "transcendental" consciousness of the Higher Self. We go beyond the perception of ourselves as an isolated ego-self. We don't experience doing-to, or being done-to, but just "doing." The doer and done-to become one. This may sound removed from any consciousness that you have experienced, or may even care to, but the Witness center is actually the most important of them all in our work on ourselves.

The Witness becomes our main vantage point; we awaken it first, before getting into the suppressed contents of the lower centers. Lower-center material is more easily integrated through the capacity of *non-identification* and the healing power that is realized through the activated Witness center.

You will see that once you have become familiar with the principles involved, activation of the Witness is not a remote mystical possibility, but a concrete, practical, accessible form of consciousness that can easily be used in everyday life. The activation of the Heart makes it possible for us to love ourselves, but the Witness marks the true beginning of TRANSCENDENCE.

7. Spiritual

The Spiritual, or Crown chakra, as it is also known, is located at the top of the head, just outside the body. It is the center of cosmic consciousness, where the individual self realizes its oneness with the Universal Self.

To approach the Spiritual, you must be integrated in all the centers below, and be living completely in the moment. Any desire is enough to bring you out of the moment, and back into your time-based existence.

You are fortunate if you can experience cosmic consciousness for even a brief period. It is in the future for the majority of us. To attempt to describe this essentially indescribable experience would be a misplaced effort. It is enough to know that such a consciousness exists, and that it is the culmination of human evolution, the experience of ONENESS.

PART II

INTEGRATIVE
PROCESSING

THE STEPS OF
INTEGRATIVE PROCESSING

I. AWARENESS

FOCUS ON THE PRESENT
DO NOT SEEK UNDERSTANDING
MAINTAIN FUNCTIONAL AWARENESS
IDENTIFY YOUR FEELINGS
IDENTIFY THE DUALISTIC PATTERN
OWN YOUR EXPERIENCE
AFFIRM THAT YOU ARE PROCESSING

II. ACCEPTANCE

ACCEPT YOURSELF
ACCEPT YOUR FEELINGS
ACCEPT THE EXTERNAL
BE NON-REACTIVE
IDENTIFY SELF-REJECTION
ACTIVATE YOUR HEART CENTER

III. DIRECT EXPERIENCE

ENTER THE FEELING
USE BREATH AND BODYWORK
INTEGRATE FEELINGS BEHIND THE ADDICTION
EXPERIENCE FEELINGS DURING MEDITATION
BRING UP UNRESOLVED ISSUES FROM THE PAST
BRING YOUR FEELINGS TO A CRISIS
OBSERVE YOUR TOLERATION POINT

IV. TRANSFORMATION

ACTIVATE THE WITNESS CENTER –
BRING IN HEALING ENERGY
ALLOW PSYCHIC ENERGIES TO BALANCE
OPEN YOURSELF TO TRANSFORMATION
TRUST
UNDERSTAND PSYCHIC CLEANSING
RECOGNIZE THE HINDRANCES
TAKE PART IN GROUP WORK

I enter complete awareness of my feelings.
I realize that many of my feelings are
negative and painful. I take
responsibility for my feelings,
understanding that the purpose of the
events of my life is only to make me
conscious of these feelings that I carry
in my subconscious. I choose to work
with these feelings as they come up,
and not to suppress them again.

6

Awareness

Awareness is the capacity beyond the mind that can observe both thoughts and feelings. Awareness, the first of the four steps of Integrative Processing, is part of that function of the individuality called the intellect.

Many people confuse the functions of the mind and intellect, making no real distinction. The mind is that part of us which thinks and reasons in a somewhat impersonal manner, almost like a machine. The intellect is that part of us which knows. The intellect is closer to our real identity, although it would be a mistake to consider either of these functions the real person.

Awareness is not an end unto itself, as some may believe. You may be aware of your real feelings, but if you do not know how to handle this awareness, you may still be immersed in self-rejection and suppression, not allowing the feelings to complete their cycle and be released. Awareness is only an intellectual function. The intellect does not connect to life's experiences. It does not have the capacity to be "in the moment," perceiving and responding spontaneously. Nevertheless, you can make no real progress on yourself until you become aware. It is the first step.

FOCUS ON THE PRESENT

Much of the focus of traditional psychotherapy involves going back into the past to try to uncover suppressed feelings, but in our work, probing the past becomes secondary to working with the present.

Our present feelings are, in fact, formed by the past. Our past subconscious conditioning is what determines how we perceive what happens to us, through the mechanism of projection: suppressed emotions are projected onto present situations. Therefore, looking at the present is also looking into the subconscious.

When you realize this deeply, the world will become fascinating, because you understand that your subconscious programming is right here – this very moment – right in front of you. There is no need to attempt to push into the subconscious. On the contrary, you cannot avoid it. Your interactions with the world, and even with yourself, serve as the stimulus for bringing up your blocks. You experience your energy patterns in the present. Of course, the blocks were formed in the past, but it is not necessary to analyze the original cause. Processing is a *present-centered* self-therapy. Although you may also work with present feelings about a past event, you do not necessarily analyze the event.

DO NOT SEEK UNDERSTANDING

At one time, psychology believed that understanding the cause of the blocks in the personality was key to the elimination of the blocks. Acceptance was considered essential in resolving the condition, but it was assumed that one had to understand before one could accept. The psychological schools of analysis were founded, where years were spent investigating the subconscious. People caught up in analysis became intellectual, articulate, and knowledgeable about their blocks, but remained blocked, because they avoided functioning on the feeling level, where integration takes place. Indeed, both analyst and patient became characterized as lifeless and non-spontaneous.

Understanding is not
required for acceptance

Most contemporary schools of psychotherapy agree that understanding the cause of blocks in the psyche is not required for their release. Psychology has evolved into what are called the humanistic and transpersonal schools. These current schools deal much less with analysis, although there may be some, and focus primarily on other forms of therapy.

This therapy brings about the surfacing and experience of suppressed emotion, without necessarily elaborating on its cause or origin. Understanding the cause is not considered essential for the acceptance of emotions. You might think you understand why you are unable to love, based on childhood conditioning, for example, but that does nothing to solve the problem. Integration with the hostile, hating self within will cause the catharsis, and enable you to go beyond being blocked at the love/hate level.

Yet, many people still mistakenly feel that in order to work on themselves, they must go into the past – either remote or recent – and understand what happened. The urge to understand is popular in our culture because of the misplaced emphasis on the intellect, and lack of comprehension concerning the feeling side. Even seasoned spiritual travelers can still be unclear about the proper role of understanding.

Do not confuse understanding with awareness. Awareness means being conscious about a feeling; it does not imply that the origin and history of the feeling are understood. Understanding is not to be considered valueless, only that it is not essential for integration and healing. Integration occurs as a result of acceptance, not understanding. Understanding is likely to occur spontaneously, without effort, at the proper time, *after* integration has occurred, along with a catharsis of blocked energy. Insights will flash into awareness, connections will be apparent, and the emotion that accompanies catharsis will show that suppressed energy has been released. Understanding can then be used to make any required changes, or to insure that past mistakes are not repeated.

Nevertheless, you should not expect integration to come from understanding, nor should you seek understanding directly. The very effort keeps the mind preoccupied so that integration cannot take place. The mind takes on a tremendous and futile burden when it insists on understanding.

Moreover, when you try to understand, your biases keep you from clear perceptions. Suppose you try to understand the cause of any current psychological condition within yourself. You may go back to childhood; but since you are searching for a specific link, you will choose from all your childhood experiences the ones that seem to provide the causal connection. You probably had many other strong experiences that did not "result" in a current condition. Why did you react traumatically to certain ones? You ignore the possibility of the condition being latent, and the event merely activating it. If causes are to be traced to a past existence, which is usually not part of conscious memory, you can appreciate the difficulties involved in relying on understanding original causes. Your current feelings are exactly the same as the ones you suppressed sometime in the past, probably extending into past lives. They reappear, in apparently different circumstances, but the suppressed energy that is attempting to cleanse is the same. There is no need to go into the past to analyze, search, or understand what happened. If you are in touch with your feelings *now*, you have all the information you need to begin healing, which will happen if you just accept and experience those feelings.

MAINTAIN FUNCTIONAL AWARENESS

In working on ourselves, our main focus is on our feelings. Functional awareness is simply the ability to be in touch with your feelings, to be conscious of what is happening in your inner world as you function in the outer world. It is the recognition of feelings as they occur. Functional awareness may seem a simple matter, but in fact it is a difficult step for most people. This is one of the places where the objectivity of a therapist can be helpful.

Self-awareness
must be a priority

One of the reasons for difficulty with functional awareness is our sense of priorities. The lifestyle of the average person is such that little time is available for self-awareness. Our lives seem to be incessantly busy because we are caught up in the endless quest to satisfy addictions, which requires time, energy, and money. Or, we may feel that we have legitimate responsibilities, such as a family. Either way, even though it seems that we are acting to satisfy needs, we become goal-oriented.

Preoccupation with goals necessarily makes us less conscious of what is happening within; self-awareness becomes secondary. You may think it is possible to maintain goal-orientation and still be aware of your feelings, but the subtle priority of goals over feelings conditions you. In the long run, the ability to feel what you are experiencing is diminished. Feelings simply do not enter the threshold of conscious awareness. You become unaware of your inner condition because it does not matter; you become engulfed in the rush for results.

Feelings become repressed. They occur, but there is no awareness of them. The result is stress. We must change our priorities and become more sensitive to inner feelings. Many times we learn to do this only after a breakdown, such as burn-out, a heart attack, alcohol or drug addiction, which results from this kind of inner neglect. Then, we finally get the message. As we turn our attention to feelings, giving them the priority they deserve, we discover much more than was expected, and that the underlying emotional entanglement goes deep.

It's not goal-orientation alone that makes us insensitive to our feelings. The simple and often involuntary habit of avoiding unpleasantness gradually erodes both the willingness and ability to be in touch with ourselves.

Another reason that we allow insensitivity to ourselves to build is that we don't know what to do with negative feelings when we do become aware of them. We may think that we are handling them by ignoring them or by escaping into various diversions, but instead, we suppress.

Some people think they are being selfish if they take their own feelings into consideration, and may, in fact, consciously or unconsciously pride themselves on their "unselfishness" when they pay no attention to their own feelings. A parent, for example, may put children or spouse first, and not consider his or her own feelings equally valid. This kind of martyrdom is sometimes an unconscious power maneuver, calculated to instill guilt in others, but not always. It may simply be another way of avoiding one's own feelings.

Feelings become denied

Denial is common, and is one of the first hurdles to therapy and emotional growth, whether you are working alone or with a therapist. In denial, you simply do not know that you have certain feelings. The feelings are repressed, and do not come within conscious view. You must be very careful that you do not deny your real feelings. Becoming aware of your feelings is a skill that will develop as it is exercised, but you must begin to exercise it.

You must expect that as you look within, pain and chaos will be encountered. However, knowing how to handle this turmoil will bring you the confidence to face it with courage instead of doubt. As the pain emerges and you clear it instead of again suppressing, you will experience the elation that comes from the release of buried and traumatic tensions.

What needs to be emphasized is a sense of *priority*. When you give priority to inner feelings, you begin integration; you become feeling-oriented instead of goal-oriented.

This shift in values may be thought of as the beginning of spiritual life, and the turning away from materialistic life. You learn that what is within is most important; that you can dissolve the compulsion and pain that has been suppressed in the past but has not been eliminated from your life.

IDENTIFY YOUR FEELINGS

Feelings usually occur in relation to an event or circumstance in our lives. Any recurring or strong feeling signifies that suppressed material is coming up, and that processing is appropriate. We are concerned with several types of feelings:

> **Pure Feelings**
> **Emotions**
> **Moods**
> **Attitudes**
> **Impulses/Desires**
> **Addictive Compulsions**
> **Body Sensations**

You should always take care to identify the feelings *behind* the event. If you are encountering hardship, you must integrate the feelings that the hardship brings up in you. You may be feeling the pain of not having certain necessities, but behind this is the fear of survival. Both the sense of lack and the fear are to be processed.

When you start processing the most apparent feeling concerning an event, as the feeling becomes integrated usually other, linked feelings will emerge. It is important to keep tracing back to all the linked feelings behind any event. However, linked feelings usually cannot be uncovered intellectually. They must be allowed to reveal themselves as you process.

For example, if you have an argument with someone, you may be impatient and angry, but behind these feelings are other, more basic ones. Your sense of personal worth may have been challenged – the feeling of inadequacy emerges to be processed. Behind this yet may be other, more basic feelings. All these feelings must be integrated. It is not always easy to trace back to all the feelings behind an event, but being familiar with the characteristics of the chakras that we discussed in Chapter Five will give you the tools to identify and not deny feelings as they occur in any experience.

Feelings are not caused
by outer events

Usually, we assume a causal connection between the internal and the external; we think that the outer event causes our feelings. As we progress in our work, it becomes evident that the assumption of causality is false, even though it may not be obvious now. The inner and the outer occur simultaneously; one does not "cause" the other. Understanding this makes self-acceptance easier, especially the dropping of blame.

Learn to distinguish
between thoughts and feelings

Feelings are not always accompanied by outer events. Instead, a feeling may be accompanied by a thought, and sometimes we may purposely use a certain thought to bring up a feeling for integration. The thought serves as a stimulus for the feeling, just as the outer event does. Even so, it is not primarily the thought that is being processed, but the feeling. It is helpful to distinguish between thoughts and feelings, and to understand that we are working with energy, as it manifests in feelings. A thought that has no charged feeling associated with it would not even hold our interest. Feelings are energy-based.

They occur in the chakras, get blocked in the chakras, and the ultimate purpose of all growth therapy is to loosen the energy blocks.

Learn to recognize your feelings

Pure Feelings are feelings that are not filtered through the personal belief system, and may be physical, physiological, or psychological. You may be tired, alert, hungry, or filled; you may have encountered loss, gain, rejection, or welcome. Pure feelings have no emotional content. They are matter-of-fact sensations of objective/subjective experience. If you are aware of a pure feeling, there is no need to process; you are already in the moment with your experience, and you will not experience stress.

Emotions result when pure feelings are filtered through beliefs. Because you believe you should not be tired, you become depressed; because you believe you should not be rejected, you become unhappy. Emotions indicate a significant underlying belief when they recur with forcefulness. They may be clarified by relating them to the center of consciousness that produces them. The kinds of emotions we are concerned with include: fear, anxiety, sexual impulses, food and substance addictions, anger, power compulsions, sadness, depression, loneliness, possessiveness, helplessness, relationship dynamics, and any other emotion you can identify in yourself. If it is at all possible for you to see how you create emotions by filtering pure feelings through beliefs, it will help you integrate your emotions. However, this is not normally possible, because beliefs are largely unconscious. In our work, as I have said, we do not attempt to intellectually confront and change beliefs, because beliefs are maintained by suppressed energy and are difficult to deliberately change. Instead, we integrate the emotion produced by the belief. Integrating the emotion brings about a clearing of the suppressed energy, and the belief is let go of in an unforced way.

Moods are vague feelings of discomfort or distress that are not severe enough to be thought of as major problems, but stay with us, almost as repeating themes. You may have the feeling that you don't look good, that you are never comfortable, are unsure of yourself, not at ease with others, hate to spend money, are abnormally hungry, nervous, never satisfied, etc. Seemingly innocuous moods represent other, more basic, energy patterns. Moods should not be dismissed. They can generally be traced back to the first through fourth energy centers, and will relate to suppressed issues such as insecurity, sexual imbalance, low self-esteem, loneliness, etc. Working with moods will probably contribute as much to self-integration as working with the heavy emotional events in your life. Meditation is the best time for working with recurrent moods.

Attitudes are energy-based, and so may be processed. Attitudes represent our defenses, our opinions, and in general, suppressed patterns.

Impulses and **Desires** relate to motivation; they are the inner urgings to satisfy perceived needs. Rather than acting on it and running after the illusion of satisfaction, you can release the energy of a negative impulse or desire by processing it. Impulses are generally more irrational than desires. With desires, we think we understand why we need something, even though many of our desires are compulsive and can never really be satisfied.

Addictive Compulsions are impulses concerning addictions. We are compelled to seek out the object of addiction to avoid other feelings, but processing gives us an alternative. Working with the *feeling behind the compulsion* can provide a release without having to yield to the addictive pattern. This is our basic approach in dealing with addiction. For example, if you experience chronic anxiety when you are alone, which leads to the impulse to be with other people, you may decide the impulse is compulsive and an addiction. If you work with the anxiety itself, instead of being motivated by it, you can eventually be freed of the addiction.

Body Sensations form a class of feelings by themselves. They may be thought of as physical, but actually they occur in the energy body. Hence, body sensations indicate energy status, and a recurring sensation indicates energy blockage. When we have a severe sensation, we call it a "symptom." It is important to tune into the body to enable sensations to come into awareness before they reach the level of being classified as symptoms. Sensations may be processed, and will lead to an unexpected amount of emotional clearing, because the energy body is the origin of the emotions. Body awareness is central to certain meditation disciplines, where practice consists of sitting and being aware of body sensations. Working with body sensations is very helpful in developing the capacity for feeling, since feeling occurs in the body. As you become more sensitive to yourself, you will discover that emotions and sensations occur together. This is the interfacing of body/mind that we discussed earlier. The beginning of a pattern is noticed first in either the emotions or the body. Focusing on whichever of the two you are aware of will bring the other aspect into awareness.

After you have isolated the feelings you are working with, you should identify what you are perceiving in the simplest terms possible, and which chakras are involved: I feel anger in the Solar Plexus when I get into a certain situation. I feel lonely in my Heart when I am rejected. I feel anxiety about money in the Survival center when new expenses come up. I feel sexual frustration in the Second Center under certain conditions, or even all the time. Try to clarify the feeling or sensation and link it to the apparent triggering stimulus if there is one; i.e., the external event or inner thought. What is important is to look for the feeling *behind* the event.

Any event that occurs with emotional impact should be given priority. Sometimes you may become aware of a feeling but then dismiss it, thinking it insignificant. As you start getting into yourself, you will find that these feelings, which you have probably had for long periods, are really problems calling out for attention. You just never realized their significance. If you don't stop to experience and release the feeling, you suppress.

Many feelings represent attempts of the subconscious to clear. There are no insignificant feelings. When feelings come up, try to condition yourself to automatically stop and recognize that something worthy of your attention is happening. Processing doesn't necessarily require a lot of time; you can learn to quickly handle feelings so they are not suppressed.

A therapist may be helpful at the beginning to assist you in identifying your feelings and patterns, but there is definitely no need to be tied to one for any length of time. You learn to view *life* as the therapist, and life is designed with absolute precision to bring up exactly what needs to be surfaced from your subconscious. This is the purpose of life on the Earth plane. All you need learn is how to use your circumstances to facilitate a therapeutic result.

IDENTIFY THE DUALISTIC PATTERN

The basis of emotional stress is lack of integration. We become addicted to one side of any dualistic experience in an effort to avoid the other side, establishing a pattern of behavior. Patterns tend to function on an unconscious level. Nevertheless, they influence us tremendously, distorting our perception of reality, and generally leading us to act in self-limiting ways.

Associated with each recurring negative feeling is a pattern of behavior. In turn, behind each pattern is a belief. We may not be aware of the pattern or the belief, but usually we are aware of the feeling, unless it has been repressed. In our work, we start with what we are aware of, which is the feeling.

When a feeling is processed, two results are achieved. First, the suppressed negative energy that has been manifesting as a feeling is cleared. Second, the dualistic pattern that produces the emotion is eventually revealed. This will happen spontaneously, as the pattern is integrated, and does not need to be pursued actively. In fact, searching for the pattern can be used as an escape from having the feeling.

Identification of patterns
is helpful, but not essential

After you have worked with your feelings, you may become aware of some of your patterns, and possibly the underlying beliefs. You are not yet free of them, but you are on the way to integration. However, identification of patterns is not necessary for processing to be effective, and may not actually come until a fair amount of clearing has taken place.

For example, suppose a man has a problem with authority. He continually finds himself in situations where he is in conflict with various authority figures, because he unconsciously seeks out or attracts these situations, and even unconsciously creates them. He will do things like park in no-parking areas, becoming angry and indignant when ticketed.

More serious signs would include periodically recurring conflict on the job, such as his becoming resentful whenever the opportunity arose, thinking that he was being controlled, manipulated, and used. Such is the power of the mind to project the conditions held in the subconscious, that many times the conflict will have a real basis. The subconscious energy becomes powerful enough to actually create oppressive circumstances. In less severe instances, the oppression would be only the person's perception, and would manifest less in objective reality.

The conflict with authority is a Power center affliction. The unconscious and irrational belief at the bottom of the conflict might be that all authority is negative, manipulative, and limiting. The belief gives rise to the dualistic pattern of addiction to rebellious self-determination because of his contempt for authority. He tries to escape into "freedom," rejecting any and all authority. A more integrated perception of this duality would be reasonable self-autonomy balanced with respect for authority as the representation of the cooperative nature of society.

He feels, most probably, rage that his life is being controlled by others. The person does not normally have the
insight or background to identify the conflict, and may easily go
through his entire life unconscious of the source of his pain.
Much anger has probably been suppressed, resulting in a chronic condition. Anger, by the way, may be caused by other patterns. The chronic presence of this emotion does not necessarily
imply an authority problem.

If the person is taught an effective method to clear the
suppressed anger, he can realize therapeutic benefits without
understanding the source pattern that is causing the anger.

Not until a certain point is reached in clearing will the
knowledge of the authority conflict have any significance for
him. He may have been exposed to this information previously,
with no comprehension. Awareness of the pattern is reached
naturally, as long as processing therapy continues. When recognition of the pattern occurs, he does not automatically gain
sudden freedom from it. Clearing therapy must continue,
although it is now likely to proceed at a faster rate, because the
pattern itself can now be worked with.

You should handle your self-awareness similarly. As you
integrate feelings, you are making real progress in your work on
yourself. When the time is right, the underlying dualistic pattern
will become evident, and eventually, the belief behind the
pattern.

When you are aware of them, patterns of behavior may be
meditated upon. You will increase your knowledge of the
pattern and release suppressed energy. Emotions will come up,
to be integrated. You can go deeper into the awareness of how
the pattern influences your behavior, and weaken its influence
through acceptance.

When you start to become aware of your patterns, you will
be able to sense an emotion coming before it builds. The
awareness will enable you to neutralize the emotion, if you want
to. Processing becomes unnecessary, because no energy builds
up, and suppressed emotion is not called up or has already been

cleared. Still, you must be careful not to become too intellectual, thinking that you are controlling your emotional reactions
because you know your patterns. It is better to process any
feeling that starts to comes up, rather than assuming it has been
neutralized because the pattern has been recognized.

Patterns are reflected by
the astrological birth chart

Because I have a strong background in astrology, whenever
I am consulting with a client I often use the client's chart to
assist in identifying patterns that need to be integrated. The
formation of the planets at the time of birth represents the
energy potentials of the inner self, and broadly corresponds to
the energy relationships between the chakras. Blocks in the
chakras can be immediately identified, and then worked with
directly, through breath and bodywork.

The chart gives insights that go beyond, but include, forma-
tive events of the present lifetime, especially parental relationships. The chart also substantiates one's experience. If one has
potential for a compulsive sexual problem or an anger problem,
for example, it clearly shows in the psychological interpretation
of the chart. Even so, astrology does not provide the solution;
it only identifies the problem.

Integration of patterns, not elimination, is our central purpose. Of course, integration can take place without the aid of
astrology. When the birth chart is not used, we begin without
knowledge of the patterns, working with the actual energy that
is felt. The patterns will emerge over time. In practice, we do
largely the same when we use the chart, but we have a head
start on intellectually identifying the patterns.

We come into life with but a few major patterns. Our life's
work is the integration of these patterns that cause us so much
pain. We must understand that progress will proceed slowly.
Slow but steady progress is actually the most powerful kind of
transformation, because when we get overnight results, the
results go as quickly as they come.

OWN YOUR EXPERIENCE

One of the most important principles of processing is the need to "own" experience. Because of suppression in the past, we have created our Karma, the subconscious reservoir of negative energies, which we project outward. We then interpret in distorted fashion, perceiving negativity as being directed toward us from other persons or circumstances. These outside agencies act like mirrors, reflecting back our own negativities. They are actors in the play we are directing. They function in just such a manner as to bring up the suppressed feelings we carry inside. That is the purpose we unconsciously assign to them.

To understand this, and to take responsibility for whatever negativity you are faced with, is to own your experience. You can go nowhere in transforming any feeling or experience until you own it. Granted, this can often be challenging and difficult. You may think you are being treated unfairly; you may feel anger, bitterness, or heartbreak, but if you do not take responsibility, you miss the point. You must assume that you have created your negative experience through projection of suppressed energies.

*Realize that you
are projecting*

The realization that you are projecting is the most important aspect of awareness. Until then, you are asleep. You react to your projections blindly. When you become aware, you stop reacting – you own your experience instead of rejecting it and being driven by it.

Actually, when you are in this first step of processing, you will not generally be able to do any more than make the assumption of owning – you will not feel it on a gut level because you are still in the intellectual stage, and your sense of owning will necessarily be no more than an intellectual assumption. You must understand the theory behind owning thoroughly so that you will be able to proceed on faith, especially during times of emotional stress, when it is not easy to keep a clear perspective.

Whenever you begin to process, make the assumption that you are responsible for what is before you. In other words, do not blame any other person, thing, or situation. Also, *do not blame yourself*. Because owning is essential to self-work, let's take another detailed look at exactly how we create the negativity we encounter. This may be thought of as happening in four ways:

1. Duality

In simple dualistic experience, there is no subconscious Karma at work. The perceived negative is an inherent part of the perceived positive – both must be experienced.

For example, pleasure soon loses its glitter. It does not last, and seems to bring with it other negative aspects that were not anticipated. We create the other aspects, assigning negative values to them, to balance the interaction. This is dualistic projection; it is not based on clearing previous Karma.

Dualistic projection is greatly intensified when we are attached, or – in modern terms – addicted. When we are addicted to something, it means we are compulsive about it. We must have it because of our mistaken beliefs. We have arranged our needs so as to be dependent upon the energy exchange with the object, whether a form of security, a substance, power, or a person.

If we were not addicted to the experience, we would not go through alternating pleasure–pain. In the first place, we would not find the same kind of pleasure as when addicted. Our pleasure in a relationship, for example, would be one of sharing and mutual support, rather than clinging to the relationship out of fear of loneliness. Addicted, we become dependent; we must be with and control the other. Unaddicted, we allow the other their freedom, but enjoy spending quality time together, without compulsiveness.

The same difference exists in the manner we relate to anything. We can abuse or not abuse. Of course, addiction is not a conscious choice, but we must be aware of how it works.

2. Projection–Clearing

In this stage, subconscious energy and patterns are projected onto reality, and things are perceived that simply aren't there. We perceive what we carry inside – what we unconsciously project in order to clear.

An incident occurs. The subconscious recognizes what it has been waiting for; it projects onto the incident, and we experience emotion out of proportion. We are irrational. Projections can range from simple and amusing misperceptions to schizophrenic paranoia.

Your neighbor carries out his garbage, and you become angry because he is making too much noise, or doing it at the wrong time of day, or making a mess, etc., ad nauseam. You are projecting and clearing anger, possibly based on your belief in a self-image which demands that your street look a certain way. If you were to react without loading the incident with subconscious anger, you would probably laugh at the neighbor for being such a slob (you could still love him as you laughed at him), and there would be no annoyance at all.

You buy a new car, but decide that you got the wrong kind, that something is wrong with it, or that you got cheated. You are projecting and clearing insecurity.

You feel that no one can ever love you, that you will always be alone and lonely, and that even your partner will never understand you because of what he or she just did. You are projecting and clearing loneliness.

These emotions are being cleared because they were previously suppressed. They come to the surface *when conditions are right* – when there is an event or the negative side of a dualistic experience that will support the projection. The neighbor may actually have been inconsiderate, and so on, but your reaction is out of proportion. You over-react.

In more advanced cases, we unconsciously provoke others and then react to their reaction. Your neighbor is careless about his garbage because you are such a fuss-pot; you actually did buy the wrong kind of car, against the suggestion of the sales-person; you made an unreasonable demand of your partner, and then react with resentment and despair when he or she refuses. You set yourself up to fall.

Cases such as these can be difficult to recognize as they are happening. That is why you must always make the assumption, whenever difficulty arises, that you are projecting and clearing negative emotions.

3. Projection–Manifestation

The next stage of creating our experience is less obvious, but more extensive than the previous stages. Subconsciously suppressed energies have built up enormously, actually creating the conditions we encounter in the seemingly "outside" world. If we continually suppress emotions that come up in stage two, we will come to this stage, as most of us have in many areas.

The condition of projection-manifestation is much talked about in the New Age field. I'm sure you have heard "you are what you think" or "change your thinking and your life will change." Our beliefs create our world. The problem, however, is that most of what we think remains on the subconscious level, and is not easily seen and changed, even with whatever reprogramming techniques you may have heard about.

It is not the beliefs themselves, but the suppressed subcon-scious energies that result from the beliefs, which go out into the world, form our experience, and come back at us. We attract the very same energy we suppress. We do this to bring our subconscious energies into awareness and to clear them. A very angry person may suppress anger to the point where he or she will be the victim of someone else's irrational outburst, violent assault, or even an impersonal car accident. The fact that suppressed energy is carried over from past lives will help to explain why an apparently innocent person will suffer such calamities.

This is the essence of the Karma theory as it relates to events that come to us for no apparent reason. Being born into poverty, enduring hardship, loneliness, bad luck, and so on – all these conditions result from energies that have not been released properly, but have been carried inside.

Relationships are particularly susceptible to Karmic carry-over. It can be assumed that major difficulties we undergo with another are because of incomplete exchanges with that same person in a previous life. We maintain our connection because we are attached, through dualistic love/hate, tending to repeat the dynamics of a particular relationship until its energy is properly released.

Past-life therapy is, in fact, now being practiced by certain psychotherapists. One who comes to mind is Roger J. Woolger, whose excellent book, *Other Lives, Other Selves,* I would recommend to anyone wanting to become familiar with the realities of past-life influence. The premise of past-life therapy is that re-experiencing the suppressed pain in the context of the past life will cause the unblocking.

Past-life therapy is logical and effective, but my feeling is that you don't necessarily have to go back into the past to release suppressed emotions. This would include your childhood past, as well as past lives. The past has formed the present, and the problems and feelings that you face now are the very same ones you faced then. The point is to release the energies through acceptance and experience of them, and to cease the self-rejection that prevents the release. This can be done quite effectively by working with negative feelings as you perceive them today. In contrast, you can go back to a past life, maintain self-rejection, and still not release or integrate feelings.

What is important, whether in past or present life, is to take responsibility for your experience as the first step to clearing it. Understand that *you* have created it, and it is still following you because you have not assumed responsibility.

4. Spontaneous Clearing

The last way we create our experience comes about through no external interaction, but occurs during meditation, or bodywork, or anytime. Once we begin to work on ourselves, we set the stage for spontaneous clearings.

Spontaneous clearing will take the form of negative emotions coming up for no particular reason. Sadness, anger, depression, sexual feelings, moods, whatever – these feelings may even temporarily get worse than before you started working on yourself. This is common once deep inner work is begun. It should be interpreted positively, knowing that your psychic garbage is being released. When it is released, you have to experience it; if you resist, you only suppress it again.

How long does clearing continue? Once you understand what you have been doing to yourself – probably for your entire life as well as previous lives – and you make the shift to a spiritual, or feeling orientation, you can no longer be the same person. You become unsettled in the world, because the old, materialistic goals do not attract you, yet you are under siege from the release of psychic toxins from within. Furthermore, you have no real grasp of what life will be like in the future, when your higher consciousness is developed. This awakening is indeed, a very fragile period, and you must be gentle and caring about yourself. How long? For as long as you need.

AFFIRM THAT YOU ARE PROCESSING

The intellect is the home of the decision-making capacity. An important function of the intellect is the conscious decision to go ahead with processing and not fall back into unawareness and self-rejection, which makes integration impossible.

When you affirm that you are proceeding with processing, you automatically call into operation the skills you have learned. Thinking about what to do next is not necessary; you simply watch as problems take on the new perspective that leads to integration.

I accept myself, my feelings, and my life circumstances as they are. I blame no one, understanding that I have created what I perceive. In no longer trying to avoid my experience, I make possible the eventual transformation. My love for myself grows because of the courage I show in accepting and facing myself as I am.

7

Acceptance

Acceptance is the second step in Integrative Processing. At this point, we have become aware of a negative feeling or condition, and have made the intellectual assumption that we are responsible for it. We may not yet understand its full depth and significance; still, we are aware of something painful that needs to be resolved.

The painful feelings have not cleared; they remain strong because we have habitually rejected them. Rejection of feelings is self-rejection, because on a certain level we are our feelings. We find ourselves in an endless cycle of pain and self-rejection, the opposite of self-love.

Rejection of feelings is also suppression. Pain stays suppressed, and whenever it breaks into our awareness we again suppress it through self-rejection. In this chapter, we will explore how we self-reject, even when we don't want to. Self-rejection is a critical issue, and we will examine it in detail.

There is something almost automatic in us that tends to self-reject, or suppress. It would be conjecture to try to fathom the reason for this, but it seems a part of human nature. Suppression is a requirement of existence as we know it. If we didn't have our Karma, our suppressed subconscious, there would be no reason for the world to exist, in the metaphysical model. The world is our projection, and projection has to have suppressed contents. You might think this concept is irrelevant to working on yourself, but it has proven helpful to me; it makes it easier to maintain a more level perspective, and not get discouraged because there is so much in the subconscious to go through.

Self-rejection is a
function of the mind

The mind is the gate that opens or closes, thereby allowing or preventing direct experience. Any action of the mind that blocks direct experience is self-rejecting; conversely, any action of the mind that allows direct experience is self-accepting.

Self-acceptance is more of a passive quality than an active or aggressive quality. It comes into being when the mechanical mind reaction of self-rejection has ceased. As such, there is nothing really to do, only to stop doing. We are conditioned to be aggressive in pursuing goals in the world. Often, we turn toward inner growth with the same kind of aggressiveness and impatience for results. This very attitude is self-rejecting. Acceptance happens when there is no active seeking, when there is no expectation or striving, when the mind has come to rest.

When something is accepted, the barriers of the mind to direct experience – to the *feeling* of the event – are taken down. When you are feeling, you are not suppressing; you are in the moment. Whether you intellectually prefer the moment to be as it is has nothing to do with your acceptance of it. If you are self-accepting, your mind does not block your feelings.

The intellect remains free to have any preference it might. You don't have to like something to accept it. Your preference that the event be different may take the form of actively initiating change, but your preference does not influence your acceptance of an event.

ACCEPT YOURSELF

When I first became interested in working on myself, I was attracted to teachers and methods which seemed to offer an approach to help me change myself into a better person, without the "faults" I found objectionable. I also tried to develop skills that would help me acquire what I thought would make me happy. I was attracted to growth therapies as a means of self-improvement.

I am still attracted to growth therapies, but my motive is different. I now seek to accept and integrate, not to change. In accepting, I become aware of parts of myself previously unrecognized; my individuality expands and is enhanced; patterns become balanced; growth occurs.

I hope I have been able to communicate that trying to avoid or change the perceived negative, trying to be better, even more loving is, in the end, all self-defeating. You may attempt to change yourself, but you only strengthen the negative when you fight it. In fighting the negative, you fight yourself, and you cannot win. You only suppress negative energies through self-rejection. Unconscious conflicts are not resolved, and conditions recur, in a different time and place. Of course, we are not justified in continuing to *act on* negativities; we simply do not attempt to force change.

Growth occurs through integration, not change. You cannot seek growth directly. You cannot seek to change yourself directly. Integration happens after you truly accept who and what you are *right now, without seeking to change* any part of yourself. Seeking to change is the subtle state of mind that self-rejects.

ACCEPT YOUR FEELINGS

To become integrated and to grow, you must accept and experience your feelings, whatever they may be. If you have failed at something, and are disappointed, you must accept and experience your disappointment. If you are angry about something, you must accept and experience your anger. If you are compulsive, you must accept and experience the compulsiveness. Note that I am not saying you should act on or be motivated by any of these emotions; I am just saying that you must not resist feeling the emotion.

Self-rejection does not come about because
you have negative feelings – Self-rejection
occurs when you reject the feelings

In other words, feelings are never self-rejecting or accepting, even feelings of hatred toward yourself. It is the attitude toward the feelings that is accepting or rejecting.

If you discover subconscious feelings of disapproval, resentment, or hatred toward yourself, you must handle them carefully. Such feelings certainly might be thought of as self-rejecting but, paradoxically, this is not so if you can accept the feelings. It is when you reject the feelings, and become motivated by them or against them, that you self-reject. Feelings of self-hatred are what we project onto the world. We hate ourselves, we suppress and then project. We perceive others as hating us, or we hate them.

Self-condemnation represents stored negative energy, just like other negative emotions. It must be cleared somehow. When you consciously accept and experience the energy, clearing can take place. Allow feelings of self-hatred to exist without guilt. Bring them into consciousness, allowing them to work out their energy cycles. As you accept the feelings, entering into direct experience of them, they will clear. You will have a catharsis of the trapped energy that has been adversely affecting you. You will spontaneously understand the history and how the patterns behind the hatred formed, possibly even going into past-life circumstances. But this happens only when you start with acceptance.

Acceptance means accepting that
you will be unhappy some of the time

Unhappiness is easier to accept if you can grasp the dualistic nature of existence. Dualism means that happiness and unhappiness always go together. If you can accept both dualistic happiness and unhappiness, you begin real transformation. You begin to grow, to transcend the issue. Paradoxically, you start to experience a different, non-dualistic kind of happiness, a happiness which does not depend on circumstances. Happiness becomes *unconditional*.

This is the pattern for real change. Real, and lasting, transformation occurs when you integrate the dualistic experience within. You no longer cling to one side of any duality and resist and suppress the other side, rejecting yourself.

The concept of integration of duality was probably first incorporated into contemporary psychology by Jung. His formulation was that we must accept the *shadow* side of ourselves, the dark and negative aspect that we suppress because of its painful nature. His opinion was that we all have such a nature. Making peace with it was one of the central aspects of his work. Processing is an approach that will enable you to do this.

If you are to accept your negative side – your misery, if you will – how can you be sure that it will be resolved? Asking the question implies the motive of avoidance. This motive will impede acceptance and integration. Such is the fragile nature of acceptance. You can't accept to get rid of; you have to accept to make part of yourself.

Surrender

Acceptance is a more modern term for what is called *surrender* in classical terminology. Surrender is a complex subject, and I have encountered people who have, in my opinion, a distorted understanding. Does surrender mean blind obedience to the guru, complete submission to external events and persons, resignation to personal circumstances, the attempt to destroy the personal ego through renunciation, or simply indifference? Or does it mean total compliance with your own impulses? It is none of the above, but these are the traps that are available.

Surrender is a personal concept that will grow and change as you engage in an active spiritual practice such as processing. It is basically *ceasing resistance to what is,* both in terms of inner feelings and outer events. We harbor resistance on deep levels, for no rational reason.

I have found it easiest to begin cultivation of surrender on the body level. Becoming aware of physical sensation, which is really energy sensation, and accepting without choice teaches us how to accept emotions.

Surrendering to emotions will gradually become easier as you continue working on yourself. In my own work, I remember coming to the point of acknowledging and accepting the inevitability of painful experiences. As I surrendered to the eventuality of my anger, which was what I was working on, I released my resistance on a deeper level, and the judging, analytical, protective ego loosened up. I no longer feared my anger. I didn't care as much if I was angry or not, and I saw that the attainment of a perfect state of non-concern would be liberation. The anger would not necessarily have disappeared, but in not caring about it, I was no longer bound to it. I set up the proper condition for a possible final cleansing, but I was not relying on this, knowing that it might never happen.

The final condition of surrender is when there is no resistance at all to inner or outer experience as it happens. All concepts that dictate how things should be have been dropped; there is no critical self that evaluates life as it happens, trying to avoid certain parts and cling to other parts. Of course, we still have a personal identity, but our feelings are not inhibited – we allow them to be as they may, without having to act on them. We are *real.*

Being real is an important part of emotional self-acceptance. It means tactfully allowing your true feelings to show when appropriate – being what you are, instead of trying to be what you or others might prefer or expect. Being real only becomes possible when you have taken responsibility for your feelings. Until then, others will become alienated or threatened when you show negative feelings, sensing that you blame them or circumstances outside yourself for your condition. When you take responsibility for your feelings, others will not be threatened, but will welcome and appreciate your honesty. You don't have to broadcast the fact that you have taken responsibility, either. Others will sense this as well.

ACCEPT THE EXTERNAL

Experience can be broadly divided into two classes: inner and outer. Often, experience will consist of both elements. It may appear that the outer causes the inner. Something happens, and we seem to respond with an emotion. However, the inner and outer actually occur simultaneously; one does not cause the other. Moreover, we create our experience, through the mechanisms we have discussed. We continually overlay simple reality with our projections, creating our *perception or interpretation* of what is happening.

Because we project onto appropriate screens, there is always an element of what we have projected in the person or circumstance which serves as the screen. We don't try to sort this out before processing; it would be difficult in our subjective state and would impede integration, keeping us in the mind. Therefore, we assume we have projected all of our perception. Later, after integration has occurred, we will gain a more objective understanding of what each party has brought to the event.

Acceptance of the external
is self-acceptance

Since what we perceive in the external is our creation through projection, accepting it results in self-acceptance. For example, when you perceive qualities in others that you dislike, you are largely projecting those qualities. If you can accept the qualities without trying to change them or your feelings about them, you are self-accepting. To do this, you may have to accept your dislike.

In other words, don't try to force yourself to like something in order to accept it. Remember, acceptance means opening to your feelings, whatever they are. Accept your feelings as they are, accept your dislike, but don't act on it. Since your dislike is the result of your projection, do not hold another person responsible for the dislike. If you can take responsibility for your dislike, you will be able to relate to the other person constructively, going beyond the dislike.

Similarly, with any actual happening or circumstance that affects you, you accept yourself if you accept the event. Do not blame anyone else, or take refuge in thinking it "happened" to you. Your unconscious psychic forces mold circumstances to fit your needs exactly. You project your suppressed energy onto the world and perceive it as coming to you from the outside. It follows that if you resist what is happening, or simply, *what is,* you are self-rejecting. If you fight the event, you fight yourself.

Understanding this puts all our struggles into a different perspective. If we have created the event through projection, fighting it has a certain self-defeating aspect to it. When we struggle against ourselves, who can win?

Acceptance does not
imply complacency

You should not be complacent about confronting conditions calling for creative response. Acceptance means only that you accept conditions *now;* acceptance has no bearing on the future. Accept responsibility for conditions, accept the pain associated with them, but also take action to improve or change conditions, if necessary.

Much of our Karma is such that confrontation and change are necessary. We are presented with real problems, and we must deal with them in constructive ways. The difficulty is that if we have not cleared the subconscious, we will go on to create or attract the same conditions all over again when we take action. If the problem is approached through acceptance, the required change will take place without struggle. You must therefore strike a reasonable balance between action and acceptance, with the emphasis on acceptance.

I would like to emphasize a point about acceptance that many people misunderstand. They think that to be accepting, they have to resign themselves to negative circumstances, and then try to force themselves to like the circumstances. This is wrong. Intellectually, you are free to have preferences. What you need to accept are your *feelings, as they are,* about the circumstances.

If you accept painful feelings associated with a certain event, you eliminate self-rejection, even though you might prefer not to have the feelings. You may continue to dislike the actual event, and this would, of course, be appropriate under many circumstances. However, if you accept your feelings concerning an external event, you also accept the event in a certain way, and this will lead to the eventual integration of the event. You arrive at the paradox of both accepting and disliking an event at the same time. You dislike on the intellectual level; you accept on the mental level; you feel on the body level; but you also take steps to make necessary changes. This highly practical metaphysical position should be the point you eventually come to in your self-acceptance regarding events that are clearly destructive.

For example, if you suffered abuse as a child, you should *not* try to intellectually accept the abuse. Instead, you have to accept your feelings about being abused. You felt pain, outrage, humiliation, abandonment, sadness – these are the feelings you must accept. The feelings were already hidden within your subconscious and the purpose of your experience was only to bring them into consciousness in order to clear. If you process the feelings by going back into the past, you can release them.

With events not blatantly destructive, but just annoying or bothersome, you will find that accepting the feelings that come up will change your opinion about the events. They will no longer be thought of as problems. Your opinion will change naturally, coinciding with the release of negative energies through your self-work, and it is not something you can do directly.

In other words, whether you like something or not has nothing to do with your acceptance of your feelings. Liking or disliking is irrelevant to feeling. Accepting your feelings, as they are, is what self-acceptance is all about.

BE NON-REACTIVE

Non-reactiveness is the necessary complement to acceptance. You cannot accept negative feelings and then think that you are free to act on the feelings, or to extend them into the universe in any way. This would be a serious mistake. Acceptance makes sense only when you become non-reactive.

Non-reactiveness means that you do not react to, that you are *not motivated* by negative feelings and emotions. It does *not* mean that you should try to resist, limit, control, or not have the feelings in the first place. Feelings come up spontaneously, and the attempt to control them is suppression. You should allow feelings to come up as well as any accompanying physical expression that is part of the inner release – like laughing or crying – but then you should not react to the feelings.

Non-reactiveness does not result in suppression because the feeling is allowed to express itself fully in your consciousness when you enter direct experience. Direct experience of the feeling is all that is required to eliminate suppression. You do not have to act on or act out the feeling to avoid suppression. When emotions come up, you are in a precarious position. You have not yet released any of the tension of the feeling that integration brings. The temptation is to act on the feeling to relieve tension.

Don't act. Don't be motivated by the feeling. Don't extend the negativity into the universe by doing or expressing anything that would probably be self-destructive in the long run. You are learning sophisticated techniques that will enable you to dissolve negative emotions without having to act on them, but you must exercise will power and self-discipline at first. Will is an important function of the intellect, which must be used now.

Non-reactiveness is essential in regard to the active emotions, like anger, possessiveness, jealousy, or inappropriate sexual impulses, but it is also needed in working with the more passive emotions, like fear, sadness, or loneliness. When we give in to negative emotion, when we are motivated by it, we reinforce its power over us, and strengthen the negative pattern. By not reacting or being motivated by it, we loosen the pattern.

Not reacting is most difficult when you are under attack and have to defend yourself. If you have been practicing non-reactiveness at other, more meditative times, you will gain the ability to maintain it during stressful times. You can defend your rights much more effectively, because your emotions are not in the way, even though you are still feeling them.

Non-reactiveness does not mean that you become passive to anyone else's aggression; it just means that you do not blame them. Though it may not be apparent now, you have created or attracted what appears to be coming to you through the other person. You should intellectually acknowledge this, but do not refrain from defending your rights.

Thus, if another person appears to block you, it is you who block yourself. You will feel anger because the Power center is frustrated, but do not think the other has made you angry. Take responsibility for your anger, and dissolve it through processing. You can then go on to work with the other person to make the necessary creative changes regarding the situation. You will be immensely more effective at implementing change because you are not coming at the other out of anger. The situation is likely to have changed automatically anyway, because of your acceptance.

Blameful expression does
not release negativity

It is generally agreed among psychologists today that unrestrained blameful expression of negative emotions is counterproductive to the release of the emotions. By blameful expression, I mean confronting others, arguing, accusing and blaming them, yelling at them, and so on. Considering the overall effects of unrestrained blameful expression, there is no question that it is self-destructive.

First, it reinforces the misbelief that the other is responsible; you condition yourself into victim consciousness. Second, what you put out comes back to you, usually intensified. There are plenty of unconscious people who are just looking for others to exchange negative energy with. Third, it doesn't really do anything to dissolve the emotion, which still sits with you in a more agitated state. Fourth, in attacking others, you hurt them; they become alienated from you, often irreparably.

I would even question the value of energetic "releasing" in therapy sessions, where the client acts out emotions, beating on pillows, etc. In the case of anger toward parents, for example, it is usually not made clear that the parents are not responsible for the hurts the child has suffered. As we have discussed, the child chooses the conditions that will activate its character in accordance with the suppressed subconscious. This therapy may only serve to condition and reinforce the sense of blame, which may be the primary reason that the suppressed anger cannot be released. Still, after an energetic therapy session in which catharsis has been achieved, blame has dissolved as well. But how often is real catharsis achieved, and which comes first, the catharsis or the dropping of blame?

Do not confuse spontaneity
with emotionality

The first step in avoiding the problems inherent in unre-strained expression comes with non-reactiveness. It is totally erroneous to think that you are becoming less spontaneous or more inhibited by doing so. To be spontaneous means to be able to respond in a positive and creative manner to what is happening, not to be chained to any predetermined emotional response, like a robot who jumps when its buttons are pushed. To be so lost in your drama that you have no control over the outward expression of negative emotions is nothing but uncon-scious emotionalism. When you practice non-reactiveness, you train yourself to become the kind of person you want to be. When you fail to maintain non-reactiveness, you self-reject.

IDENTIFY SELF-REJECTION

We often find ourselves aware of a particular feeling, or confronted with a recurrent event, but we are at a loss to resolve the issue. We linger with emotions, dwelling on them perhaps for years. We don't know how to get rid of them.

These feelings and events stay with us because they are not cleared. When we have direct experience of something, we clear it. The cycle of energy is released and finished. Direct experi-ence means staying with a feeling long enough, and in the right way, so clearing can take place. However, direct experience is prevented by self-rejection, and the feeling never clears. We "wallow" in our misery and self-rejection. The feeling comes up again and again, and is suppressed again and again.

You must watch your
mind carefully

Self-rejection takes place because of the activity of the mind. We mentally react to our feelings, instead of staying non-reactive. Of course, not all activity of the mind leads to suppression, but we often misuse our mental powers in the unconscious intent to avoid feelings. Since self-rejection is a product of the mind, the intellect – a higher function – can identify it and make the decision to stop doing it by exercising its discretionary power. We stop self-rejection simply by making the conscious decision to do so.

But to stop self-rejection, you must first become aware of how it works and what it does to you. You must become very attentive to how your mind works. This is the "mindfulness" of Buddhism. Self-rejection is part of our basic conditioning, and can be changed through education and awareness. When we become aware of how we self-reject, the actual awareness begins the freeing and outgrowing of the self-rejecting mechanism.

Affirmations

An aid in breaking self-rejection cycles is the use of *affirmations*. To understand how affirmations work, let me first summarize our approach to self-therapy.

Processing is a technique for the uncovering, integrating, and controlled releasing of traumatic and negative feelings that have been suppressed in the past and continue to plague us. Suppressed feelings are composed of *energies* that are kept locked in the body, in latent form.

Self-rejection, however, is not an energy-based feeling; it is of the *mind,* not the body. Self-rejection is a conditioning of the mind, a means of shutting out experience. Processing techniques that release emotions will therefore not help to change conditioned mind-sets, such as blame or guilt. In fact, trying to process blame or guilt will not work, and holding blame or guilt in your consciousness as you do feelings will only reinforce the blame or guilt. Affirmations can be used to change conditioned mind-sets.

On the other hand, affirmations cannot be used to integrate or change suppressed feelings. No matter how many times you tell yourself you are feeling great, you will stay depressed if this is the feeling that is surfacing. If it has any effect at all, the affirmation will only serve to *suppress* the negative feeling. Feelings must be experienced. We will study the proper use of affirmations in another chapter, and explore reconditioning the subconscious mind to be self-accepting. For now, remember: **Processing integrates feelings; affirmations recondition the mind.**

The principles we are about to discuss concerning self-rejection have always been central on the traditional path to enlightenment. In contemporary society, the principles remain the same, but perhaps the emphasis will be different from what might have been appropriate in previous times. Still, there is one problem that remains constant – the appearance of the principles as being negative in nature.

Pointing out exactly how we reject ourselves can become tedious. Moreover, when we fall into habitual self-rejection, we tend to become dependent upon the mental conditioning that keeps us suppressed. When the conditioning is challenged, we become anxious, possibly enough to make us turn a deaf ear to what is being said. We resist hearing because our basic ego formations are being threatened. We remain in denial. It makes no difference that we are miserable with ourselves, because we cling to our misery. We fear that we will be nothing when our self-destructive conditioning is taken away.

This is not entirely irrational. Our self-rejecting habits support us; they limit us, yet they get us through. When they are taken away, we have no suppressive mechanism to defend ourselves from the possibly overwhelming negativity that lies close in the subconscious. We feel like our supports are breaking under us, our anchors are no longer holding, and we become temporarily lost until new frames of reference are established.

*Maintain the spirit to
break through self-rejection*

Resistance to the loosening of self-rejecting mind-sets becomes a secondary problem when you begin inner work. If you are working with a therapist, the therapist takes it for granted that resistance will be encountered; handling it is part of a therapist's skill. You may become defensive and resentful toward the therapist, or toward anyone who points out your self-rejection. If you are working by yourself, you must remember that unconscious resistance can keep you from making progress, and that you must maintain your intention to cut through self-rejecting conditioning. Once you understand that self-rejecting habits keep you in misery, you will gain the "warrior" spirit necessary to advance in the inner quest.

It's possible you may feel that our discussion of self-rejecting modes of behavior has no relevance to the work you would like to do on yourself. You may feel you need depth work of a particular type, etc. You may be justified in thinking this, but you may also be putting up just another type of resistance. Modes of behavior, while mundane in a certain respect, affect us deeply. The *attitude* behind the behavior is what influences us, and we are apt to overlook the attitude, thinking it insignificant. We miss the forest because of the trees.

We don't see that we reject ourselves almost every minute of the day, from the moment we get out of bed. We are conditioned, and we keep re-conditioning ourselves to self-reject, and we don't understand why we are miserable. You may think that a particular attitude you have is not a problem, that you can live with it, that you're only human, but remember: You cannot accept self-rejection.

Self-acceptance does not mean that
you may keep yielding to self-rejection

Self-rejection must be understood and changed with gentleness and love. Self-rejecting supports must be broken, and there is often real pain in the breaking. You must understand what is happening, and neither be too reluctant to give up your supports, nor too hard on yourself as you look at your behavior structures. You must be gentle with yourself, as well as with others.

Even though we may discuss self-rejection in detail, it is sometimes difficult to be objective about ourselves. This is another area where a qualified therapist or even a sensitive friend can be helpful.

When we discuss self-rejection, please remember that what is being said is not negative, even though we are discussing negative behavior patterns. Many of the concepts may be new and difficult for you. As you continue to entertain these ideas, the logic will eventually become clear.

These are the ways we reject ourselves and suppress emotional experience:

Repression

Repression is unconscious suppression. In suppression, there is always part of us that is aware that we are suppressing; we just don't know any better. Chronic suppression lapses into repression, where awareness is lost of both feelings and the act of avoiding them. Repression is the most serious type of self-rejection because we become totally out of touch with ourselves. Eventually the build-up of negativity results in neurotic behavior and self-destructiveness such as chronic depression or hostility, illness, or physical calamity such as accident or assault.

Most of us engage in a certain amount of repression, especially if we lead active lives. I feel there is no cause for alarm, however, as long as we begin to work on ourselves. When we start addressing the issues and feelings that are conscious, we gradually change our threshold of awareness, and previously repressed material will come into view to be integrated.

Resistance

Resistance to feelings is the first way we consciously suppress. Because aversion to pain is instinctual, it is not hard to see why we want to avoid negative experience. Not knowing any better, we assume pain can be avoided by turning away from it. Resistance is probably the basic cause of suppression, resulting in the creation of the subconscious. It is one of Nature's traps, having us create our Karma in order to project the world.

We simply have to be aware of the implications of resisting our feelings, and I hope our discussion has made that clear. Even so, you do not have to be constantly ill at ease, waiting anxiously for the next moment when you will suppress. You should just remain aware of the tendency to resist, and gradually condition yourself to confront, accept, and experience fully your feelings regarding the more important issues that come up.

As you condition yourself to confront feelings rather than resisting, your personal boundaries will grow. As you accept pain instead of avoiding it, its nature will change, and it will become neutralized. By raising your threshold for pain, you effectively lower the amount of pain in your life. If you run from pain, you lower the threshold, and you find that you can never get away from it.

Blame

Blame is the next most common way of rejecting ourselves. We blame because we want to avoid responsibility for what happens to us. When we blame any person, object, or circumstance for our experience, we essentially become blind to reality. Self-acceptance is impossible, and we simmer in self-rejection. This includes blaming ourselves, which is called guilt, a special form of self-rejection. Blame is essentially the same as complaining.

Blame is so common that it is seldom questioned. It is almost a form of bonding ritual among certain people to blame somebody for something every time they speak. If you want to support your friend, you support their blame. People blame their job, various authority figures, the government, the economy – the list is endless. Blame can be the common element that binds spouses, lovers, or partners together. When I encounter a person who is heavily into blame, I almost feel as if I am watching a stand-up comic routine.

People who are intelligent and educated believe that their spouses do things that make them furious. Or their children. Or their employees or boss. These are cases of projected emotion. There is no reason to assume that whatever triggered your emotion was the cause. You just took that opportunity to bring up your feelings.

Self-work is not possible when blame exists

In Eastern philosophy, a person is considered unconscious when into blame, becoming conscious when moving past blame and understanding the true cause of the problem. As we have discussed at length, *the person* is the cause. Understanding this does not eliminate the problem; it just means that work can begin.

When we take responsibility for our emotions, we begin to make significant headway toward inner healing, but the difficulty is that even when we intellectually own our experience, we continue to *unconsciously* blame. We remain stuck in self-rejection, preventing true acceptance, integration, and release of negativity. One of the essential challenges of any therapy is getting past unconscious blame.

You may try to enter into direct experience of your feelings, thinking you are past blame, but energies are not released because you are still blaming on a deeper level. The free flow of energy is inhibited. Instead of integrating, you are stewing in your negativity. I suggest that you be particularly aware of this possibility when working with feelings concerning relationships. Occasionally, I'll find that I've gotten nowhere with processing until I finally become aware of and deliberately let go of the blame that is holding back the energies. Dropping blame becomes easier as integration proceeds. Even though blame impedes integration, it can be intellectually put aside as direct experience is entered.

Unconscious blame is not part of our subconscious Karma as suppressed energies are. Blame is a conditioning of the mind, not an energy-based feeling. Therefore, you should not try to accept or process blame to get past it; this will reinforce blame instead of releasing it. Blame is handled by being deliberately dropped. However, the feelings behind the blame are definitely Karmic, and will need to be integrated.

Unconscious blame must be brought into awareness, because it influences how we perceive reality, creating a blame-suppression cycle. We perceive an emotion, we unconsciously blame, self-acceptance is not possible, and we self-reject. We suppress the feelings, and also our blame. The same scenario exists for guilt. It is largely unconscious, making it hard to get at.

These are sensitive and difficult issues to address in psychotherapy. In traditional therapy, it is assumed that blame will eventually go away as therapy proceeds. I know of therapists who have not even confronted clients with the notion that they should take responsibility for their feelings and what has happened to them, because the client would resist and resent this. Instead, forgiveness is suggested.

*Forgiveness is the realization
that blame is a mistake*

Forgiveness is, of course, a very desirable quality, but often we misunderstand what it means. Forgiveness means finally seeing that the other person was not really responsible for what we thought came from them. Sometimes we try to force ourselves to forgive, thinking we are being spiritual or loving, or simply in the attempt to avoid pain. We continue to believe that the other is responsible for what has happened to us, but now we have pardoned them for their behavior.

Such "forgiveness" is intellectual, pseudo, and self-deceptive. We become even more out of touch with inner experience. It can even inflate the ego, because we think we were generous enough to forgive. True forgiveness means understanding that the original blame was wrong, not the granting of a pardon for what we mistakenly believe someone has done to us.

Blame is particularly relevant in parent/child dynamics, which traditional therapy focuses on heavily. We are encouraged to forgive our parents, often without understanding that we should own our past. This kind of therapy can work in the long run, but the question is, would another, more realistic approach work more effectively? We have already discussed that we choose our parents and early environment to serve as a catalyst for our character. The events of childhood activate what is already latent in the child's subconscious, a viewpoint being discussed and supported by transpersonal psychologists today.

We often don't want to let go of blame because of nothing more than pride. Unconsciously, we understand the truth that we are responsible for our experience. The conscious ego, however, wants to blame because it is defending itself. It does not want to feel that it could be stupid enough to cause harm to itself. The nature of the ego, and of highly ego-centric people in particular, is to always be right, and blame is usually how self-righteousness is maintained.

Self-blame, or guilt, is a variation on the basic blame dynamic. By blaming ourselves, we protect ourselves at a deeper level, just as blaming others will protect the ego from the realization of its responsibility for its experience.

Self-blame is not the same as taking responsibility

This is a very important concept. Spiritual seekers, when first realizing that they are responsible for their experience, may fall into the trap of blaming themselves, rather than others. The result is still self-rejection, preventing them from going further in their work. You must realize that your Karma has been formed out of ignorance, not deliberate intention. Blaming yourself is inappropriate; it is another mechanism to avoid owning and feeling on a deeper level.

If you feel self-blame because you think you are responsible for someone else's condition, you should realize that you are reacting inappropriately. Relationships are always mutual, meaning there is mutual consent. Others also have their Karma, and have chosen the relationship to bring their experience to themselves. Of course, this does not condone deliberate mistreatment of others, but guilt is misplaced, and is probably self-serving.

Guilt may start because we want to blame someone else, but that may not be possible. Having no other outlet, the blame is redirected to the self. In Gestalt, this is called "retroflection," and can occur with other aggressive impulses as well.

For example, if a child is unloved, the child may feel guilt about not being lovable enough for the parents. The belief, "it's my fault," is activated. In addition, the child feels frustration about not being loved, and wants to blame the parents for this. However, it is too threatening to blame the parents, because the parents might become angry and withdraw life support. The child redirects the blame back to itself, creating more guilt. What is happening is that guilt is unconsciously created by the child as a shield from the deeper realization that it does not feel love for others. Instead, the child is locked into a previous-life

Karmic pattern of dependency/resentment. The resentment is unconscious because it has been suppressed, but it is one of the factors that originally brought the child into a relationship with these particular parents. The child projects the unconscious resentment onto the parents, and experiences them as unloving, or even hating.

As an individual coming into birth with this Karma, the Karma is harder to accept than the idea that the parents don't offer their love. If the child can feel that the parents hate the child, the ego is protected from the realization that the hatred is coming from within; the awareness of the hatred within remains suppressed. The child's ego grabs at the idea that the parents will not provide love, choosing parents who will comply, or else behaving so as to invoke their disapproval. The child projects their non-love, and then avoids responsibility by feeling guilt. The same pattern extends to adult relationships.

Intellectual therapies, in particular, take a long time to resolve unconscious blame or guilt. How should this be handled in processing? The guilt of the mind needs to be *reconditioned,* not accepted. The principle of affirmation can be used effectively here.

The final, and possibly most important realization about blame is that, when we are blaming, we give up our right to autonomy. We are slaves to the other if the other is really responsible for what we are feeling; we have no self-determination in the most vital sense. When we finally take responsibility for our feelings and what happens to us, we are obviously no longer being controlled by agencies outside ourselves. We cease giving our power away to others. Taking responsibility means that we control our own destiny. We are no longer the victim.

Blameful Expression

Unrestrained blameful expression does not release negative feelings. The old idea of blameful expression as a means to "get it off your chest" is now considered to be erroneous and damaging by most therapists – except possibly within the therapy session – even though a few decades ago contemporary psychology did support "expressing your feelings" as a means to clearing negative emotions.

Although the act of expressing and returning our hurt to the source from which it apparently came seems to be a natural impulse, this is only because of the unconsciousness from which we are emerging. When we finally understand that the other is not responsible for our experience, it becomes obvious that taking out our emotion on them is completely inappropriate. You may have felt that someone was "making" you angry, but now that you have a better understanding of what actually happens, I hope it is clear that blame is a distortion of the truth, and that blameful recrimination is nothing less than ridiculous. In our passion, however, we often lose objectivity.

Confronting, yelling at someone else, acting
out your emotion as if others are to blame
is totally wrong, and will get you nowhere

It won't even give you the pleasure of venting. Trying to vent by emotionally confronting someone does give some movement to the energies, and so may appear to provide temporary relief, but the eventual result of unrestrained expression is further suppression, not release of the energies. You may have verified this in yourself or others by observing that emotional outbursts only become worse once they begin, even if you "express yourself" in a quiet, calm manner. In addition, there is damage to the relationship, and ultimately to yourself.

When you express negativity in a blameful and accusing manner, you undermine the trust that exists in any close relationship. The other person is hurt, sometimes deeply and traumatically. They may have no choice but to back off, and may keep backing off, if your expression is continually blameful and harsh. They may be able to see what you can't: that you are creating and reacting to your own distorted perception of reality. You end by driving away the ones you love.

Moreover, when you release negative energy into the universe by expressing it, you set up conditions for it to come back to you, which it will do, magnified. The actual physical expression is what starts the cycle. Before it is expressed, negativity is in a more potential form, and may be more easily handled. Blameful expression *affirms* the negativity. If the person at whom you have expressed negativity happens to be unconscious and vindictive, the negativity will return through that person. If the person is not vindictive, the energy will find another path back to you, often surprisingly quickly. This has been called "instant Karma."

Of course, you may share your feelings in a non-blaming way with someone who will be understanding enough not to become threatened and defensive, but this is much different from the motive sought in active, blameful expression. Blameful expression is a vindictive attack. On the psychic level, hostile energy is sent out to penetrate the aura of the attacked person. This is why anger, for example, is so painful to contend with. What we don't realize is that to hurt someone in blameful attack, we must first hurt ourselves. The attack is as debilitating to the sender as to the receiver, and vindictive people end up destroying themselves.

Still, blameful expression may appear easier than non-reactiveness, because when we express, we avoid really facing and experiencing our feelings – we suppress them. This is the real motive behind blameful expression, and why "expressing" can feel like feelings are relieved. However, the negative energy is merely driven deeper into the subconscious. If you can observe how this works in yourself, you will take important steps to gaining control of your emotions.

When strong emotions are felt, there is movement of energy in the energy body; this is what an emotion is. If expression of negativity is ultimately self-defeating, how is the surge of energy to be handled?

Strong emotions are to be
released by processing

By using breath and bodywork, entering into direct experience of the energy; by not avoiding it but simply feeling it, any emotion that comes up can be cleared instead of suppressed. There are times when this is not easy, but these are the times when the most may be gained: when deep subconscious pain is surfacing. Significant change can take place now.

One point is critical: If you continue to mentally blame, even though you may refrain from blamefully expressing your emotion, you will still suppress instead of cleanse. You will be locked into blame, and self-work will not be possible. In other words, if you continue to blame, it really makes no difference whether you express or don't express. Either way, you are still suppressing, and rejecting yourself. It is when you can see past blame, and understand the destructive results of blameful expression, that self-acceptance occurs.

Acting Out

Acting out means that negative energies are extended into the universe by being included in our personal drama. Instead of being aware of, accepting, and not reacting to negativities, we affirm them and their power to influence us by acting them out. We remain unaware, self-rejecting, and reactive.

For example, if you act out fear, you allow it to influence you. You project fear needlessly, becoming fearful of the objects onto which you have projected. You react to those objects, not perceiving that you are reacting to yourself.

Awareness would help you recognize that the fear comes from inside you, and that you unconsciously project it. Acceptance would help you not try to avoid the fear by running from it. Non-reactiveness would further your capacity for integration, and the eventual de-sensitization and clearing of the fear.

Motivation / Acting On

In motivation, we act on negative impulses, trying to satisfy them, instead of confronting and dissolving them. Motivation is a large area for investigation, made difficult because most motivation is unconscious. Normally, we are not especially aware of what compels us to do what we do, although we could be if we watched ourselves closely or if someone helped us clarify our motivation.

Motivation covers a wide range of human needs, mostly comprising the energies of the first four chakras: Security, Sensation/Sex, Power/Significance, and the need for Relationship.

What all motivation has in common is that we are coming from a sense of *lack*. We feel that something is missing, and we go out to get it. The assumption is that a sense of balance, or happiness, will be achieved when the missing something is found. Taken to its logical conclusion, this orientation has resulted in the consumer society. Motivation based on a sense of lack is not questioned; nor is whether our needs are valid or not. Of course, we do have valid, basic needs that must be met, but as I have pointed out, many of our needs have grown to the point of being artificial and compulsive.

The sense of lack can never be satisfied, but only transcended

How does motivation relate to acceptance? This is subtle, and may have to sit with you a while before it sinks in. When you are motivated to satisfy any desire that comes from a sense of lack, you are essentially rejecting yourself because you are attempting to avoid the feeling of lack. The nature of the dualistic experience is such that no amount of "satisfaction" will be satisfying, and the lack is affirmed and perpetuated, instead of being finally transcended.

The attempt to escape from lack through satisfying it in one form or another is often not apparent to us. We assume we act normally, we think we have needs, we rationalize our behavior, but the truth is that we are attempting to avoid the feeling, rejecting ourselves. After blame, wrong motivation is the next largest area of blindness that keeps us in suppression.

This type of motivation is referred to in the classical literature as the problem of desire. Most desires are considered as keeping us in bondage. Release from desire, not the satisfaction of desire, is a major part of liberation. Release from desire comes about by processing the desire impulse instead of being motivated by it.

Much of our motivation is unconscious, but we can become aware of it if we start with what is conscious. As we accept and experience impulses that we are aware of, we begin to uncover other, deeper motivation.

To give a basic example, suppose you are lonely and depressed. If your habitual response to this feeling is to suppress it through diversion in the form of relationships, entertainment, or substance abuse, you are being motivated by your depression, or by your lack of happiness. In seeking to avoid depression, you are rejecting it, and rejecting yourself. Integration of the feeling is not possible, and you will not get rid of the depression, except perhaps temporarily. You are locked into a cycle of depression/diversion. If you were to face the depression and begin integrating it, the depression would gradually go away. It wouldn't go away immediately, because you are likely to have a lot of suppressed feeling needing to be cleansed, but eventually you would become clear.

The same logic can be applied to all the centers of consciousness. We seek to avoid insecurity by grasping for psychological and material supports. We seek to avoid helplessness by going for power and prestige. We seek to avoid sexual tension by mindlessly chasing after sex. We seek to avoid feelings of inadequacy by going for approval. Our efforts are all self-defeating because they affirm and perpetuate the very thing we are trying to avoid. We are trying to avoid one side of dualistic experience by escaping into the other. Integrating these impulses is what will bring them into balance.

When we are motivated by the desire to be rid of body sensations we classify as "pain," we also self-reject, although this may be more difficult to comprehend. Our physical symptoms correspond to our psychic imbalances, as well as our emotional imbalances. Emotional problems are therefore related to the sensations in the body.

If you accept physical sensations, you do the most possible to integrate the psychic imbalance behind the discomfort. Accepting and experiencing the pain will lead to a balancing of energies. When you resist the pain, you strengthen it by feeding additional energy to it.

We also self-reject when motivated by moods of uncertainty, restlessness, irritation, etc. We become motivated into all kinds of evasive, self-destructive behavior. Simply be aware of your negative moods; accept and experience them. Let them dissolve by neither opposing nor being motivated by them.

If you understand that you cannot avoid the negative, you will cease to be motivated by it. You will accept it and end its compulsive influence.

Worrying

Worrying is the condition of thinking about feelings, instead of feeling the feelings. Often, there is a strong component of blame present. Worrying uses up much psychic energy, draining us and encouraging addictive tendencies to replace the energy.

You can cease worrying by first becoming aware of your worry, then consciously dropping the thoughts and blame about the feelings. Embrace and enter the feelings, no matter how difficult this may be. When you stop thinking about your feelings, you stop rejecting yourself because the thinking prevents direct experience of the feelings. You take the first steps to clearing the feelings.

Activity / Excitement

We need a balanced amount of activity, including physical exercise, to keep our energy from becoming lethargic, but sometimes we engage in activity for no other purpose than avoiding ourselves, resulting in self-rejection and suppression. The simple act of constantly doing something draws the attention outward, away from inner awareness. Since no real goal is involved, "keeping busy" becomes compulsive. Or else, unnecessary goals are created; workaholism prevails. We immerse ourselves in activity, and when the newness wears off, we assume we need a new activity. We run from one diversion to another, but we are really running from ourselves.

Excitement also draws us from inner awareness. We become thrill seekers. Because of the suppressive power of excitement, our pain or anxiety is made to disappear. We vibrate with the thrill. Excitement can become an addictive cycle. We oscillate between the up of the thrill and the down of having exhausted our energy, trying to get out of the down through more excitement. Since the old is no longer exciting, we are forced to find something new; we become desperate in our search. We become addicted to loud rock music, dangerous sports, violent entertainment, etc. We put ourselves into perilous situations for the thrill of it, becoming self-destructive.

As we survey modern life, it is hard to escape the conclusion that much of the frenetic pace that is common fits the above descriptions. We have actually lost the ability to just sit and do nothing, which is what meditation is. Trying to be still brings up anxiety or other feelings, often masked by boredom. Confronting these feelings is the first obstacle to any spiritual journey, and most people never get past it.

If compulsive activity or excitement is a problem for you, you must realize that the feelings you attempt to avoid are the result of past suppression. Continued suppression will result in eventual stagnation, and no amount of activity or excitement will do any good. There is no other way to regain contact with yourself except to begin to confront these feelings, through accepting and experiencing them.

Ambition

Ambition is one of the most common attributes of the isolated ego. The pain of isolation is felt, and it is assumed that release will come when personal success, wealth, possessions, or fame are acquired or achieved. This is the essence of materialism and the still popular American dream. Ambition is very much socially acceptable.

We become conditioned from childhood to reject ourselves and our present condition, whatever it may be, and to want more. We enter the race to nowhere, sometimes never waking up from the madness.

Ambition is one of the more acute forms of self-rejection, because a great deal of energy is mobilized to achieve goals. The same energy then serves to form the suppressing shields around feelings. We become highly goal-oriented, and out of touch with ourselves.

Note that it is not the actual working toward goals that comprises ambition; we must achieve certain goals to survive. Ambition is the addiction of the ego to the attainment of goals. The ego thinks it enlarges itself when it achieves. Goals become non-humanistic. We become selfish and isolated. Yet, ambition seems to be part of growing up.

We may delude ourselves that we have gone beyond ambition when we have merely made a shift in objectives. We stop being ambitious about materialistic things, becoming ambitious about artistic expression, recognition, or spiritual growth. Ambition for any of these has the same self-rejecting effect.

Dropping ambition involves learning to be happy as you are, in the moment, with no projections into the future. Happiness results from the acceptance of all of life – the life lived holistically.

Impatience

Impatience is another form of self-rejection that goes almost unnoticed. Impatience implies the rejection of what is happening right now. Because what is happening is our projection, self-rejection is the result. If you are impatient, you can never be in the moment, which is where direct experience takes place.

Impatience is the same as *rushing*. Realizing that most of our lives are spent in rushing to achieve goals gives us another perspective on the level of self-rejection that is common. Rushing means we are not relaxed; we are not accepting what is happening. When we are constantly rushing to get somewhere, we gradually lose the ability to be in the moment, which is the only place fulfillment can exist.

The loss of the ability to enjoy the moment especially shows up in our attitudes toward work. The idea of enjoying work is almost non-existent today. Enjoying work is made almost impossible by the pressures we face; but then, how many of these pressures are our own creation?

Behind the impatience and rushing lie suppressed feelings of anger, dissatisfaction, or frustration. We are compelled by such feelings, unconsciously assuming we can avoid them if we hurry, but we inevitably learn this is not possible.

Second Reaction

If you observe yourself carefully whenever a negative feeling comes up, you will notice something that might be called the "second reaction."

The first reaction is the feeling you are working with – your subconscious material, your Karma – coming to the surface, triggered by circumstances. You have no control over the first reaction, and should not attempt to resist it. The first reaction is of the body; it originates in the blocked chakras.

The "second reaction" is of the mind. You become upset

about the feelings that are coming up. If you are feeling angry, you will become additionally angry and impatient about having to take time to deal with the first anger or the situation, etc. You become angry about the anger, but you could become depressed or sad. Similarly, you become fearful about fear, sad about sadness, and so on. With the second reaction, you inwardly react to your feelings and reject yourself.

When you allow yourself to react to your feelings, you self-reject because you don't permit the free expression of the feelings into consciousness. Clearing will not occur. When the mind becomes agitated by the feelings it is perceiving, it is judging, and decides that it doesn't like what it sees. The mind is resisting, not allowing the feeling to pass into direct experience.

Moreover, when you become angry, and then angry about the anger, the second anger is directed at yourself. You are angry with yourself for allowing yourself to become angry. You falsely believe that you can and should control your feelings, and that anger is bad because it is painful.

Processing is based on the premise that we have no real control over our feelings. They come and go spontaneously as we unconsciously project and create our world. Surrendering to the lack of control over your feelings is an essential part of your self-acceptance.

I want to be sure you understand that the second reaction refers to your reaction to your feelings, not to the original feelings themselves. I am not suggesting that you have no feeling responses to the events of your life. Feelings are what you are learning to integrate. Being non-reactive means letting your feelings come and go spontaneously, without reacting to them. Accept your feelings without choice, and witness them impassively in direct experience.

Watch your feelings carefully. Learn to distinguish between the initial feeling and the second reaction. Since the second reaction is induced by the mind, you can control and eliminate it consciously, and no suppression is involved. This technique by itself can be enough to teach self-acceptance.

If you find that you cannot easily drop the second reaction – for example, if you continue to be angry at yourself for becoming angry – then process the second reaction as well. This will effectively integrate the second reaction, because you are now aware of the dynamics of what you are doing to yourself. Allowing yourself to be influenced by the second reaction is also known as "beating yourself up."

If you cultivate the ability to not react to your feelings and just allow them to be as they are, integration will begin. You open the door to direct experience of feelings, and eventual transformation.

Control

Control is an issue for many people, relating to autonomy, self-esteem, and the Power center. We feel that we like to be in control of what is happening. When things get out of control, we become anxious.

The areas that we would like to control may roughly be divided into inner feelings and outer circumstances. Control of the outer is what most people focus on, but it is the inner that they are attempting to influence.

Outwardly, we attempt to control whatever does not fit in with our mental concepts of how things should be. This amounts to self-rejection because, as we have discussed, perception of the external is always our projection; rejecting our projection is rejecting ourselves. People who need a high degree of control over their environment are suppressed, becoming threatened when events reveal their suppressed energy.

Inwardly, it is difficult to accept that we have no real control over emotions, moods, or desires. We try to control our feelings because they are painful or don't fit in with our belief systems, concepts, self-image, and goals, all of which are conditioned mind-sets keeping us from the experience of ourselves as we are.

We reject ourselves when we attempt to control our feelings. We reject ourselves when we edit our feelings, thinking that we should or shouldn't be having a certain feeling, or else attempt to actually control outside circumstances or people.

In the end, the measure of your need to control both inner and outer events is a good approximation of your addictions. Addicted people need to feel as if they exercise control over their dependencies. Addictions may happen only in certain specific areas. It is easy to fool yourself or others into thinking that you have no dependencies when you may be completely dependent on one thing: a particular possession, person, or self-image, for example. Many times we are unaware of the dependency because of its sheer magnitude.

Judging

It is normal to filter perceptions and feelings through a kind of evaluation grid. Something is presumed to be good, and some other thing bad. We have learned to judge mainly because of instinctual survival drives, but the tendency is carried over when there is no survival urgency, although there may appear to be because of our belief systems.

Whenever we categorize things as good or bad, we essentially reject ourselves because the very activity of the mind in making the classification blocks off direct experience. It does not matter that something has been judged as "good"; direct experience is still inhibited.

When we judge something as good, whether it is an internal feeling or external event, we affirm its dualistic nature, and set ourselves up for the complementary "bad" experience. We affirm our addiction.

In judging, we also affirm and reinforce our isolated self. We normally judge for our own benefit. In our culture, this is unquestioned, but we can avoid reinforcing our isolation by enlarging our sense of "I" to include others.

Judging, evaluating, and comparing are all based on the sense of the isolated self. Isolation leads us to believe that we must struggle to survive. The sense of the isolated self is the basic misconception that most spiritual practices address.

Concepts / Expectations

Concepts and expectations come into effect whenever we have an idea about how something should be, rather than accepting it as it is. This usually applies to conditions in the external world, but we maintain false concepts about our inner life as well. We feel we should always be happy, and we reject ourselves when we are not.

Our concepts, instead of helping us, actually form our limitations. We shut out reality because it does not match preconceived notions. Life is spontaneous and ever changing; our concepts can never keep up, and we reject life, simply because it does not fit in with what we know or expect.

Thus, if we are heavily into concepts, we become rigid in our behavior. We become narrow, we are not interesting to be with because we are always analyzing everything to see whether it will be good or bad for us. We are self-centered, instead of reality-centered.

Concepts are always based on addictions. For example, if you are addicted to first-center Survival issues, your concepts will concern security. You will feel you have to "own" things to serve as protection from the danger of not having. Your security is bound to objects. You become anxious about losing the objects, and obsessive about owning.

Self-Image

Concepts concerning the third chakra, the Power and Significance drives, form the special category of *self-image*. Self-image is a basic ego-concept, made somewhat difficult to recognize because it is often unconscious. We form mental opinions about ourselves and how we should be, and reject any part of ourselves that does not match. Self-image leads to the "masks" that we put on.

The influence of self-image can be felt on the most basic levels. We feel that we should be strong and reject ourselves for being weak. Feelings of weakness are then suppressed and not allowed to exist and find an integrated balance. We create the neurotic need to be strong, to balance the suppressed, but still unconsciously felt weakness. Moreover, self-image defines exactly what strong and weak behavior is, which varies according to individual and culture.

Similarly, self-image might demand that we be superior. We then suppress, affirm, and maintain inferiority. We can think we are superior for almost any reason – because of possessions, abilities, social identity, lovableness, saintliness, or success.

Self-image can be especially limiting when we try to establish personal growth goals. We think we should always be happy and successful, and we suppress perceived unhappiness and failure. The free flow of energies is inhibited. Our perception of *what is* becomes limited.

A trap for the spiritual seeker is the self-image "I should always be loving." When we are not loving, we feel as if we have failed. "Love" becomes a forced sentimentality, which later rebounds as the complement is experienced. The problem is that our idea of love is just another concept constructed by the mind; it is not real love. I am not saying you should express resentment if that is what you happen to be feeling. It's just that, as a spiritual seeker, it is easy to fall into the self-rejecting habit of judging your feelings, and becoming upset when you discover negativities you think you should not have. This is nothing less than suppression, and I have seen "spiritual" people who continue to reject themselves even though they have been in spiritual circles for years. As a result, they make no progress and become hypocritical, thinking they are "loving," when they are constantly giving out messages from their suppressed subconscious of exactly the opposite. They are trying to make themselves conform to a spiritual ideal that they have acquired.

Whenever you want to be like anything or anyone, no matter how beautiful or exalted, you reject yourself. You are trying to mold yourself in the image of something or someone else, and this never works. If the person whom you admire is a great person, they didn't become so by trying to emulate someone else, but by being themselves. Being "yourself" is what we are talking about – not trying to force yourself to conform to a concept of the mind.

The problem becomes one of recognizing what you really are, instead of what your concepts superimpose on you. This is another way of describing the nature of the spiritual quest. Self-image concepts are part of your unconscious mental conditioning. As you go further into understanding what you are not, other conditioning will surface to be released.

Processing will release you from concepts that limit you. By starting with whatever negative feelings you are aware of, you will gradually discover the underlying concepts. You may pick up the thread at any point, and eventually the complete pattern will become clear.

Identification

Identification is similar to self-image. Self-image refers to imagined or real qualities that are identified with to enhance and protect the ego. The term "identification," when used by itself, refers to the attempt to lose oneself by merging with something outside of oneself. This can be almost anything – an organization, person, idea, purpose, career, role, creation or possession.

Although most of us are probably familiar with the concept of identification, it is still one of the most common ways of self-rejection. We identify with something because we want to escape from ourselves. We try to avoid the pain that we are feeling: more specifically, the pain of isolation, loneliness, or emptiness. We become driven to find significance in the identification syndrome, but never succeed.

When we attach to something outside ourselves, we feel larger than we were. We no longer have to look at ourselves and our inner pain. I believe that an energy transfer takes place, and we feed dependently off the object, even if it is an object we have created. Examples would be attachment to corporations, groups, or a small business of our own, all of which have their own existence as entities with energy potentials and boundaries.

Identification builds a false sense of importance, and relates to the Power center. We say, "my" wife or husband, "my" career, "my" home, "my" knowledge. Anything that threatens these objects is perceived as a personal attack. If our work is criticized, we feel we are being attacked. If the work fails, we have failed.

Identification results in self-rejection because whenever we identify with something, we attempt to escape from ourselves. We also disidentify with and reject everything outside of the object. Since we usually project heavily onto whatever is excluded, we reject ourselves. This can result in extreme behavior such as racism, where inner negativities are projected onto the group that is rejected.

In the initial stages of identification, it is possible to feel a euphoria that can obscure the objective awareness of the addiction. The euphoria is all the more heightened if one has been leading an aimless existence, because it will appear that finally something has been found that gives meaning to life. The dualistic experience that awaits is not sensed.

For this is the problem with identification: In the end, it is strongly dualistic. We are addicted to and dependent upon the object, and we fear losing it. We will create our own negative experience, as we have created the positive. We are bound to the object, and growth comes to a standstill. Self-rejection continues because we do not face ourselves as we are – we try to avoid ourselves by merging with the object.

Once you are aware of the mechanics of identification, you will be able to see it in yourself. At that point, it must be treated like an addiction. Breaking the identification will entail pain, because you will feel as if you are losing a part of yourself. You will feel lost and empty. Previous negative feelings that were suppressed by the identification will come to the surface. All this has to be processed, and eventually equilibrium will be found.

The term "identification" also describes the tendency to think of ourselves as the same as our emotions, both positive and negative. The aim of spiritual practice or therapy has always been to break emotional identification. Paradoxically, we then own our feelings, but do not identify with them. Feelings are seen to be of the lower self, while our sense of identity is transferred to the Higher Self.

Future Orientation / Hope

Our culture has always encouraged holding and working toward hopes, ideals, and goals. At times, there is a real need to improve conditions, but when we are continually dreaming about the future, it becomes obvious that we are attempting to avoid the present. The unpleasant present is avoided by fantasizing about the future, even if we are being motivated by what we might think are the highest of ideals.

It is also possible to fantasize about how *dreadful* the future may be, giving full play to our fear. The point is that we live in the future in order in escape from the present, which consists of all our feelings, as they are.

*Hope takes you out
of the moment*

A certain kind of strength can be drawn from fantasies and hopes about the future. If you have a strong goal before you, you can endure hardships that would normally be debilitating. The hope keeps you going. It is possible to endure a miserable life because you think you are working for something that will bring you, or even someone else, happiness in the future.

However, the strength that comes from hope is a false strength. It is more of a strength from *tension* than from being centered.

Becoming accustomed to using this kind of energy results in chronic future orientation, and the inability to be happy now. You become "time-bound" – conditioned to look to the future for fulfillment. You become restless, and incessantly addicted to activity, thinking that fulfillment will always be around the corner; but future orientation never allows you to really experience the pleasure (or pain) of the moment. When you finally get to the future, you are still thinking about another future goal, and you again miss the present. Attachment to future goals, ideals, and hopes is so pervasive that it becomes an area of continual self-discovery. We keep finding new areas of attachment that we did not see before.

Nevertheless, there may be times when we need to rely on hope to get us through; taking away all hope from ourselves or others may be pointless or even cruel. In dealing with self-rejection, gentleness and judgment are called for, and we must not exceed our toleration point.

Past Orientation / Idealizing

Living in the past, thinking about how good or bad things were, becoming attached to people or situations in the past, are all ways that are used to block awareness of the present. The exception is when a past event is re-experienced in order to integrate it. In this case, we work with present feelings about the past event, which are often the same feelings that were suppressed at the time of the event.

If we are continually thinking about pleasant times in the past, we are avoiding the present; but sometimes the motivation may be even more subtle. Usually, the pleasantness of the past was of a dualistic nature. At the time of the experience, the negative component was suppressed. The suppressed negativity remains, and keeps surfacing in the thoughts that draw us back to the episode in question. We don't recognize that the subconscious is trying to clear, and we persist in dwelling on the positive parts of the experience, which were a projection to begin with. The suppression in held in place. This happens when we idealize someone from the past: a parent, spouse, or child whom we have "sanctified." We become attached to the projection, and avoid confronting our real feelings.

Trauma

Occasionally, we find that we can't let go of negative, traumatic events of the past. We dwell on events that have happened, we relive them, and our spontaneity becomes inhibited by persistent thoughts of the event. This may happen with victims of crime, abuse, assault, severe psychological shock or pain.

Trauma is actually suppression, in which feelings are involuntarily rejected, blocking release of the energies. This mechanism seems to be part of the instinctive defenses. Treating traumatic reactions has always been the focus of much of traditional psychotherapy. Trauma arises because the pain involved in the event has not been faced and experienced. Instead, we remain in the mind, constantly thinking about the event. Ironically, our thoughts become the shield from our feelings. Even though we think about the event, we still do not integrate the feelings, which continue to haunt us. There is no way to clear traumatic feelings except by ending resistance to them and experiencing them, as was not done when the event occurred.

Ending resistance to traumatic feelings will cause integration. You must carefully watch how you reject and resist the feelings. Enter meditation, activate the Witness, and drop resistance; allow the feelings to just be. Allow them to work out their own cycle and eventually dissolve.

Try to distinguish your thoughts from your feelings. Often, there is a strong component of blame present in thoughts. This is all that is needed to prevent acceptance. You then remain unable to clear the feelings that are trapped in the energy body.

Seeking Understanding / Searching / Analyzing / Thinking

Seeking understanding can prevent direct experience of feelings, and can therefore be considered self-rejecting. Most people are not aware of this. They think that in seeking understanding they are attempting to learn about themselves, in order to better cope with the future. The result is the incessant mental activity known as thinking.

Excessive thinking has always been considered to be a hindrance on the path to spiritual enlightenment, or mental and emotional health, whichever way you prefer to look at it. The primary aim of meditation disciplines is to quiet the mind, not to provide verbal answers. When the mind is quieted, the answers will come, but they will not be of the mind. The mind can never go beyond the known, and the known will not provide what is needed.

In other words, when the mind is quiet, direct experience can occur. We move into the moment, and the answer comes spontaneously.

Still, there are things that must be understood. The key is proper use of the mind and intellect, not their abuse. We need to understand how our energy systems work, which includes understanding their limitations. We need to eventually become aware of our patterns, our beliefs, and our motivations. We need to know how to approach our problems, how to work on ourselves.

We misuse the mind when we search for the answer that will make everything right. There is no such answer, and everything will never be right. This is what must be accepted. Then, integration will occur. Excessive analysis becomes a defense and an escape.

Escapist Behavior / Boredom

When you immerse yourself in activity with the conscious or unconscious intent to avoid feelings, you are attempting to escape.

Anything can be used as an escape. The most obvious is entertainment: the television, film, news, radio, publishing, and music industries that form such a huge business in our culture. You can escape into work, sex, relationships, humanistic pursuits, art, anything. It is not the activity that is the escape, but how it is used.

Of course, from time to time there is a legitimate need for escape from the pressures of daily routine. When escape into diversion is conscious and moderate, no harm is done. Self-rejection begins when escape from reality is excessive and compulsive.

Boredom is one of the feelings we commonly try to escape from. Boredom is the mask for any number of negative feelings that are hiding just behind: anxiety, depression, sexual frustration, and fears of all kinds, for example. When you react to boredom by trying to escape from it, you self-reject. You continue to suppress the negative feelings lying just behind the boredom. Boredom is a sign that a large amount of suppression is taking place.

Boredom often comes up in meditation or breathwork practices. It means you are disturbing suppressed energies and are unconsciously defending yourself with the boredom. Do not be defeated by boredom, but transform it. Processing boredom can be fruitful; it will lead to the feelings being covered over. You don't have to become compulsive about this either, thinking that you can never turn to any kind of activity because you will be escaping. Keep a balanced and moderate frame of reference.

A good rule of thumb is to ask yourself whether you are engaging in an activity to find happiness, or to express the happiness you feel within. Usually, there is very little we do that we could say is expressive of happiness. We remain trapped in the dualistic world, oblivious to the spiritual reality that happiness must come from within, through the reconciliation and transcendence of dualities.

Substance Addiction

Substance addiction, whether to drugs, alcohol, smoking, or food, is a more advanced form of escape. The addictive cycle provides psychic energy that is used to maintain suppression, as well as to provide energy simply to function. This condition is reached because of the habitual behavior of escaping. The constant turning away from ourselves builds the blocks that cut us off from our own energy resources, resulting in extreme self-rejection and real dependence on the substance.

The energy we gain access to in the addictive cycle is of two basic types: that which comes from within, and that which comes from without.

In all forms of substance abuse, we gain access to energy within. What we tap into, however, is of the nature of reserve energy. We use up our reserves, and the eventual end is complete psychic and physical exhaustion. Addiction to alcohol as well as to illegal and prescription drugs is rampant in our culture, although many people think they are not addicted because their level of consumption is no more than normal. They become "social" drinkers or drug users. If you have to have one or more drinks every evening after coming home from work, you may want to take a hard look at whether or not this constitutes addiction.

In other forms of addiction, we tap into energy outside of ourselves. This happens in power or sexual addictions, for example, when others are involved. Relationship dependence is a special kind of addiction, where we seek in the other the energy of the qualities we have blocked off in ourselves.

All addictions have the same deceptive quality. We think we are benefiting from the addiction because we feel more relaxed or function better when we are on the peak. We forget that the valleys between the peaks are also created by the addictive cycle.

Relationships

Romantic relationships can be an effective form of self-rejection. It is possible to escape from ourselves into the newness and excitement of the romance, leaving it when the excitement wears off. This form of self-rejection and the longing for it are epidemic in our culture. Of course, I am not saying that one should not enter into relationships. The need for relationships of all types is a genuine need. It is when the relationship is used for escape that it becomes self-rejecting. We will discuss relationships in more depth later.

ACTIVATE YOUR HEART CENTER

All of us suffer from many of the above forms of self-rejection. Sometimes we will be clear in most areas, but completely self-rejecting in another area. This is where we defend ourselves from ourselves. This is what is preventing us from breaking out of our self-enclosed ways.

You must approach acceptance slowly. Work on one aspect at a time. Be careful that as you become self-accepting in one area, you do not transfer your self-rejection to other areas.

Stopping self-rejection requires courage of the highest type. You are, indeed, approaching the work of a lifetime, and it will require all your fortitude. You now know, however, that accepting yourself is the work that you are to do.

The courage to face your real feelings will bring the first light of self-love, the birth of true self-esteem. Self-love is of the Heart center, and you can further activate it by concentrating on and breathing into the Heart as you accept yourself and your feelings. Know that self-love is not dependent upon any object.

It is dependent upon your acceptance of yourself, and of others as reflections of you.

Self-love can exist as you face any negative condition. More accurately, self-love will come into being *as you face* those conditions. You will know that what you are doing has real value, value that will stay with you forever. You are building the spiritual body, which is the only thing you take when you leave this earth.

As your respect for yourself grows because of the courage you demonstrate in facing yourself, your respect for others will also grow, because this is an extension of your respect for yourself. So too, as your self-love grows, your love for others – real love – will come into existence. Real love cannot be thought, persuaded, or imagined into being; it comes about through your acceptance.

I enter the direct experience of my

feelings. I understand that I must confront

fully what I have avoided in the past,

in order to bring myself into balance.

I experience the feelings behind my addictions

and compulsions. I enter my feelings during

meditation, observing my toleration point.

8

Direct Experience

When you drop self-rejection, you end the mental activity that interferes with the clear perception of both inner and outer events. You become self-accepting, and your mind assumes a transparent quality; it is still there, but as it is quiet, you can see through it. Perception is not colored by the mind. You enter direct experience.

What can now be experienced directly and clearly is of the nature of energy – what we have been calling feelings and emotions. Energy patterns and exchanges make up existence. When you open yourself to energy, you open yourself to life. Direct experience is possible because you have entered "the moment." This is the state that comes about when the mind has ceased its self-rejecting activity. Until then, there is always a sense of time, either looking forward or backward. The mind is the creator of time. Entering the moment means that the mind is no longer attached to time consciousness, and is content to encounter life as it manifests now. There is no resistance or desire to escape from *what is*.

This is when integration really begins. Integration means the mind has accepted, and you are in the moment with, your

171

feelings and experiences. Being in the moment is the end point of all psychological, spiritual, or true religious teachings. It has been called peak experience, cosmic consciousness, self-realization, or God consciousness, but all these names refer to the experience of the eternal "Now."

The moment is completely simple, and that is why it is so easy to miss. You can enter the moment at any time, by dropping the self-rejecting mental activity that searches, judges, clings, and avoids. The moment is a state of consciousness, a new feeling, and does not imply that you should cease preparing for the future; only that you don't live in the future. Be careful as well that you don't confuse living in the moment with living *for* the moment. This could possibly lead to becoming irresponsible, self-indulgent, or unconcerned with the rights of others.

ENTER THE FEELING

Feelings are entered by keeping them in consciousness without resistance, experiencing them fully, but without acting on them. The natural flow of the energy of the feelings is permitted to occur. If feelings are avoided or resisted, they are suppressed. By simply staying in the moment with feelings, allowing them *to be* for as long as necessary, the emotional charge is dissolved. This may be done either in activity or meditation. Allowing feelings to exist without resistance eventually results in their cycle of energy being completed.

Go into the body experience
of the feeling, in the moment

To enter any feeling, bring your attention into the body, where feelings originate. With an accepting mind, feelings can be perceived with clarity and sensitivity. You will be able to sense your body to a depth that was never possible when you were self-rejecting. Accept the feeling. Open yourself to it.

Experience it without resistance. Become *choiceless* about whether you want to have the feeling or not. Stay with the experience of the feeling until you sense a change, a break in the energy. Have faith that facing the feeling will result in the eventual integration and transcendence of the issue.

Feelings can occur in the chakras as well as in any other part of the body. Try to focus on the physical area where the feeling is occurring. If you cannot associate the feeling with a specific place, go into your body in general. Feelings can be complex, and can be the result of the interaction of two or more chakras; it may be hard to pinpoint a specific feeling. Eventually, your sensitivity will increase, and you will be able to relate different feelings to their body locations.

If the feeling you are working with is associated with an outer event, such as an interaction with another person, keep the event in your consciousness along with the feeling. Drop all forms of self-rejection, such as blame. Simply hold the scene before you in your imagination, opening to and experiencing fully the feelings that come up.

*Do not try to
analyze the feeling*

You should remember that you are not entering the feeling with the intention of analyzing and understanding it. Don't try to understand why the event happened, why you did or felt what you did, what is there to learn from the event, etc. These insights will come spontaneously *as a result* of the integration that direct experience will bring. For now, just fully experience the feelings of the event. If you persist in trying to analyze, integration is inhibited.

*Do not think you must "express"
a feeling to release it*

When you allow a feeling to enter your consciousness without resistance, it begins clearing. The feeling does not have to be expressed verbally or acted out in order to be released. Release will often be accompanied by sounds, movements of the body, or crying, which is perfectly fine, but do not think that you must express feelings outwardly to release them. Release will take place when you allow the feeling to enter your consciousness with acceptance. Bringing suppressed feelings into consciousness, *with complete acceptance,* is all the expression that is required for their release.

I find it unfortunate that many psychologists still create the impression that to release suppressed feelings, they must somehow be expressed outwardly into the world. Therapy may then involve psychodrama and role playing. This may be appropriate sometimes, in order to get the client in touch with feelings, but I feel it is not as effective as inner owning and confrontation. Outward expression may be the only recourse if the client does not have the capacity for an inward, meditative approach. Nevertheless, development of the meditative capacity is a basic requirement for inner growth, and therapy should not overlook this.

Sharing is another type of outward expression. Of course, I am not against sharing your feelings with either a therapist or a close friend. Sharing can be helpful at the right time, but don't think that you have to share in order for integration to occur. Sharing can be abused, and become a dependency and another way to avoid your feelings.

Keep a clear distinction between
feelings and self-rejecting thoughts

Even though you dropped self-rejecting thoughts when you accepted yourself, you are still likely to oscillate between self-rejection and acceptance. For example, suppose you are integrating a painful feeling that you had previously rejected because you blamed someone for causing it. You will probably tend to fall in and out of blame as you work with the feeling.

As long as you are holding blame in your mind, you are not really in direct experience. You have fallen back into self-rejection. You are trying to process the blame along with the feeling, but remember, self-rejection such as blame can not be processed. Self-rejection is a function of the mind, not of the energy body. Processing applies only to suppressed energy.

When you catch yourself falling back into self-rejection, you must deliberately shift again to focusing on the feeling, and away from the self-rejecting thoughts. Keep bringing your attention from the blame back to the feeling whenever necessary. Keep separating the blame from the feeling. You could focus your attention on either one, but when you focus on the feeling, the blame will not be present in your consciousness. You can develop this ability with a minimum of practice, and will be able to stay with the actual experience being integrated, avoiding the self-rejection.

USE BREATH AND BODYWORK

If you are working on integrating a serious issue, you will want to set aside some time for incorporating breath and bodywork. We have not discussed breath and bodywork since Chapter Four, but that does not mean that they are of secondary usefulness; in fact, they can be instrumental in bringing about integration.

Working with the body brings us into
closer rapport with the feelings

Feelings are composed of energy and occur in the body. When the energy gets stuck in the body, in the chakras, we experience emotional problems. Working with the body can be instrumental in loosening the stuck energy and quieting the self-rejection of the mind.

I would recommend a basic routine of Yoga postures as an effective and convenient approach for working with the body. Other bodywork techniques involving a practitioner might be added if you are so inclined, but I would not consider this essential.

Certain Yoga postures will work on unblocking certain chakras, and if you can identify the chakra, you can hold the appropriate postures while experiencing feelings, increasing the cleansing effectiveness. A Yoga session can last anywhere from ten minutes to an hour or two, but even a short session will be invaluable to get you into your body. Please remember that exercise in general does not serve the purpose of bodywork or Yoga.

After loosening the energy flow with Yoga, breath will be helpful in breaking energy blocks. Breathing into the chakra is especially effective. As you are breathing, continue to integrate the event, by being with it without resistance. The prana that you are generating through the breath goes directly into the energy block.

This serves two purposes. First, correct breathing will bring suppressed issues to consciousness, allowing you to become aware of them and begin conscious integration. Second, breath will implement the integration of the issue, which may not always happen quickly with acceptance alone.

INTEGRATE FEELINGS BEHIND THE ADDICTION

Confronting addiction is central in inner work.

First, you must realize that you actually have an addiction. You may think you only have needs, but there is a subtle distinction between needs and addictions. Addictions are compulsive; you are attached to the object. You escape into the object, and become anxious when denied the object, whether it is a person, possession, or substance. True needs are more in line with the natural cycles of being.

Let's summarize the types of addictions, as they relate to the various centers:

FIRST/Security: Anything that represents security and serves to mask fear or anxiety. Wealth, material possessions, work, activity.

SECOND/Sensation: Substances, including alcohol, drugs, tranquilizers, smoking, food. Tactile and sensual sensations, including sex, luxury, entertainment.

THIRD/Power: Status, self-image, significance, influence, importance, accomplishment, approval.

FOURTH/Heart: Relationship dependency.

FIFTH/Creative: Creative expression.

If you have any such addiction, there will be many times when you will be compelled to satisfy it. This is when you can set yourself free. Unfortunately, there is no other way to proceed except to confront the pain and anxiety that will come up now.

Now is the time to use the principles we have been discussing. Use your knowledge to accept the anxiety, depression, and pain. Refuse to reject yourself any longer by rejecting these feelings. Enter them, and experience them as they integrate and dissolve. Use Witnessing techniques to absorb the negativity, instead of yielding to it and being motivated by it into the addiction.

Learn to distinguish between the
impulse to satisfy an addiction
and the feeling behind the addiction

For example, suppose you have a food addiction. The food cravings are the impulse to satisfy the addiction. Behind the addiction are the feelings that you are suppressing with the addiction. You may not even be conscious of those feelings.

You may have unconscious fear that you keep suppressed with the food addiction.

Begin by working with the impulse to satisfy the addiction. This impulse is a form of energy tension, which will respond to the techniques you are learning. The strong concentration on the impulse will reduce it without your having to act on it. In the case of food or any other kind of cravings, allow the cravings to be without acting on them. Do not fight having the feelings; fighting gives more power to the cravings. Do not try to escape from the cravings by ignoring them or distracting yourself from them. Confront and integrate the cravings, using the powerful help of breath and bodywork. You can beat cravings with acceptance. Cravings are cyclical. If you can face them for a short period, they will retreat until the next time. The time between attacks will become longer, and you will start gaining the upper hand.

If the impulse is too strong to resist, practice accepting the impulse for a while before giving in to it, gradually increasing the direct experience time. Substitute something harmless for the addictive substance. If you have a severe addiction problem, a support group will be invaluable, but in the end, confrontation in some form is what it comes down to. The feelings must be faced.

Eventually, you will become aware of the feelings you are suppressing with the addiction. When this happens, you know that you are making progress. Sometimes, just becoming aware of these feelings can provide the catharsis necessary to break the hold of the addiction, but usually further integration of the feelings will be needed. Confronting your addiction is no easy task, but remember, this is essential work for you. You are working on your evolution into higher consciousness.

EXPERIENCE FEELINGS DURING MEDITATION

Direct experience of feelings can be best accomplished during meditation, although it can also be done in activity, when the event is taking place. If you regularly practice meditation, I would suggest adding processing to the other techniques you now use. If you are not practicing meditation, processing is an excellent way to start developing meditation skills. The concept of processing is, in fact, essential to any meditative discipline.

In meditation, brainwaves slow down to the Alpha level of activity. This state induces relaxation and healing. If you work on yourself while in Alpha, you have a tremendous advantage. Integration proceeds almost by itself, and the Witness is easily activated.

An important part of meditation is the cleansing that takes place. Just sitting still gives the subconscious the opportunity to bring its suppressed contents to consciousness. Various feelings will come up as the subconscious cleanses. If you don't practice meditation, the sole alternative for cleansing is the projection mechanism, which results in a distorted perception of the world.

*Do not re-suppress feelings
that come up in meditation*

When feelings come up in meditation, they must be handled properly if cleansing is to be effective. When I first began to meditate, I didn't understand this. My intention in meditation was to calm the mind, expand my consciousness, and enter more blissful states. In other words, to escape.

Whenever disturbing emotions came up, I assumed I was having a bad meditation. I tried to avoid the feelings, by bringing my attention back to the object of meditation. I became upset, and would get angry about the anger, fearful about the fear, and so on. Meditation became a fight to try to control my thoughts and feelings. What I was doing, I understand now, was re-suppressing negative energies as they came up for clearing. I had no concept of integration, as we have been discussing. I thought that I would eventually get past negative intrusions, but I never did, and my attitude about meditation became pessimistic. I was unknowingly practicing what is called "suppressive meditation."

Eventually, I came to understand that the problem was in my approach. This insight had much to do with my decision to write this book, because I feel other people probably make the same mistake. By emphasizing integration and clearing, perhaps the pitfall of suppressive meditation can be avoided.

Processing, then, can be thought of as an essential preliminary to depth meditation. When negative material comes up, in activity as well as meditation, it means the subconscious is trying to clear itself. You must take time to accept and experience whatever is coming up.

Even though I have been practicing meditation for many years, I have benefited most in the more recent years, when I understood cleansing and did not resist being with negative feelings. Much, if not most, of my meditation time is still spent working with negative feelings. I know that I have benefited from this therapy. I know that I have integrated and left behind compulsive patterns.

When I sit to meditate now, I first enter Alpha and the Witness. I go into my body. I start gentle breathing, and watch for whatever body sensations may occur. I assume any pains that appear in the body are just negative energies releasing themselves. I witness these. If I feel an emotion, I go into the corresponding center, breathing into the center to free the energy. I let the emotion or feeling build without reacting to it – I simply watch and feel. Soon, that particular feeling will have dissipated, and something else may come up. After a while, feelings and emotions will have spent themselves. I begin to lose awareness of the body, and enter other stages of meditation. There is no fighting, no controlling, no intention, no expectation. I am fine with whatever happens.

BRING UP UNRESOLVED ISSUES FROM THE PAST

Even though our main focus is on our feelings as they are right now, sometimes it is helpful to work with feelings about past events. Many painful, unresolved issues have a past-time reference about them. We have sustained hurt and loss in the past, and these feelings must be cleared. Actually, we are dealing with present feelings, but since they have a connection to the past, the feelings can be precipitated by going into the past. This is simply a therapeutic technique, and does not mean that you are living in the past.

You can go back to any painful incident, recent or remote, and bring it into your field of awareness as you sit in meditation. Relive the incident from the Witness vantage point. The trapped subconscious pain will be triggered. As feelings come up, welcome them. If there are certain issues that you consider too painful to go into, they are obviously the very ones that need attention. They are likely to be influencing you in ways you do not suspect.

Remember that you are not going back into the past to try to understand. You are bringing up feelings for acceptance, experience, and integration. Allow understanding to come as a *result* of integration. Searching for understanding during meditation will prevent you from going into meditation, Alpha, and the Witness.

Remember to stay aware of the distinction between the feeling and the self-rejection that originally suppressed it. Deliberately drop the self-rejection. Don't sit and re-suppress the feeling by reliving the self-rejection.

As we have discussed, parents should not be held responsible for childhood trauma. Even so, reliving events from childhood can serve as a valuable hunting ground for bringing up suppressed energies, if you feel so inclined. Working with the wounded inner child, for example, can be an important part of self-healing for some people, although it is by no means the only approach. Other areas of the past will become apparent to you. Try to connect past incidents with current problems.

You may question whether going back into the past is pertinent to living your life now. It is, because the past becomes *symbolic* of the present. In one sense, it does not even matter if your memory is accurate or not; you are only recalling your subjective view anyway, which may be very different from someone else's. It is still effective because your memory is a symbolic drama, a metaphor, which triggers the subconscious.

You are doing therapy to yourself with this technique. Don't be afraid of going deep into traumatic issues. Past events are the most common format in which feelings come up during meditation. Don't resist memories that recur – it means that something is crying out for release. Accept the memory, no matter how painful, and stay with it until all negativity is released. You can assume this has happened when there is no longer an emotional charge associated with the memory. If something is especially hard to face, it is a major issue for you, and represents much more than you probably realize. Working with it will integrate more than you expect.

In therapy, this kind of approach is similar to what is known as *desensitization,* which is used with phobias, obsessions, and compulsions. Gradually and gently increase your exposure to the threatening issue, and open to whatever feelings come up.

BRING YOUR FEELINGS TO A CRISIS

If you enter the experience of a negative emotion, and do not give in to outwardly expressing it, or in any other way try to avoid the feeling, it may build within you. You may begin to tremble, feeling the energy as it moves around your body. You may become lost in emotion; your sense of identity may alter; you may begin weeping. In not avoiding the emotion, by accepting it, you permit it to build to the point of crisis. This is the *healing crisis.* Crisis should not be pursued too actively, but if it happens, you should know what to do.

Allowing your feelings to come to a crisis does *not* mean you are not "letting your feelings out." Of course, feelings must be released, and not allowed to accumulate in the energy body. What actually happens, however, is that whatever method we choose for letting feelings out usually involves self-rejection. The feelings are re-suppressed, and not really let out at all.

When feelings are accepted, they are not suppressed. The very act of keeping them in consciousness means they are being cleared. If they can be kept in consciousness to the extent that a crisis builds, this represents a catharsis and healing. Allowing crisis to build calls for the warrior spirit. Try it if the opportunity arises. You will push back some of your personal boundaries, I can assure you.

If you enter a crisis, meditation would be the best format. The crisis should not be prolonged beyond the period of meditation, but you may break from the sitting pose to assume any Yoga posture that will work on the chakra or any other part of the body involved. Alternate between sitting and the posture.

Breath control becomes important. Use the Integrating breath, which we study in Chapter Eleven. The breath will keep the energies manageable. Breath will allow easier access to the Witness, which provides a calm vantage point to observe the crisis that is happening, usually in the lower four chakras. The breath need not necessarily be fast or deep, just steady.

The crisis will always pass, and any shaking or trembling will cease. You will know that you have cleared a considerable amount of negativity from your subconscious because of how you now feel. I have never been hurt from allowing my feelings to build to a crisis, nor have I known anyone who has. Our fears of emotional crisis are usually unfounded, but you will have to decide if this kind of intense work is appropriate for you. If you have a history of mental or emotional imbalance, allowing a crisis to build would probably *not* be advisable, and you should consult with a therapist before proceeding.

You might also want to be cautious in allowing inner emotional crisis to build when working with an active emotion like anger. Anger produces adrenalin, making the body ready for fight or flight. Physical release like beating pillows, sports, manual labor, etc., may be helpful if you have not yet fully developed the capacity for inward releasing.

However, I have found that active emotions are not deeply affected through physical "releasing," but only the most superficial aspects of the energy are touched. I have been able to accomplish more of a physical/emotional release with Yoga postures. I have devoted considerable time to passively allowing anger to build to a crisis in meditation, and have achieved substantial clearing. The adrenalin has always been able to dissipate, and even aided, I have felt, in breaking up the congested energy in the solar plexus chakra.

Other, more passive emotions, like fear, sexual impulses, loneliness, and addictive impulses do not have the same motive power as anger and may be safely brought to an inner crisis.

OBSERVE YOUR TOLERATION POINT

Even though we have just discussed the integration that a healing crisis can provide, you should also be aware of your own personal toleration point.

As you drop self-rejecting habits, you open to the possibility of real growth, but growth does not come without a certain stress. When you look inside, you are likely to become aware of chaos. Fear, anger, sexual impulses, loneliness, which have all been suppressed, are now coming to the surface for integration. You may even think you are getting worse instead of better; this is common on the path to self-individualization. You are not getting worse, but are just noticing what you have been hiding in your subconscious. You cannot return to the blissful state of ignorance about yourself; you must go forward, through the negativity that is surfacing.

When you stop self-rejection, you are left confronting the negativity that would normally be suppressed through the self-rejection. You are learning to integrate this negativity, but because you are still learning, it may not be possible to integrate as fast as necessary to handle all that is coming up. You reach the condition of *overload*. Overload is stressful, and to find an escape from the energies, you will self-reject, possibly in a different manner from what you have just dropped.

Do not exchange one kind of
self-rejection for another

For example, suppose you have become conscious of how you have been self-rejecting through blaming others. You might then shift to blaming yourself to re-suppress the excess energies that cannot be integrated. Or, you could shift to escape through excessive activity or entertainment, movies and novels, etc. Shifting methods of self-rejection is common and often unconscious. You exceed your toleration point for integration, and compensate by creating new habits of self-rejection to take the place of the old.

Being aware of this syndrome will help you to avoid it. You should try to get a sense of when you are approaching your toleration point, and not exceed it. You may have to stop inner work and fall back into old habits of self-rejection, but this is better than unconsciously creating new habits of self-rejection. Just being aware of the self-rejecting pattern will in itself help to loosen it. Gradually, your ability to integrate will increase. You should not feel any impatience with yourself for having such a limitation. If you accept the limitation and work within it, you establish a groundedness that will be of great value.

I invoke the healing power and the

self-love of Witness consciousness.

I feel its presence as I surrender

the outcome of my experience to the

Higher Self. I allow the Higher Self

to work in my behalf. Transformation

occurs that I could not anticipate, and

I am taken to a higher plane of existence.

I have transcended. I have grown.

9

Transformation

Transformation is the fourth step in Integrative Processing. In order to reach this step, you must have passed through the previous steps: You have become aware of your feelings regarding any event or condition, and have taken responsibility for them; you have ceased any self-rejection concerning the feelings; you have entered direct experience of the feelings.

Transformation involves the spiritual component of the individuality, or what is called the *transpersonal* in contemporary psychology. Don't be misled into thinking that the transpersonal is something outside yourself. Transpersonal, to me, only means that part of myself which is beyond my ordinary, lower-self awareness. The Higher Self is the transpersonal.

When we are not in direct contact with the Higher Self, we project and experience it as a power outside of ourselves. There is nothing wrong with this; it corresponds to a stage of evolution. However, an important part of self-realization is the awareness that the power is within. It is this inner power of the Higher Self that guides transformation.

There is a difference between change and transformation. Change implies a willful, decisive move. The intellect decides something needs to be different, and action is deliberately taken. There are times when change is necessary.

Yet, there are times when the aggressiveness of deliberate change will not, and cannot, be effective. The intellect eventually realizes that to find fulfillment, experience must become new, and the unknown must be entered. Willful determination fails, because the intellect can only chart a course to what is already known.

Transformation becomes the recourse. Transformation implies the natural outgrowing of one set of circumstances into another, guided by the power of the Higher Self. There is no forcing to be something that appears to be more attractive, or more valuable. Surrender to the present unfailingly brings about transformation into the future. Growth takes place without effort; the Heart opens without knowledge; transformation comes without asking.

ACTIVATE THE WITNESS –
BRING IN HEALING ENERGY

Witnessing is the traditional term used to describe the detached attitude that is acquired when the sixth chakra, the "Third Eye," is activated. Certain meditation techniques, which we shall discuss in Chapter 11, involve concentrating on this point to invoke the Witness capacity.

Witnessing means just what it implies. We cultivate an impassive stance toward what is happening. We become the detached observer, watching without choice or comment as the flow passes before us. Witnessing applies to inner feelings as well as to external events, implying a sense of "being with" painful feelings, instead of being the feelings.

The Witness exists
only in the moment

Self-rejecting activity of the mind must stop before the Witness can come into existence, but *shifting to* the Witness will also stop mind activity. Some teachers have said that thoughts should be witnessed, but what they actually mean, in my opinion, is that *feelings* should be witnessed. I have always found that thought inhibits the Witness state.

The Witness center may be consciously activated to help integration. Bring your consciousness to the Third Eye center. Bring yourself into the moment. Shifting to the Witness is an ability that will grow with practice. At first, you may not be sure if what you are sensing is really Witness consciousness, but soon, you will recognize the feeling – it is almost a physical sensation.

Witness consciousness breaks the identification with what is being witnessed. This may appear to be in contradiction to what we discussed earlier: the need to own our experience. There is no contradiction, because these functions take place on different levels of our being, which are called the lower self and the Higher Self.

The Lower and Higher Selves

The lower self is the one we are familiar with, the one we have been talking about, the personal ego. This self can be approached through psychology and growth techniques. This self must definitely take responsibility for what it feels and puts out into the universe. The Higher Self is something else – it is what we discover as we go within. When psychology includes the Higher Self in its format, it becomes transpersonal.

The Higher Self is indescribable, at least for me. I would just say that it corresponds to the Witness. It is our true identity, which we lose sight of in the identification with the lower self. Breaking identification with the lower self, and the desires of the lower self, is the purpose of spiritual practice. Note that we do not try to destroy or change the lower self. We merely shift our sense of identification.

As we learn to shift our sense of "I" from the lower to the Higher Self, we are increasingly liberated from material bondage. When in the Witness, we no longer are troubled by addiction, chained to duality, or have dualistic preferences. We understand that pleasure and pain sit side by side. There is no getting one without the other. We accept both. The lower self may still operate in the world of duality, gaining and losing, but the Witness is content simply to observe it all.

The nature of the Witness is euphoria

The Witness has no requirement for anything to be any particular way – just *to be* is enough. Activation of the Witness is a primary goal of esoteric teachings. When we live in this euphoric center of consciousness, we feel transcendental love. Our feeling of well-being simply overflows and those who are close to us can't help sharing that feeling. There is no effort involved in trying to love, or in deciding to do so. We are truly detached from the self-centered preoccupation of the lower self.

The understanding of the Witness concept is of immense importance. Great psychologists like Jung and Perls have always said that to become whole, we must suffer. They are talking about what we have been talking about – the need to integrate the suppressed, painful part of ourselves. The concept of the Witness, however, brings everything to a new plane. We understand that, yes, we must experience our suppressed pain, but on the level of the lower self. When the Witness is activated, we enter the Higher Self, and we view our pain with detachment, love, and even euphoria.

This is what acceptance is. There is no magic involved in simply suffering. Suffering has transformational value when it is embraced, not rejected and resuppressed; when it is viewed from the Witness; when it is experienced with love.

Are you accepting
with love?

One of the tests of acceptance is to note whether you are accepting with love. No matter what conditions you are facing, you can activate the higher centers, the Heart and the Witness, and enter the experience from the vantage point of higher consciousness. If you are not accepting with love, you have not yet reached your full potential and effectiveness. I am not referring to the love of the lower self, which is attached and dualistic, but the love of the Higher Self, which is unattached and choiceless. You can feel love even when you are integrating a painful event. This may seem impossible, because we normally feel one emotion at a time. How can one feel love and pain at the same time?

The love that comes from the Higher Self is not an emotion. It is a state of being that is open to the cosmic, ever-changing Now. The euphoric nature of the Witness is the true experience of love. It is based on the principle of acceptance, not choice. It is not dependent upon any object, it just *is*.

As you activate the Witness center, you awaken the healing power of love, coming from within. You can then direct it to any chakra or condition. Don't deny the negativity that you are facing, feel it, but also feel the love from the Higher Self, melting the pain of the lower self. Love will provide the transformation.

ALLOW PSYCHIC ENERGIES TO BALANCE

Direct experience of negative energies in the Witness state creates optimal conditions for clearing and balancing. This happens automatically, under the direction of the unconscious aspects of the Higher Self. We don't have to give any more thought to clearing than we give to our bodies' physical systems, such as circulation or digestion. Indeed, the stopping of thought is what makes integration possible. We stop thought when we drop self-rejection, and enter the Witness. Until then, thought inhibits the natural healing cycle.

The key healing attitude of the Witness is non-identification

Whatever is manifesting, whether an emotion, desire, addiction, or physical symptom, although it is part of our lower self, it is not really us. We mistakenly identify with attributes of the lower self. We are more like the Higher Self, the part that just witnesses. If we cultivate the sense of non-identification with the negative side of the lower self, we allow the sense of the Higher Self to grow.

As we drop identification with the negative condition, we still allow it to exist in our consciousness. We experience the condition, with love. We feel as if we are "being with" the condition, in the moment, instead of being the condition.

There is an element of time involved in integration, even though in the Witness the sense of time is different. Integration does not usually come immediately. If you realize that you are working on integrating material that has possibly been suppressed for lifetimes, you will have more patience with the time factor.

Usually, our Karma will come to us in pieces. Incidents will happen, emotions and moods will occur that are all caused by the unconscious energy we hold. Each occurrence is the opportunity to either integrate or re-suppress negative energy. Each time we successfully integrate the appearance of a negative pattern, we carve a little more off our subconscious load, but there will be many incidents before the whole load is dissolved. Certain periods of our lives may be spent in meeting one particular suppressed aspect of ourselves.

However, each time an incident is successfully integrated, you will feel the results. Your boundaries will have expanded. You will gain more freedom. You will not be as compulsive.

You will not be moved as easily to react to or be motivated by negative patterns. Addictions will start to come under control. Issues that before were difficult to bear will not be as much of a problem.

You are now not projecting as much into events as they occur; you have begun to release negativities. You perceive that life is going better, or that others are not causing you as much trouble. But it is you who have changed.

As you continue to integrate events, you will gain a clearer view of the objective nature of interaction. You see the other's side much more easily. You see the positive side of an occurrence that before you had been loading with negativity. Situations will be *reframed* spontaneously.

Reframing is a technique which means finding the proper context for any event, so that it is perceived positively rather than negatively. When reframing happens automatically, it is a sign that integration has occurred, but you should be careful about deliberate reframing. It can easily serve as another way of suppressing feelings. Don't ever talk yourself out of your feelings.

OPEN YOURSELF TO TRANSFORMATION

When you allow energies to balance themselves, you invite the transformational power of the Higher Self to work in your behalf. This power cannot be commanded, controlled, or anticipated. It is the "grace" that comes when you do not ask – when your mind is calm and in the state of acceptance. The Higher Self will enter, and will direct the outcome of both your feelings and the circumstances that you are surrendering to. This happens automatically, when you accept your experience as it is.

The Higher Self is another part of ourselves that may have been inactive until now. We are usually not conscious of the Higher Self, but this intelligent power is behind all healing, whether physical or psychological. The Higher Self, more super-conscious than subconscious, works on the psychic planes, in turn affecting the material plane. In ways that appear miraculous and magical, transformation is effected.

We connect to each other
on the psychic levels

Because of the psychic connection between us, you don't have to confront someone directly when you are processing. When you integrate emotions that concern another person, changes in the relationship will spontaneously occur. The other person will be affected, and will change their behavior, possibly without even knowing why.

When you stop blaming, you no longer put out the negative psychic energy that others unconsciously feel. You no longer buy into their game. You also no longer buy into your own projections. In no longer fighting the other, you absorb their energy as you receive it. You don't send it back mixed with your own hostility, which just fuels the other's aggression. You don't allow the other to take advantage of you, but neither do you return their negativity with more negativity.

The negative energy that you must absorb from the other corresponds to your Karmic debt to yourself – it is part of your projection. Don't be resentful about having to absorb it. Don't become angry about the anger. When the debt is paid, the other person's negativity that you perceive as being directed toward you will disappear.

With regard to external circumstances, the intelligence of the Higher Self initiates transformation on the psychic planes, which manifests on the physical plane. The shaping of events is guided in practical and creative ways that cannot be foreseen. Transformation occurs, and another phase of life is begun.

*You must maintain a choiceless
position about outcomes*

One of the requirements for transformation is that you must have no personal agenda for the outcome. When you have expectations, concepts, self-image, or self-interest to maintain, you inhibit the working of the balancing forces. It has been my experience, however, that the outcome is always satisfactory – many times in ways I could not anticipate. I go beyond the duality in question, integrating the "negative," and no longer clinging to the "positive." A particular boundary is pushed back.

When you approach a problematic situation with a particular solution in mind, you don't allow the opportunity for real growth to occur. Your solution is based on what you already know, and is likely to be merely the pleasant dualistic complement to what you would like to avoid. To go beyond, you must go to a place that is unknown. When you drop all concepts of what the outcome should be, you allow the higher intelligence to bring about the appropriate transformation. You make room for the new to happen, and real growth occurs.

Many believe there is a religious power that comes into play. This is a personal matter, but my feeling is that we are just accessing another part of ourselves – a new ability. This does not necessarily mean that a power outside of ourselves is now working for us; perhaps an expanded concept of who we really are would be more appropriate. Regardless of how you view it, contemporary psychology is coming more and more to the conviction that the transpersonal element is essential in healing.

TRUST

As we begin to function in the consciousness of the Higher Self, we realize that trust, or faith, is one of the more important attitudes that we can hold.

When we trust, doubt is absent. Doubt is the negative orientation of the mind that makes inner work difficult. When we doubt, we are restricted, as in any other self-rejection. Doubt has an effect on our psychic energy, and encloses us, instead of opening us to the Higher Self as trust does.

If you are to trust, what exactly are you to trust in? In many ways, it makes no difference what you trust in as long as the object of your trust is basically a positive force. When you trust in something beyond your conscious self, you open to receiving intelligent guidance and energy from a source that the conscious ego cannot provide.

If you are of a religious nature, you may choose to trust in God. If you find the right guru, you may feel trust in that relationship, eventually extending the trust to the inner guru. If the concept of the Higher Self appeals to you, you may trust in this guiding and intelligent force, or in the concept of grace. You may trust in the intelligent and supportive Universe. If none of these is appropriate for you, you can trust in the scientific principles of processing and psychology in general.

If you feel you need some*thing* to trust in, whatever you choose as the object of your trust will only be your projection. This is not necessarily detrimental, though, and can actually correspond to a significant and fruitful stage of growth. Trust in anything you like, as long as you trust. If you are going to create the object of your trust, however, it is better to create an abstract entity than project your trust onto another human, unless that person is very qualified to receive your trust.

Personally, having experienced that the principles we have been discussing work, I feel comfortable trusting in them, as well as in the Higher Self. I feel that everything I perceive on the Earth plane is happening in order to cleanse my subconscious, and that I cooperate by just surrendering to *what is*.

I also have a sense that the Universe is large, intelligent, and will help me if I let it. I have a sense of the inner planes of existence, and just the knowledge that they exist is enough to invoke my trust in life. I trust that the Earth, in its natural state, is a nurturing and loving energy with which I can commune.

I trust that the evolution of the individual is leading to the awakening of higher capacities for love and creativity. Because I have experienced this, I want to keep going, even though I may have no clear conception of where it leads.

I trust there is an infinite power beyond my conscious self, which will work in my favor if I let it. I choose to think of that power as part of myself, with which I have not yet come into full contact – the Higher Self.

I trust, finally, in myself; in my capacity to survive and be happy, not because of what I have or what is happening, but because I AM.

UNDERSTAND PSYCHIC CLEANSING

We must realize that what we are engaged in is psychic cleansing. Even though it may not be apparent, being in a physical body presents that opportunity. When we don't yield to unpleasant feelings or resist them, but instead integrate them, we allow cleansing to take place.

In cleansing, psychic toxins are released into consciousness, becoming temporarily intensified

If you are cleansing addictive compulsions, you will feel the compulsiveness even more as it is cleansed. When you cleanse anger, you will feel more angry. When you cleanse dependency, you will feel more helpless and alone than ever. Experiencing such feelings more strongly is in itself a sign that cleansing is happening. This period ends sooner or later, depending on how much suppressed energy is in the subconscious. You must be gentle with yourself now, because you have become fragile in contrast to your former self, when you may have been aggressive and hard.

You enter a period of psychic fasting. By eliminating all the usual escapes from your pain, you bring the pain to the surface. You have to experience the psychic toxins as they are released in order to get rid of them. If you have ever tried physical fasting, you know that it is a period of discomfort as all the physical toxins are dumped into the bloodstream. Nevertheless, the result is beneficial, and you feel better after the fast. Psychic fasting is similar. Be patient and tender with yourself.

Emotional and physical
releasing may take place

Because of the body/mind correlation, there may be releases in the physical body that correspond to the releases in the psychic body. Physical symptoms of various types may appear. The interaction between the physical and psychic levels should not be described as one causing the other; they appear simultaneously. The acceptance of symptoms is the basis for holistic medicine. The body is allowed to manifest the cleansing symptoms, balancing itself as it does. Although the physical symptoms are accepted, there may be adjustments to be made on the physical level, such as changes in diet, supplements, environment, exercise, and so on. Usually the discovery of a chronic physical condition and the treatment of it on the physical level will coincide with the releasing of psychic Karmic burden.

The releasing of suppressed material can precipitate catharsis, the emotional purging of unconscious pain and blocking. Catharsis is often accompanied by weeping. If weeping ever occurs in yourself or someone you are with, you should never attempt to inhibit it. What should be done is simply to support and comfort yourself or the person, by holding them, or just by being with them. Gently encourage them to stay with or even go further into the pain. Don't encourage them to avoid it, as we are inclined to do. The crisis will eventually pass, and a thorough cleansing will have taken place.

In working on yourself, as you uncover painful past emotion, you include and experience it without avoidance. The attitude of including is exactly what makes deep cleansing possible. The energy in the chakras balances in a self-regulating manner, resulting in catharsis, but you cannot precipitate cleansing deliberately. Cleansing occurs spontaneously, when you do not seek to avoid, but when you meet the negative.

RECOGNIZE THE HINDRANCES

Buddhist texts refer to what is known as the "Five Hindrances." As you begin working on yourself, you start to bump up against old boundaries. This may be interpreted quite literally, as your auric field feels the effect of the additional prana taken in with visualizations, breath and bodywork, and inner concentration. The aura tries to expand, but meets the resistance of old, self-destructive patterns of the energy body that are being disturbed.

These patterns, being energy formations, have a pseudo-intelligence of their own, and they sense the threat to their existence. You may even think of the patterns as representing sub-personalities, if it helps you to visualize their place in your being. The sub-personalities act up because you have not accepted them.

The resistance of the patterns takes the form of the Five Hindrances, and possibly others that you may add to the list. The point is that you will meet resistance as you begin inner work. It can be handled by processing, as can any negativity. There is no way past the Hindrances except to just keep going, and to blast through – with gentle acceptance, of course. Resistance is lessened when you seek to integrate, and not eliminate the patterns. The Five Hindrances:

1. I WANT. Desires of any chakra can be stimulated, including present addictions.

2. I HATE. Resentment may increase, perhaps irrationally.

3. TORPOR. Torpor is an energy condition of sudden sleepiness, which may come up in breathwork or meditation.

4. RESTLESSNESS. General anxiety may increase.

5. DOUBT. Doubt concerning the method, the teacher, the therapist, the progress.

As you might gather, only one of these would be required to discourage the average person. It is probably the case that many people starting on the inner path never get far because of the Hindrances. The Hindrances were formalized by Buddhists, thousands of years ago, because they realized the difficulties of inner work. Make good use of their forewarning.

TAKE PART IN GROUP WORK

Working by yourself can be effective self-therapy, but you add a new dimension to your practice by participating in group sessions. There is a strong energy that builds in the group format, which you can take in and use. This is especially true if the group takes place in a healing environment, such as a place dedicated to inner or spiritual work, an ashram, or a natural, peaceful location.

On the other hand, you must be careful you don't become dependent on the group, and neglect developing your own practice; group energies can definitely be addictive. Sharing with the group can be meaningful, but you should not think that sharing is all that is required for integration. You must ultimately face yourself alone, and the group cannot be there to provide continual support.

But if you are working by yourself, the group can provide just the additional push you might need to bring an issue to completion. The ideal format would be a strong foundation of regular individual work supplemented with weekly, monthly, or even less frequent group sessions. Group work may consist of bodywork, guided visualizations, encounter work, dreamwork, or emotional releasing.

PART III
LOVING YOURSELF

I recognize that love from within is

the only true source of love. I nurture

myself to allow the love within to grow.

I no longer enter relationships to find love,

but to express the love I feel within.

The ability to love myself has grown because

of my emotional self-acceptance. By

experiencing and not avoiding my painful

feelings, I have implemented real growth

and transformation.

10

Love from Within

UNCONDITIONAL HAPPINESS

We are all engaged in the pursuit of happiness. From the most basic drives of survival, to the most refined tastes for art, intellectuality, and love, we seek that which fulfills us. We naturally seem to seek this outside of ourselves. Perhaps our early conditioning as dependent children receiving love and nourishment from outside led to the view that happiness is external, that it must be pursued and attained. Perhaps this tendency is another of "Nature's traps," keeping us in the world until we become wise enough to know better.

Seeking fulfillment outside of ourselves is the materialist attitude about happiness. Whether the concern is survival, sensation, power and recognition, love or creative needs, happiness becomes conditional upon achieving, attaining, or possessing something outside of ourselves. Even creative needs depend on successful execution and recognition before fulfillment can be attained.

Successful satisfaction of needs becomes a condition for

happiness. We defend our ownership of the means to satisfy needs, whether a career, person, place to live, or self-image. We become dependent upon these possessions, fearing their loss. We become anxious and resentful about our dependence, often unconsciously. We learn to hate the possessions that are supposed to bring us happiness, feeling that they actually own and control us, instead of the other way around.

Of course, there are legitimate needs that must be met, but I am talking about something else. We have built a need system that is addictive, neurotic, and artificial. Our needs have gone beyond simple and basic human requirements, but we still look to the satisfaction of these exaggerated needs for happiness. They become the *source* of happiness.

It is unfortunate that much New Age emphasis is on learning how to more effectively get what we think we need to be happy; in other words, how to better satisfy our addictions. What is needed is to learn how to get rid of addictions.

The purpose of spiritual life in general is to get us to the point where we no longer assume that anything from the outside will be a source of happiness. It is possible to still have activities, relationships, or possessions, but instead of regarding them as sources, we regard them as *expressions* of happiness. To the extent that we can do this, we are freed from dependency, poverty consciousness, and dualistic experience.

When we know that nothing from the outside can significantly and permanently help us find happiness, we are freed from the sense of lack. When we do not lack anything, we feel complete as we are, and have entered what is known as abundance consciousness. This condition has no dependence whatsoever on our possessions – it is a state of mind. Abundance consciousness serves to attract fortunate circumstances, exactly because we do not feel that anything is lacking. We acquire material resources and harmonious relationships, but are not dependent on them and do not fear their loss.

Being human, we cannot expect to live up to the ideal of abundance consciousness immediately, and should not condemn ourselves when we don't. The pain that comes with dependency must be accepted and experienced. Inner strength will come to allow us to go beyond dependency.

If happiness is not to be found outside ourselves, where or how is it achieved? We are sometimes told to seek happiness within. Often, not much more is said, and the meaning may not be entirely clear. The phrase "seek happiness within," is actually misleading, and is a trap many fall into when they begin thinking about spirituality. They turn from worldly pursuits out of eventual disillusionment, and try to find happiness from another source, which is now supposed to be "within." Do you see the error?

The approach is exactly as before, but now it is thought that happiness will be found from a non-material source, such as the self-projected concept of God or guru. We continue to be aggressive, demanding, concerned with our own needs, and attached to the idea of "happiness."

There is no source of happiness. The very concept of conditional happiness is false and misleading. We still cling to the dualistic concept of happiness/unhappiness, grasping for one, rejecting the other. If you can perceive this truth, you will realize that all efforts are misdirected. It is possible only to create a new "source," within or without, a new invention of the subconscious from which you expect happiness. In doing this, you fall into the dualistic experience all over again, projecting both happiness and unhappiness.

If all efforts to "find happiness" are in vain, what is there to do? When you truly understand the futility of effort, you will simply stop trying to compulsively pursue happiness, whether in career, relationship, possession, or self-expression. Stopping effort is the first step toward liberation. Release from anxiety will follow, as well as the pressure to be or do anything in an addicted manner.

However, most of us are so conditioned to be achievement-oriented that stopping effort is usually impossible. Remember, I am not saying that it is necessary to be inactive. Rather, I'm referring to the motive implicit in activity. We are *searching* for happiness, instead of expressing happiness through the activity or relationship. We are victims of the core misbelief, "I am not enough."

You must realize that you are enough, just as you are. You don't need anything to be happy, you just need to *be*.

If you stop searching, you will be left with the terrible emptiness that is no longer masked by the false hope that searching brings. This emptiness must be worked with like other perceived negativities. Indeed, it is a main item we all must face.

Real work on yourself begins when you start to integrate and stop being motivated by whatever form the emptiness takes, whether it is a longing for security, sex, power, or relationship. I promise you, you will eventually become clear, and experience a freedom and exhilaration that you didn't think could exist.

I realize that this sounds like something that could never be attained, and perhaps you are asking yourself if it is necessary to go to such extremes. After all, what most of us want is just to live a basic, simple life. Why be concerned with abstractions?

This simplistic view of happiness overlooks our basic situation. We don't understand the dualistic nature of existence, and we continue to reject much of life, including ourselves. Our subconscious will not let us alone because of the suppressed energies we carry, causing us to act self-destructively. Happiness remains elusive.

Psychotherapy has been the means by which many of us have found the healing and growth that results from accepting ourselves as we are. Still, there are times when psychotherapy can fall short of achieving maximum benefit. Its intention often is to get the client functioning, which may come down to getting him or her interested in pursuing goals, perpetuating the myth that happiness will be found in the future from sources outside oneself. The real issue – the ultimately self-deceptive kind of life we lead – is not addressed.

I feel, however, that this is changing. The advent of transpersonal psychology, which recognizes the spiritual component to the psyche, includes concepts such as we have been discussing. The intent is no longer to patch up, but to understand why problems perpetuate, helping the client bring spiritual concepts into real life.

Issues of dependency in relationships, for example, are now being discussed widely. Co-dependency groups meet, just as Alcoholics Anonymous groups do, and people come to realize that the problem is their dependency, not the other person. Dependency is basically the impulse to search for happiness outside yourself. I would suggest that you become a true warrior, and attack the central issue relentlessly: give up your addictions to security, sensation, power, and relationship. Until you do, you will continue to encounter misery through the very door that you hope happiness will come.

If we are to no longer search for happiness, what do we do with ourselves? This is the point where self-work actually begins. We feel. We simply feel all that comes our way. When we are not feeling something, we exist without sensation in the Now, the eternal moment.

We will still be subject to some dualism because that is the nature of the world, but we do not cling to one side and reject the other. Dualities are experienced as integrated complements instead of warring opposites. If the unpleasant comes up, it is accepted, not rejected.

We understand that experiences are largely projected, and we own them, blaming no one. We have no preference about which side of the dualism we are now in because we know that both are inevitable. We trust in the flow, allowing negative experiences to be absorbed and dissolved without resistance, becoming positive experiences, and vice-versa.

We activate a higher intelligence within, which guides the transformation of energies. We are emotionally unaddicted to outcomes because we no longer depend on them as a source of happiness. As we integrate dualistic experience, we discover a euphoric transcendental state beyond conditional happiness/unhappiness, which is not far away or inaccessible, but easily within our grasp. This state of unconditional happiness is called love.

DEPENDENT LOVE

Although our search for fulfillment can take many forms, it could be said that what we really seek is love. This is especially true in relationships, of course, as well as in other forms of searching, when we pursue security, sensation, or power. Love, coming from a higher center, will satisfy the emotional aspect of lower needs. But we must be aware of the different types of love. Just as there is a difference between our lower and Higher Selves, there is a difference between dependent and self-love.

Dependent love comes from the lower Heart center. It is dualistic because it is based on a sense of lack. We feel empty within. We seek to avoid the pain of isolation by uniting with another person. At first, we experience ecstasy from union with another, especially if it is sexual, but various problems are created, which can eventually undermine the relationship.

The first problem is that dependent love is highly conditional. The partner is chosen carefully to begin with, and once a relationship is established, we become upset if they do not meet our expectations. Our expectations are really addictions, which we rationalize as "needs." A relationship based on mutual satisfaction of needs is a business partnership – we give in order to get. It is difficult to cultivate a loving attitude when you are concerned primarily with the satisfaction of your own needs.

Addictive needs vary somewhat between the sexes, men usually placing sex high on the list, and women usually being concerned with material security. This difference in itself does much to account for the endless battle that seems to exist between the sexes. Then come the unconscious needs that impel us to relationship, when we seek in the other whatever we block within ourselves. You might say that mutual satisfaction of needs will always be a part of relationships. My opinion, however, is that the more expectations, needs, and demands you have, the more your relationships will suffer and be a source of pain instead of love.

When you look to another to satisfy your needs, there will

be times when they fail, sometimes unintentionally. If you are conditioned to feel satisfaction when your needs are met by the partner, you will also feel dissatisfaction when they are not. Unless you can release the dissatisfaction – by processing, for example – you can quickly become resentful, and the dualistic love/hate syndrome begins.

Another problem is that the sense of lack is not eliminated when we are motivated by dependent love, but only suppressed. An addictive cycle begins. The excitement of the relationship covers the emptiness for a while, but the emptiness continues to build in the subconscious. We need more and more of the energy of the relationship to suppress the emptiness, becoming compulsive about sex, for example. Eventually, the relationship reaches the point of exhaustion, and the emptiness becomes felt again because there is no more energy to suppress it. We become disillusioned, thinking that the partner is the cause. We may even project feelings of isolation onto the partner, resulting in additional alienation.

It might be possible for a dependent relationship to last if we could accept that closeness will be balanced by alienation. Instead of blaming the partner for the anxiety or pain we feel, it is accepted and worked with.

Dependent love is the complement to unintegrated emptiness, isolation, and loneliness. We reject ourselves by rejecting these inner feelings, seeking escape in the relationship. Escape does nothing to end the emptiness, however; it only suppresses and affirms its existence. We essentially buy into and give permission for the emptiness to continue, becoming locked into a cycle of dependency/emptiness, never seeing that the existence of one depends on the other.

In seeking escape in a relationship, we may become compulsive about certain "needs." Some may focus on sexual needs, hoping to find escape there. A pattern of compulsive sexual searching is set up. Since it is only the newness of a relationship that serves to hide the inner emptiness, the sexual attraction soon dissolves. The person continues to search for the illusive satisfying partner, not understanding why lasting fulfillment is never possible. The same scenario exists with regard to security, or any other compulsive need that we strive to satisfy through relationship.

Dependence creates other problems. Because we depend on the other to avoid our inner emptiness, we fear losing the person. The fear results in anxiety and possessiveness. We cling to and try to control the other out of fear of loss or even of their temporary absence. We become resentful that we are dependent, and can't help project the resentment on the partner.

Fear itself may also be projected onto the partner, so that we consciously or unconsciously fear them, and become anxious and afraid in their presence. Fear becomes a major part of the negative side of the relationship; the fear of losing the person is in direct proportion to our "love." Much of the fear is suppressed, but eventually it becomes a significant source of additional resentment, often unconscious, completing the love/hate syndrome.

Resentment from all these sources becomes the motivation behind the fighting that is always present in dependent relationships. Negative tension builds up, and the partners try to clear it through fighting. They fight, each blames the other, thinking everything would be all right if the other would behave properly. Because they blame, tension does not dissolve with the fighting, but is suppressed. Fighting continues, getting worse as previously suppressed tension again tries to clear along with new tensions that have accumulated. Eventually, the level of suppressed resentment is such that there is no alternative except for the relationship to collapse. Processing the negative resentment and tension here instead of reacting to it with blame would be of great value.

I am not suggesting that you should avoid intimate relationships. I am only trying to point out the pitfalls. Don't think the other is causing your pain – take responsibility for it. Realize that your addictions are what is causing the pain, whether it comes up in the form of sexual frustration, financial insecurity, anger, inconvenience, or whatever. *Process* the painful feeling, instead of reacting.

Dependent love is difficult to get past if one is not aware of what it is and how it is perpetuated. Even in non-romantic relationships, when we think we are acting out of brotherly love or even being spiritual, there is often a good deal of dependency present in our motivation.

We know that love is the answer to our problems, we all want it and try to maintain it, but we never can, in spite of our best intentions. Many spiritual spokespeople simply keep urging us to be more loving, as if this could be done intentionally. We try, only to fail, and feel guilty. We develop a negative attitude toward loving, thinking that it is not possible. We have to understand that we are not going about it correctly.

The mind can never generate love. No matter how hard you try to talk yourself into feeling love, you will never succeed; you are setting yourself up for continual failure. Your "love" will be a creation of the mind, and will have no basis in your being. You will construct a fantasy world, possibly based on "spiritual" ideals, and you will suppress and remain cut off from your real feelings. These feelings will continually try to clear through projection, and you will end up behaving hypocritically.

You can become freed from the cycle of dependent love by processing the isolation and loneliness that is felt in the Heart center. By ceasing to be motivated by it, you will eventually gain balance. Instead of fearing isolation, and being driven by it into relationships that are often destructive, you integrate the pain of isolation, allowing it to dissipate. Isolation will transform into self-reliance, self-contentment, self-individualization, and self-love. The pain is only the birthpain of the Higher Self.

LOVING YOURSELF

When the expressions "loving yourself" or "self-love" are first heard, there may be confusion about what they mean. This is because we think in terms of the love we are familiar with, dependent love. If we try to love ourselves, we may take an approach similar to that used in dependent love, using ourselves as the object of our love. We may try to escape into ourselves, as we escaped into others. We may become self-absorbed and self-indulgent, putting our own needs first. The motive is still to escape. We still reject unhappiness, and in so doing, reject ourselves.

Self-love has nothing to do with using yourself as the object of your love. Self-love means that your love *comes from within,* is generated from within, not from "loving" any object because it may please you tremendously, whether someone else or yourself. Self-love is a condition of awareness, a way of perceiving, an attitude, which results in an integrated perception of the world.

The art of loving yourself begins with self-acceptance. They are essentially the same. You begin loving yourself when you stop rejecting yourself. When you practice self-acceptance, you will experience real changes in consciousness. You no longer try to juggle people or possessions in the external world in order to find fulfillment. You find fulfillment from within, simply by integrating the opposites of experience.

Do not underestimate the importance of self-acceptance. It can end the emotional pain that you feel, or lead to the spiritual experience you want. Starting with the mundane, you will reach the highest of inner realization. In welcoming all your feelings, you become whole; life becomes holistic. You experience oneness. You no longer compulsively search for oneness in the external world, whether with another person or an achievement. You accept and love yourself.

Relationships with others change dramatically when you access the self-love within. Not until then will you experience anything approaching real love with another person. Even if you are with a person who is genuinely trying to love you, you will reject their love if you are not in touch with the love within. Their love will not get through. Love must come from inside. The love that you perceive coming from another is just the reflection of your own inner love.

Love becomes primarily a relationship with yourself. It means being able to live with – and possibly even by – yourself. It means finding fulfillment within, not from any source or person outside. Turning inward whenever there is pain has always been the message of the masters; processing is a specific method through which this may be done.

Concepts that you have about love are likely to be erroneous. You should drop all concepts and wait until the capacity builds within you. Trying to force your feelings to match false concepts creates anxiety. Love may not be what you think it is.

What is love? Love is the experience of the Higher Self. Love is the euphoric nature of the Witness, simply watching all that happens. Love is of the body, the feeling nature, not the mind. Love is the unconditional acceptance and experience of all feelings. Love of another becomes the unconditional acceptance of your perception of the other. Love of another means making the other truly non-defensive because you accept them as they are, just as you accept yourself as you are. You have no selfish motivation, or hidden agenda they are required to meet. You are protecting nothing, because you welcome both the positive and negative. In an environment of total acceptance, love will enter your consciousness.

You perceive yourself and the other as you are. You no longer expect anything or make comparisons because you are not evaluating through the mind – you perceive the other directly. You sense that you are the other, that we are all one. This knowledge is emotional. You want to exchange energies because it is the joy of life. You want to care for the other because you care for and nurture your own growth as you do. You give because you increase yourself. You have gone beyond a limited sense of personal ego.

A key concept to self-love is whether you are living in the moment. When you are in direct experience, in the Witness state, you are in the moment. You are no longer doing with a sense of looking for future satisfaction. Satisfaction comes from being with *what is*. Of course, there will always be external purpose to activity, but in the Witness, your primary pleasure comes from the activity itself, not from the eventual result. You choose activities that have the potential to be enjoyable now, as well as in future outcomes.

Nevertheless, you do not confine your experience to pleasurable events. If experience swings to the other pole, and you meet unpleasant or challenging situations, you get equal satisfaction by taking responsibility and integrating them, keeping in mind your toleration point. Acceptance of negativities becomes a source of fulfillment.

You find happiness by simply being with whatever is manifesting in your consciousness right now. Fulfillment is found in the moment; you are not as concerned if the results of your work do not turn out as expected. You may still make choices about what you desire, and what you are going to work toward – we cannot live our lives otherwise. However, through self-acceptance, you are no longer compulsive about the results of work. You are no longer attached to any one outcome; you can accept other outcomes.

I am not so much referring to material outcomes as I am to feelings about the outcome. If you are disappointed or frustrated, you integrate these feelings. You maintain the Witness to your feelings, allowing them to be what they are, without extending any negativity into the world.

Inner equanimity becomes the basis for self-love. You are thus not concerned about whether you have found the proper object to love. Your fulfillment overflows, and anyone near will feel the influence.

THE HIGHER SELF AS TEACHER

In Chapter One, we saw how a teacher might help us learn to love ourselves. The role of teacher could be performed by any enlightened person, whether guru, therapist, parent, friend, spouse, lover, even child. In light of what we have since discussed, let's expand our understanding of that relationship.

In learning self-love, we ultimately awaken the teacher within. The teacher within corresponds to the Higher Self and the Witness. We access intuitive knowledge and find acceptance and love inside; but because we are not yet in contact with the inner teacher, we enter a relationship with an external teacher to stimulate those inner qualities into awakening. We experience those qualities with the external teacher that will later come from within.

When a relationship is formed with the external teacher, it is felt emotionally. A connection is made, and it may be hard to describe why or how this happens. Perhaps it might just be assumed that at various points of our lives, we might enter into such a relationship, or even serve as a teacher for another. When the link is formed, the healing relationship begins.

All varieties of emotions are experienced with the teacher. At first, there is a strong positive attraction, corresponding to the "honeymoon" stage, but soon, negative emotions begin coming up as well. If there is love, there will be fear and resentment; our love for the teacher is dependent love, even though we may not like to think so.

The teacher appears responsible for causing our feelings, positive as well as negative. What we do, however, is to project feelings onto the teacher. The teacher functions as an especially clear mirror, reflecting what is held in our subconscious. This happens exactly because the teacher has no expectations of us. *If we maintain awareness of ourselves* as we function in the relationship, we can see ourselves clearly.

The unconditional acceptance of the teacher is what causes the mirroring. The teacher accepts all feelings directed toward him or her, love as well as fear and anger. Usually, when we love others, they respond with conditional love. When we resent others, they return our resentment, they do not accept it. In neither case do we receive unconditional acceptance. The teacher accepts our resentment as well as our love. Acceptance is the key to the healing relationship.

Acceptance makes us conscious that we are projecting. We become aware of how we actually create our experience. At the same time, we become aware of the real love being extended to us through unconditional acceptance. We feel, possibly for the first time, unconditional love. We learn that acceptance *is* love.

The teacher becomes a surrogate for working out unfinished emotional issues. We bring all our patterns into the relationship. We project attitudes concerning authority, security, approval, love, and so on. We work out our Karma in a therapeutic relationship with this one person. The relationship with the teacher becomes intense, but the stance of the teacher continues to be non-reactive, not buying into anything we do, not reacting to our love or our fear, simply accepting. Of course, the teacher will appear to react to our love, but the love we offer is not of the level as the love we receive from the teacher. We think we offer love, but we offer a mix of our positive and negative Karma.

Acceptance has a deep correspondence on the energy level, which is why it is effective as therapy. The teacher knows how to accept all that is directed towards him or her, which can amount to substantial energies. The method of acceptance is no different from what we have been discussing. The teacher only has an expanded capacity for accepting energies.

Once we have had the experience of unconditional acceptance from the teacher, we may develop the capacity to give the experience to ourselves. The teacher serves as the model for how we can relate to ourselves. Our Higher Self, the Witness, becomes the teacher within.

This kind of relationship is the foundation for psychotherapy. Here, the projecting of the client onto the therapist is called "transference." Freud is credited with this discovery. His, and Jung's, opinion was that therapy did not take place until transference began. Until then, there was no real interaction between therapist and client. The analytic schools would analyze the transference, to make the client aware of the patterns, but the humanistic therapist simply accepts. Acceptance is the more powerful form of therapy because of the subtle effects on the energy level, where blocking occurs.

As I have said, I do not believe it is essential to have a relationship with an external teacher to awaken the Higher Self, although there is no question that it can be helpful. You must decide for yourself. In modern short-term therapy, where the emphasis is on results, such a relationship is not common anyway.

I have done most of my inner work by myself, using the principles I have discussed. Twice I have been privileged to enter a relationship with a teacher. The approach that I have described in this book has formed the foundation for my work, with the external teacher appearing at certain points in my life. Perhaps this approach would also work for you.

LOVE THROUGH THE BODY

Awakening the feeling capacity is primary in developing self-love. The feeling center has become underused and we substitute thoughts for feelings. We linger in the mind when we should be with our feelings.

One of the best ways to develop the feeling capacity is through work with the body, including breath, bodywork, and meditating on the chakras. You can begin self-love by accepting and experiencing body sensations that come up during these sessions. You will start to get in touch with yourself. You develop the capacity for sensitivity by being sensitive to your body. The feeling nature grows so that you sense your body as yourself, but also as a friend. This is a friend who has always been with you, and has always worked to help and sustain you. The relationship with yourself can be thought of as starting with the relationship with your body. Of course, you have other dimensions besides the material, but the material reflects and represents the other aspects, which may be approached through the body. I have found working with the body to be a most fulfilling path to the Higher Self.

When you nurture the body, do not become self-indulgent.

You are not trying to find pleasure through the body, but are providing the body with optimum conditions to establish a fundamental condition of well-being. The sense of physical well-being can build to become a basis for emotional health, since body and feelings are so closely connected.

Begin with the basics concerning what the body needs: proper nutrition, exercise, safe and clean environment, and attitude. The attitude of self-love is the attitude of acceptance of all aspects of the body. When you accept physical sensations as cleansings in progress, you are loving your body. When you accept and experience feelings *about* your body, whether positive or negative, you begin cleansing those feelings that affect you subconsciously.

You should not try to love your body as an object. That would be an extension of the idea of dependent love. Accept and experience whatever feelings exist without trying to control or change them; it will lead to the transcendence of dualistic feelings and the beginning of self-love.

As you enter your body more fully, you become aware of a new sense of emotional being, a new connectedness with life. You become one with your body, and simultaneously one with your experience. Emotional growth coincides with your connection to your body.

PART IV
WORKING ON YOURSELF

I devote a regular period each day to practice. I understand that bodywork, meditation, and breathwork are instrumental in bringing about self-integration. I joyously look forward to my practice as a time of relaxation and recharging. I feel my powers growing as I consciously use these special techniques.

11

Techniques and Breathwork

PRACTICE

In this chapter, we will discuss specific techniques that can be of immense help in our work. In all of the traditional approaches to enlightenment, the emphasis has always been on practice. Practice is a regular routine of specific exercises through which the capacity for integration and growth is activated.

Practice balances the energy system and unblocks the chakras. The effects are felt on all levels, including physical and psychological. Stress evaporates. Sensitivity increases. The psychic capabilities awaken and come into play. Feelings and emotions become integrated. Addictions are outgrown.

Practice is the means to clear the subconscious. Negative emotions will appear in consciousness as they are released from the body during practice. You can expect that the tendency to project will continue, or even temporarily increase, as buried feelings are loosened. Practice must be approached with the understanding that integration of suppressed material will be required as it is released. However, practice will be instrumental in helping to integrate the material.

If you are serious about working on yourself, you should consider getting into the habit of devoting time, on a daily basis, to practice. Regular practice will develop your capabilities more quickly than just an intellectual acquaintance with self-work. Practice becomes a scientific way of activating, cleansing, integrating.

Practice is also helpful because you learn the principles of working on yourself in a controlled environment. You will then be able to more easily apply them during the activity of everyday life.

A practice routine needn't amount to a large infringement on your schedule. What's important is to do it every day. Short sessions performed daily will do more then longer sessions done irregularly. As you start to enjoy practice, you will increase your session time automatically. You will look forward to it as a period of relaxation.

WORKING WITH THE BODY

Work with the body is of two basic types, both of which are important.

The first is exercise. Any kind of exercise is good: manual labor, aerobics, dance-kinetics, sports, jogging, etc. Exercising only a few times a week will keep you in shape and serve as the basis for a healthy body.

The second is bodywork. Bodywork should not be confused with exercise. They serve different purposes. Exercise serves to vitalize the body, while bodywork is of a psycho-physical nature, affecting the chakras and the consciousness.

There are many types of bodywork available, but I feel that Yoga postures (asanas) are among the best. I would encourage you to become familiar with the principles of Yoga, if you are not already. Include a short session at the beginning of your practice. The stretching and loosening of the body is very relaxing, opening the feeling centers, and making it easier to enter the meditative states that are desirable for inner work. Relaxing the body directly affects the pranic energy system, and therefore, the feelings. A stagnant energy system leads to stagnant feelings, encouraging depression and compulsiveness.

If you need technical information on the performance of Yoga postures, books and classes are available almost everywhere. Often, however, the basics of approach are not correctly explained or understood, which I feel makes all the difference between mediocre and outstanding results. If you have tried Yoga and didn't feel like it was working, possibly you were overlooking an essential point. In making these recommendations, I am drawing on my exposure to a variety of Yoga schools through the years, my personal practice, and my experience as a Yoga teacher myself.

Maintain an effortless
inner attitude

Do not think of Yoga postures as exercise, but as meditation. Enter with a meditative attitude; drop all intention and effort. The object of your meditative focus becomes the feelings in your body. As you stretch muscles and loosen chakras, focus on the feelings that come up. Feelings will be both physical and emotional. Witness physical sensations, choicelessly accepting. You should push the body to the point where you are experiencing a comfortable amount of strain; this can actually be enjoyable and relaxing. You are training yourself to be self-accepting, getting into the body's feeling centers and out of mental self-rejection.

Other feelings that come up will be emotional. You may experience a variety of negative emotions, along with their associated thoughts. You should welcome these feelings, because they are cleansing. Be with the feelings in the Witness, neither reacting to nor rejecting them.

Relax all parts of the body except the muscles that are

tensed in holding the pose. Do not feel that you have to do any posture perfectly, or that you are competing. Do not judge yourself either good or bad. Relax deeply into the posture.

Hold the posture

Learn to hold the posture for a significant length of time. This will be subjective, but most people do not hold poses long enough. Of course, be careful not to cause physical damage, but stay in the pose until you feel some physical or emotional release taking place. You will go through stages of release. You will think you have stretched out and are relaxed, and suddenly you will notice muscle tension that you have been holding. You can then consciously relax that part of your body, and stretch out further. Keep scanning your body as you hold, looking for areas that are tight.

Usually, holding for one to five minutes will be enough. However, if you really want to work on a certain part of your body where you think the muscles are holding suppressed energy or on a certain blocked chakra, you could hold for fifteen minutes or longer. Try to maintain the effortless attitude, even though certain muscles will probably be under great stress. Witness this. Before beginning an extended holding, always make sure the body is warmed up, by doing basic warmups or other postures, and always be careful. You probably shouldn't do extended holding until you are somewhat advanced in Yoga. Don't strain the body to the point of injury, but also be aware that the body can usually endure more than you think. You have to use your inner sense to find the right balance. The stress that is put on it during holding is needed to cause the release.

Extended holding can precipitate a crisis. The body may begin trembling and shaking, and your emotions may become intensified as deep cleansing in the chakras takes place. Hold the pose for as long as you think reasonable, but after you release the pose, continue opening to the feelings until they dissolve. I have had healings occur as a result of extended holding.

Maintain the breath

Keep breathing as you hold the pose. Do not hold the breath. This is most important. As you breathe, focus your awareness on the areas that are being stretched out and strained. Breathe into the area. Expand and contract the body in those areas, if possible, as you breathe into them. Healing energy will be focused and will cause the release of body-held negativity. Use a gentle Integrating breath, which we will discuss shortly.

Work on specific chakras

Certain poses will work on certain chakras, releasing suppressed material in those centers. This is a key function of Yoga that is not usually appreciated. Bioenergetics employs the same principle, using physical poses to release emotions. In addition to a balanced series of postures, then, you may want to emphasize poses that are appropriate for you. If you feel that you have a good deal of a certain type of suppressed negativity, work on the corresponding chakra. Hold the pose, and keep breathing into the chakra. Here are specific Yoga postures that work on certain chakras:

First (Survival): Forward Bend, Hero, Spinal Twist
Second (Sensation): Bridge, Boat, Peacock
Third (Power): Cobra, Camel, Bow, Peacock
Fourth (Heart): Bow, Camel
Fifth (Creative): Shoulderstand, Plow
Sixth (Witness): Shoulderstand, Plow, Headstand
Seventh (Spiritual): Headstand

INTEGRATIVE BREATHWORK

Breathwork is a major tool in the psycho-physiological aspect of our work on ourselves. Breathwork has dual capabilities. First, it calms, relaxes, and promotes healing. Second, it brings suppressed material into consciousness and greatly helps to integrate the material. Psychological therapies with breathwork can be non-intellectual and non-aggressive, and will bring about healing gently and spontaneously. Breathwork has always been a central part of Yoga. The mystical path of Yoga brought the science of breath to its peak thousands of years ago.

I first learned Yoga and breathwork in 1968, when I was initiated into the Kriya Yoga tradition, as passed down from the spiritual master, Babaji. "Kriya" means "cleansing." The Yoga of cleansing is what I learned, but I did not understand the full significance of what "cleansing" meant until later, when I became more familiar with the concept of the subconscious, and the need to bring its contents to light. As you might guess, cleansing refers to suppressed energies. A basic effect of the Yoga breath is to bring up and integrate the suppressed subconscious.

Now, I see the breath as a most powerful tool for both individual and therapist/client work. When we enter into a state of consciousness suitable for deep emotional work, we want to be in deep relaxation. The state of deep relaxation is called the alpha state, or even the hypnotic state. When working with clients now, I always begin the processing part of the session with some breathwork in which I resonate with the client, attempting to bring us both together into a deep, quiet place. I believe this accomplishes essentially the same as a hypnotic induction would do, and indeed, I see the alpha trance induction that I describe later to be essentially a powerful hypnotic induction, with the difference that our primary goal is not to reprogram ourselves, but to access and integrate the subconscious.

There is also a Kundalini aspect to this breath. The Kundalini is the evolutionary force lying dormant at the first chakra, which can be activated through Yoga practice. This force, in turn, completes the awakening of the other chakras. You need not fear that it will get out of control, however. Yoga practice must become strenuous for the Kundalini to be fully activated. What you may expect is a gentle awakening of chakras, cleansing and healing of emotional issues, strengthening of the aura and energy body, and a distinct improvement in how you feel.

We have spoken of prana, the invisible energy that is contained in the air. Prana is really what we are working with in breathwork. As the breath is drawn in, prana is also drawn in. Visualizations are used to send the energy to various parts of the physical/energy body to perform cleansing and healing. When you practice with the breath regularly, you set up conditions for cleansing and healing to occur, over a period of time.

We will discuss two basic breaths, the CLEANSING and the INTEGRATING breath.

THE CLEANSING BREATH

The Cleansing breath is performed in sitting meditation, as part of regular practice.

Blocks in the breath reflect
blocks in the chakras

When practicing with this breath, you should watch yourself as you breathe. Watch the body. Sit quietly. Witness. You should try to breathe in a smooth, continuous fashion, but you will probably find that this is not possible. Your body will jerk, and your breath will be uneven. You may feel slight pain or discomfort in certain parts of the body. These irregularities are caused by the blocks in the chakras.

As you fill your lungs from bottom to top, any unevenness or discomfort you encounter corresponds to a block. There is nothing to do about these sensations but to accept and experience them. Continue the breath, making sure to breathe into all parts of the torso, especially into areas that may be difficult to breathe into, or even into areas where you may never breathe. In time, the unevenness and discomfort will diminish, corresponding to the blocks in chakras diminishing. As cleansing proceeds, you will also experience various emotions that will come up to be integrated.

Maintain an attitude of acceptance throughout breathwork. All feelings should be accepted. You will become aware of physical and emotional feelings, but make no attempt to change them; instead, surrender to them. Enter the Witness, and allow the Higher Self to direct the balancing of the energies.

Yawning

During deep and regenerative breathing you may feel the need to yawn. Yawning is a physiological response to the prana that is being taken in. Do not be confused by this impulse, but rather regard it as a sign that recharging is taking place. Allow yourself to yawn, but try to maintain the flow of the breath as you do. It is usually easier to do this on the exhale. Do not perform breathing exercises immediately after eating; wait an hour or two, until digestion is complete.

There are several elements to the Cleansing breath:

1. **Nose Breathing**
2. **Posture**
3. **Progressive Filling**
4. **Tongue Positioning**
5. **Throttling**
6. **Inner Sound**
7. **Connected Breathing**
8. **Ratio**
9. **Rate**
10. **Depth**
11. **Alternate Nostril**

1. Nose Breathing

Breathe only through the nose.

2. Posture

The most critical aspect of posture concerns the spine. The spine must be held in an upright, relaxed position. It should not be forced absolutely straight, but kept in alignment with its natural curvature, so that a sense of delicate balance is achieved. You may have to shift vertebrae, moving some forward or back. The head is loosely held upright. The shoulders, as well as all the muscles, are consciously relaxed.

Correct alignment is important because the chakras connect to each other through the nerves that run through the spine. Small changes in the alignment of the spine will affect the electrical exchange between chakras, influencing the energy flow and the feelings.

The best position to achieve alignment is sitting with no back support, not leaning against anything, including a wall or backrest. The reason it is hard for many of us to do this is because sitting with an unsupported back immediately begins releasing tensions around the spine. If you accept the pains and strains that come up, you cleanse the blocks in the chakras. Sitting in this manner for breathwork and meditation is the main practice of the Buddhist Vipassana tradition.

Over the years, my capacity for sitting has increased, and I feel there has been a correlation between this and my inner cleansing. A practical approach for you if you are a beginner might be to start sitting unsupported for as long as you can. When you feel you have reached your toleration point, lean back against a support to continue. You will gradually build your capacity.

Easy Pose

Kneeling Pose

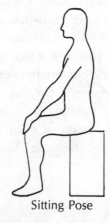

Sitting Pose

I have become used to sitting in the traditional crossed-legged position. I find it induces more of a grounded feeling than sitting in a chair. The overall energy pattern of the body is optimally configured, with no leakages out of arms or legs. Prana that runs down the limbs is returned to the body. Circulation in the legs is reduced, and more blood goes into the brain.

Cross-legged sitting is easiest in the so called "easy" pose, where the legs do not actually cross. There is no need to strain to get into the half or full lotus positions. Sitting on the *edge* of a firm cushion with your pelvis tilted forward slightly will make it even more comfortable.

If your legs are too stiff for cross-legged sitting, you can use the kneeling pose, sitting on your legs and ankles, perhaps with a pillow between your butt and your ankles. This pose is perfectly fine, although not considered quite as energy retentive as the easy pose, and harder to maintain for long periods. The grounding of the first chakra is also not as good.

If neither of these suits you, you can use a chair. Just make sure you sit on the edge of the chair, and do not lean back. In all of the poses, your hands should be either on your knees or clasped in your lap.

3. Progressive Filling

When taking a breath, fill the lower part of the body first, progressively working upwards until the very uppermost lungs are filled. You should fill in stages, each stage corresponding to one of the first five chakras:

Body Location	Chakra
1. Anal Area	Survival
2. Lower Abdomen/Perineum	Sensation
3. Solar Plexus/Navel	Power
4. Mid Chest	Heart
5. Upper Chest/Throat	Creative

Of course, air is not actually sent into the lower areas, but you can expand them during the inhale because of the action of the diaphragm. The diaphragm is the muscular horizontal membrane under the lungs. As you push air down into the lower lungs, they in turn act on the diaphragm, and expand the abdominal and anal areas outwards. You feel as if you are sending air into those areas, but a large part of what you are feeling is the *prana*. When filling, you must keep the abdomen from becoming bloated. Some tension must be kept in the abdominal muscles, allowing the abdomen to push out slightly as the lower lungs are filled.

The upper chest corresponds to sections of the lungs that actually extend upwards toward the shoulders, where we normally don't fill. You should fill the upper chest consciously, relating it to the throat center.

After the lungs have been progressively filled, you exhale in opposite order, emptying the upper lungs first, and then the lower areas.

You can get a sense of how to begin progressive filling by first exhaling. Empty the upper chest, mid chest, solar plexus, navel area, and lower abdomen, contracting each area as you exhale. You then have to bring into play another diaphragm of the body, the *perineum*. This is not usually taught to beginners, but I think that knowing about it is to your advantage.

The perineum (per-i-ne'um) is on the bottom side of the abdomen, running between the genital and anal areas, right in the crotch. If you experiment, you will find that you can contract this diaphragm independently of other areas of the body. The sensation is that of lifting and tightening the muscles of the crotch.

As well as contracting the perineum, you can also contract the anal area. You tighten and lift the area, which can be done separately from the perineum. Control of these areas is part of advanced Yoga, and is instrumental in activating and clearing the lower chakras. The anal contraction corresponds to the first chakra, the Survival center. The perineum contraction, along with the lower abdomen, corresponds to the second chakra, the

Sex center.

If this is getting too involved for you, you may skip over contracting the lower areas individually, and just contract the lower abdomen as a whole. This is how the breath is usually taught to beginners. However, doing the lower contractions is beneficial for cleansing the two lower chakras.

To complete the exhale, contract the perineum, and then the anal area, pushing out the last of the contents of the lungs. You should have a tight, solid feeling in the lower body.

As you inhale, release the lower contractions, expanding the body and allowing air to rush in. After filling the anal and perineum areas, the lower abdomen fills, followed by the navel, solar plexus, mid chest, and upper chest.

4. Tongue Position

The tongue acts like a switch in the energy circuit of the body. When the tongue is pressed against the roof of the mouth, as far to the rear as comfortable, the switch is closed and energy will circulate. This position should be maintained at all times while doing the Cleansing breath.

This position of the tongue stimulates the flow of saliva, which is regarded as beneficial and a help to circulating energies. Try to develop the ability to swallow whenever necessary without disrupting the flow of the breath. It may be easiest to do this toward the end of the exhale, but before the turning point to the inhale is reached.

5. Throttling

After the tongue is in place, you may further adjust the muscles of the throat, resulting in a partial constriction of the air passage. If you experiment with the muscles of the throat, around the vocal cords, you will eventually find the proper positioning. You will know you are constricting the throat correctly when you are able to accomplish two functions: throttling and inner sound.

As air is both inhaled and exhaled, the constriction of the air passage serves as a throttle to control the rate of flow into the lungs. The feeling is a steady flow into and out of the lungs, with the constriction doing the throttling.

6. Inner Sound

At the same time, the constriction of the throat causes the air to make a sound as it passes through. The sound has a vibratory influence on the energy system, raising and purifying the vibrations. In modern times, this principle has been rediscovered and called "toning." As you add the toning element to the breath, you add a new dimension to the effectiveness of your practice.

On the inhale, adjust the muscles of the throat to make a deep "aah" sound. On the exhale, make a hissing "ee" sound. The sounds originate from the central throat region, not in the mouth or nasal cavities. If you can make these sounds, you are constricting the air passage correctly.

The sound should not be too loud, but should not be faint, either. It may vary in your breathwork, depending on whether you are emphasizing it. Sometimes, you may wish to focus entirely on the sound, increasing the benefits of the vibration. Try to physically sense the high-frequency vibration as it travels though the energy body. Send the vibration to chakras you are working on by visualizing it happening. The inhale sound encourages the inflow of prana to that area, and the exhale sound is the outflow of stagnant energy from the area.

7. Connected Breathing

In connected breathing, inhaling and exhaling are joined so that there is absolutely no pause between them. The inhale follows immediately after the exhale and the exhale immediately after the inhale. There is no resting of the lungs between expansion and contraction. This does not imply rushing or hurrying between inhale and exhale. On the contrary, the breath is taken slowly and steadily. It's just that there is no sense of pause.

Why connected breathing has the effect that it does is something of a mystery from the physiological standpoint, but linking inhale and exhale will take you into deeper mystical experiences with the breath. The physical breath, with its in and out movement, represents the Yin/Yang, dualistic nature of the universe. Connecting inhale and exhale serves to integrate our experience of duality, connect left and right brain, and make our experience whole.

There is also something about linking inhale and exhale that augments cleansing effectiveness. This is one of the most important parts of the breath cycle. It is an area where your expertise and realization will continue to grow. It can be the focus of your meditation. Linking inhale and exhale will continually take on new meaning and experience.

8. Ratio

Ratio of breath refers to the relative length of the inhale and exhale. In a ratio equation, the inhale is always first, and exhale is second. In the Cleansing breath, the ratio is 1:2, which means the exhale is twice as long as the inhale. You may inhale to the count of eight, for example, and exhale to the count of sixteen.

9. Rate

When you are counting, the length of each count should be about one second, although you don't have to exactly time your breath with a watch. Start with whatever lengths of cycle are comfortable, but keep the 1:2 ratio. You may start with 4:8, inhaling for four seconds, exhaling for eight seconds. You may then go to 5:10, for example. Gradually build up to 8:16 as the final ratio.

During the exhale, suppressed energies are released from the chakras. Be patient during the long exhale, and watch as feelings may jump into consciousness to be integrated; do not resist them. I find that I get a better sense of being in the moment with the exhale if I sometimes imagine that I am actually holding the breath instead of exhaling, although of course, I continue to exhale. The exhale is so slow that it just feels like holding.

10. Depth

Depth of breath is controlled by the volume of air that is taken in. Depth will vary from a very full breath to a very shallow breath, depending on where you are in your breathwork.

At the start of a breathwork session, you will probably want to use a deep inhale, which expands all the areas of the torso. Filling to maximum capacity brings in maximum prana, but be careful not to strain too much. A comfortable sense of fill will be adequate.

As meditation continues, your requirements for breath will change, and you will learn to adjust automatically. Your breathing may become very shallow as you go deeper into a breathwork meditation. This can be an exquisite and delicate feeling, when you are sensing energy movements in the chakras with almost no physical breath.

11. Alternate Nostril

The alternate nostril breath is an important basic Yoga technique. Although not primarily for cleansing, occasionally using this technique will help to integrate the left and right sides of the brain, establishing a sense of calm. You can alternate nostrils as you do any or all of the above steps to the Cleansing breath, increasing the benefits of your practice.

Use your fingers to block one nostril as you breathe through the other. Start by inhaling in the left. Then, exhale through the right, and inhale through the right. Exhale through the left, and inhale through the left. Exhale right, inhale right, and so on.

THE INTEGRATING BREATH

The Integrating breath is the second type of breath we will study. We use it in two ways: First, this breath is used whenever suppressed feelings or emotions are coming up strongly and there is a need for larger amounts of prana to help integrate them. This can happen either in practice or during stressful events.

Second, if we push this breath more strenuously, we can use it when we wish to go especially deep into emotional clearing and integration during our practice. The oxygen and prana build in the body, dramatically bringing suppressed emotions into awareness and at the same time implementing integration. Sessions can reach the point of radically altering consciousness, shifting through levels of inner awareness rapidly. Emotional issues integrate, self-love is intensified, and body/mind healing augmented. Catharsis can be achieved almost at will.

The Integrating breath, when used in this manner, offers an alternative to the more gentle healing of the Cleansing breath. You may choose either breath to be the focus of your breathwork, depending on your preference. The gentleness of the Cleansing breath will, over a period of time, give you a completely adequate approach to inner integration. The Integrating breath is a more active approach, tending to precipitate the healing crisis we spoke of. There is no danger in using the Integrating breath, but it does call for more of the warrior spirit. Here are the important points:

1. Nose or Mouth: Try to breathe mainly through the nose, but you may also breathe through the mouth if you need a large volume of air. Do not alternate between nose and mouth during the same breath cycle; for example, if you breathe in through the mouth, exhale through the mouth.

2. Posture: Not important. The Integrating breath is usually performed lying down, but any position is allowed. You may want to change positions during the session, even going into Yoga poses, which are particularly helpful now to work with the breath in freeing up blocked energy.

3. Progressive Fill: Do not observe the progressive fill. Instead, breathe directly into the chakra(s) involved, expanding and contracting primarily that part of the body, if possible. For example, you may breathe into the abdominal area, solar plexus, upper chest, or all of these. Experiment in different areas to see what effect it has on the emotions that surface.

4. Tongue Positioning: The same position as the Cleansing breath is helpful, but not mandatory.

5. Throttling: None. Do not close the throat. Instead, there is a sense of "letting go" on the exhale. The body completely relaxes on the exhale, and the breath is allowed to find its own way out. Relaxing on the exhale is a critical part of this breath. Do not try to control the exhale in any way. Just relax all the muscles of the chest, and let gravity push the air out.

6. Inner Sound: Do not use.

7. Connected Breathing: Connected breathing is the most critical aspect of this breath, and you must be very careful to observe it. The purpose of connected breathing here is to build the level of oxygen and prana. If you pause between inhale and exhale, the oxygen and prana are allowed to dissipate, and no energy collects to enable the breath to perform its function.

8. Ratio: Do not observe any set ratio. As the exhale is released, let it find its own rate – this may either be faster or slower than the inhale.

9. Rate: You may use any inhale rate, ranging from slow (6 to 8 seconds) to fast (1/2 second). Experiment to see what effects the different inhale rates have on you – this varies with individuals. Do not try to control the exhale rate, let it happen by itself.

10. Depth: Vary from shallow to full.

11. Alternate Nostril: Do not use.

A typical breathwork session with the Integrating breath will last about one hour. When you begin the session, you want to use a full and fast breath to bring in as much oxygen and prana as possible. As you proceed, you will change the rate and depth to control your experience.

Breathing in this manner gets the energy moving in your body. You will feel various physiological sensations as well as emotions. The first sensation is usually that it becomes difficult to keep up the fast breathing rate required for the breath to have any effect. You will feel like you have to push very hard; be careful you don't slow down your rate to the point where the breath is ineffective. You might become sleepy and drift off, forgetting to breathe for a short period. This is not dangerous – you will always wake up when you need more air.

Other sensations may be tingling in hands and body, a sense of the energy rushing about your body, pressures or pains in parts of the body, or similar occurrences. These are all energy sensations, and mean that you are proceeding correctly.

Negative emotions will start to come up intensely, and should be processed. You should be ready for feelings that you may never have confronted before. For all these reasons, you should be somewhat experienced in inner work before launching off into a heavy session with this breath, and you may want to have a therapist or other breathwork professional with you, such as a Rebirther or Vivation specialist.

After clearing negative emotions, more blissful states of consciousness will come about. Feelings of universal love, oceanic oneness, heightened and expanded consciousness are all possible. This breath can lead to truly altered states of consciousness. In fact, one of the pioneers in the field, Dr. Stan Grof, has researched into the possibilities of creating LSD types of experiences with stepped-up breathing.

The stepped-up form of the Integrating breath is too intense to be used on a regular basis, even though the benefits are great. Using it in a more gentle way, not pushing as much, will be easier to manage and will also be beneficial to integration, along with the Cleansing breath. You should incorporate both of these breaths into your practice; they each serve to activate you in a different way.

Hyperventilation

In using the Integrating breath, the only possible physiological difficulty you can get into is hyperventilation. In hyperventilation, the oxygen/carbon dioxide ratio in the body becomes unbalanced, and you get too much oxygen in the blood. The symptoms include involuntary tightening of the muscles, dizziness, light-headedness, rapid or forced breathing, and in rare instances eventually passing out, in which case you will always come back to consciousness.

Hyperventilation occurs because the exhale is tensed and controlled, instead of being relaxed and uncontrolled. If you feel like you are hyperventilating, keep breathing but slow down your breathing to a normal rate, and be very careful to completely relax your body on the exhale. Relax all muscles, and just let gravity take out the air. When you pass out, you do this instinctively, and then you recover.

CHAKRA BREATHING

Chakra breathing is one of the most important techniques we use. This technique is effective with either the Cleansing breath, when you are in quiet meditation and wish to heal a certain chakra, or with the Integrating breath, when strong feelings are surfacing.

In chakra breathing, you breathe directly into the chakra you are working on. With any chakra located in the torso, expand and contract the area of the body which corresponds to that chakra. There may still be some sense of progressive filling. Visualize healing energy going into the chakra as you breathe; don't reject the feelings that come up.

For example, try breathing into your Solar Plexus. As you breathe into that particular area of the body, carefully sense the motion that takes place. Feel the body gently expanding on the inhale, and contracting on the exhale. Use a 1:1 ratio of breath. When you have sensed the expansion and contraction clearly, you are breathing into the center.

After breathing in this manner for a while, reduce the volume of air, still sensing the movement in the body. Keep reducing the volume of breath to only the slightest possible amount, and then to the point where there is no air actually entering or leaving the lungs, but only the suggestion of breath. You may still be able to sense a large expansion/contraction in the area of the solar plexus, even though there is no comparable motion in the physical body. What you are sensing is the motion of the chakra. Or rather, the energy of the chakra, since the chakra is composed of energy. You have reduced the volume of air to zero only for the purposes of this exercise; when you normally breathe into a chakra, there should be some amount of air entering and leaving.

You may now sense the Third Eye and Crown chakras in the same manner. Of course, you can't expand the body at these centers, but you can still feel the motion of the chakra itself.

To be able to sense the chakra directly requires sensitivity. If you succeed, you can assume that you already have a fair amount of psychic skill. If you can't sense the chakra, don't worry. The ability will come with practice.

When you are meditating, you may choose which breath and ratio you need. If strong emotions are coming up, go to the Integrating breath, breathing into the appropriate chakra. It will be helpful to break from your sitting posture, and assume a Yoga pose which will further open the chakra. You may increase your breathing rate slightly. Change positions, going to a different posture or back to sitting. Continue until the feeling is integrated.

You may also connect any chakra to the universal energy source above, and the grounding earth below as you breathe into it, which we will discuss shortly. Visualize strong white light coming from above, entering the chakra as you inhale, displacing negativity to the ground as you exhale.

INTEGRATIVE PRACTICE

Set aside a regular time, no matter how short it may be, for your practice. Practice can start with bodywork, followed by breathwork, and then will naturally transition into meditation, where no attention is paid to the breath. Let's briefly discuss meditation, for those who may be unfamiliar with it.

Meditation

The essence of meditation is to bring the activity of the mind to a halt. Thoughts are considered to block the meditative experience. In our work, we distinguish between thoughts and feelings. We allow thoughts to cease, so we can accept and experience feelings. When the energy of the feelings has dissipated, meditation can go into deeper areas of inner experience.

Even though we want the activity of the mind to cease, trying to willfully control the mind will prove futile. The best way to meditate is to develop the Witness ability, not attempting to stop or control the mind directly. Activating the Witness results in calming the thoughts and self-rejection of the mind. You may then enter direct experience of your feelings.

Begin your practice by entering meditation. Sit quietly, in the position you learned for the Cleansing breath. Be still, prepare to enter the Witness and activate healing energy. But first you must learn to visualize.

Visualizing

To do inner exercises effectively, you must call into play a new skill. You *visualize,* in order to direct energy in certain paths around the body. What you are actually directing is the pranic energy taken in with the breath. You are moving it in the energy body, but the sensation is physical. Visualizing actually has two components, seeing and feeling.

If you want prana to move in a certain path, you *see* it happening. This is different from imagining a picture in the mind. Instead, use your inner sight. For example, if you want to visualize the navel center, you could imagine it in your mind's eye, creating a mental picture. It is better, though, to see it as if your eyes were inside your body, at the navel. Inner seeing is developed by using the imagination at first, but the faculty will become more and more real as you practice.

As you are seeing inside, you may also *feel.* Sense the prana in the physical-psychic body. You might feel a current, a warmth, an expansion/contraction, a pressure, a vacuum, or other sensation. You may have your own way of feeling, but you should feel something. Again, you may have to start with imagination, but after a short while, the feelings will be real.

In the end, your intention is what enables you to direct prana. If you intend that the prana perform a certain function, it will, sensing the intention. You do not have to doubt whether

you are visualizing well enough. Doubt will impede the effectiveness.

Our practice consists of three parts:

> I.   ACTIVATING HEALING ENERGY
> II. MEDITATIVE BREATHWORK
> III. SPECIFIC PROCESSING

I. ACTIVATING HEALING ENERGY

Learning to activate healing energy is the same as invoking
the Witness and entering the Alpha level of consciousness; with
it comes the experience of self-love. It is a most important skill,
providing the power for the clearing and transformation of the
negative energies that are being surfaced.

You should activate the healing energy of the Witness
before, during, and after all processing sessions. You will become familiar with the sensation of being in the Witness, and
will know when you have to re-activate it in order to maintain
the energy and the sense of *disidentification* that is so important when working with lower chakra feelings.

Two kinds of healing energy

There are two kinds of healing energy: positive (Yang), and
negative (Yin). Both kinds are considered basically positive
healing forces. As you become familiar with them, you will
automatically draw whichever is needed for any particular
healing; there is no need to make a conscious choice.

As you activate healing energy, you enter Alpha. Alpha
refers to the rate of electrical vibrations of the brain. The
normal rate, in the Beta state, is from 13 to 30 cycles per
second. In the Alpha state, brainwaves slow down to between 8
to 12 cycles per second. You can even go deeper, as you acquire
expertise in meditation, entering the Theta state of 4 to 7 cycles

per second. There has been much research done on the benefits of the Alpha state. Healing is natural in Alpha. The conscious mind is relaxed. The body is relaxed and feels different. Meditation begins: the Higher Self and the Witness begin to function. The psychic abilities are awakened. Sensitivity to the energy flow, meaning the feelings, increases. Visualizations and affirmations are more effective. Clearing begins, almost spontaneously. Integration is facilitated.

There are three steps to activating healing energy:

1. **Aura Strengthening**
2. **Grounding**
3. **Entering the Witness**

1. Aura Strengthening (Energizing)

In this exercise, you draw upon and increase your supply of the masculine, Yang healing energy of the universe. You use this energy to strengthen your aura.

The aura is the electrical field that surrounds the body. It is made up largely of the composite blend of energies from the chakras, and is very much a reflection of who you are. If your aura is weak, you are low in vitality. A strong aura is needed as you practice; it will repel outside negative vibrations.

EXERCISE

Begin with a gentle Cleansing breath, with a count of about 2:2, spine straight, tongue in position. Continue the breath for a while before beginning the visualization.   (2 min.)

Visualize your aura around you. See an oval-shaped form, extending two feet or more all around your body, with silver-white electrical particles inside.

As you inhale, visualize a beam of luminescent, silver-white particles of light shining down from the sky, entering the top of your head, and going to your solar plexus, where it forms a large ball about one foot in diameter. Visualize the light as dazzling, powerful, dominating, burning away negativity it encounters.

As you exhale, visualize the particles flowing from the ball at your solar plexus outward to fill the space inside your aura. Visualize the particles extending to the edge of your aura, where they form the shell. Visualize (see and feel) the outer edge of your aura as strong and impenetrable. Visualize vibrations outside the shell being deflected as they try to pass through.   (2 min.)

AURA STRENGTHENING

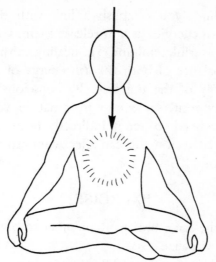

Inhale – Bring in Yang Healing Energy From Above

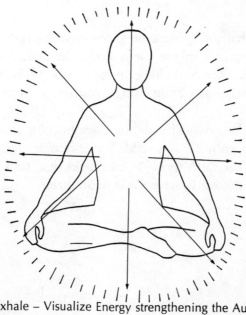

Exhale – Visualize Energy strengthening the Aura

2. Grounding

In grounding, you establish a link with the earth that absorbs negative energies as you release them. Grounding also draws in the powerful, feminine, Yin healing earth energy. Both sexes need a balance of both the Yin energy of the earth and the Yang energy of the universe. By consciously drawing in more of your opposite sex energy from nature, you can reduce the compulsive need to get it indirectly from the other sex. You'll be amazed at how this can affect your attitudes concerning relationships.

EXERCISE

Continue the same breath. Remember to both see and feel as you visualize.

Visualize a link from the center of the earth to your first chakra, the Survival center, located at the base of the spine.

As you inhale, visualize blue-green earth energy coming from the center of the earth along the link, touching your first chakra, and filling up your entire body. Visualize the energy as vibrant, warm, nurturing, loving.

As you exhale, visualize the blue-green color absorbing negativity, turning to a reddish-black color, and being pulled by the earth through the first chakra, back to the center of the earth, where it is neutralized.   (2 min.)

GROUNDING

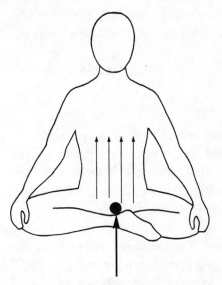

Inhale – Draw up Yin Healing Energy from the Earth

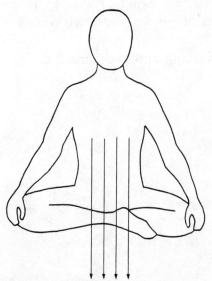

Exhale – Drain Tension into the Earth

3. Entering the Witness

If you are sensitive, or if you have been practicing, these first two exercises will have brought you at least partially into the Alpha state. This last step will bring you all the way.

EXERCISE

Continue the same breath.

Keeping your eyes closed, look up with the physical eyes to the Third Eye point. This point is between and a little above the eyebrows. You should strain the eyes slightly, looking up as far as possible. Look into the blackness with the physical eyes.

Visualize both Yang energy coming from above and Yin energy coming from below, meeting at the Third Eye as you inhale. As you exhale, you can visualize the energies spinning clockwise or just being still in the Third Eye, whichever feels best. You may want to use only one of these energies, depending on which you need most.

Continue breathing into the Third Eye.   (2 min.)

ENTERING THE WITNESS

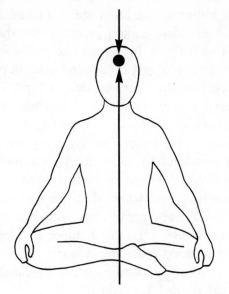

Inhale – Bring in both Yin and Yang Energy

Exhale – Hold Energy at Third Eye

Entering the Witness, using these three steps, can be a preliminary for going into deeper meditation. As indicated, the total time required is eight minutes, but you may adjust this as best suits you, either taking less time or extending and really getting into the exercise. As you practice, you should gain an appreciation of what the Witness feels like. It is a sense of being detached from what is going on around you, but also sensing your connection to it on a perhaps deeper level. Your sense of physical perspective may change. You feel the healing power and joy of your self-love.

Do the above exercises in a sitting position, as if you are meditating. It is helpful to be in quiet surroundings, and by yourself. A preliminary shower or bath will purify your aura of negative vibrations and influences that you may have absorbed.

Use a gentle Cleansing breath, but with a 1:1 ratio throughout all three steps. The 1:1 ratio is more comfortable at the beginning of a session, providing a warm-up. After you feel established in the Witness, continue with the Cleansing breath, but switch to the normal 1:2 ratio.

II. MEDITATIVE BREATHWORK

The next part of our practice is meditative breathwork, consisting of specific techniques that will help to release suppressed material into awareness. Release will happen in most types of meditation, unless you are engaging in "suppressive meditation," but using these techniques will be even more effective. The technique becomes the focus of the meditation.

The techniques are technical in nature. I have not included "guided meditations," where you are put into imagined situations that promote cleansing of feelings, because I did not want to include too much material. You may wish to include this as part of your self-healing.

You should keep in mind the basic principles of acceptance. Although the exercises are performed to achieve a certain result, you should not become compulsively goal-oriented. It is best not to look forward to results, not to live in the future, not to get nervous about performing correctly. Maintain your sense of being in the moment.

You may use either the Cleansing or Integrating breath. Start by activating healing energy, Alpha and the Witness. You may vary the rate and depth of breath as you feel.

As you proceed with the meditations, cleansing will begin. Physical, emotional, intuitive, and psychic feelings will surface. They will usually be of a disturbing nature; that is why they were suppressed originally. Do not re-suppress by rejecting, resisting, or trying to control the feelings, but accept and experience them without acting on them. You may want to occasionally re-activate the Witness. Eventually, you will find you can be doing any meditation and also be concentrating on the Third Eye.

A breathwork meditation can last from 15 minutes to an hour or more. At a certain point, you may naturally withdraw awareness from the breath, and enter deeper meditation.

There are six breathwork meditations described below. I would suggest that you establish a regular, weekly routine, using each of the meditations on a consistent day of the week. The seventh day can be used to combine all of them, or even to take a break from practice. Each element differently activates cleansing, also adding variety to practice. As you continue to practice, the different meditations become part of the unconscious mind and they will all automatically occur at once, whenever you sit to breathe.

BREATHWORK MEDITATIONS

Use a gentle Cleansing (with 1:2 ratio) or Integrating Breath for all of the following:

1. Posture / Body Sensations

Using posture as the focus of your meditation brings you into the body. As you deliberately straighten the spine, notice which parts of your body resist. There will be tightness, pain, and a sense of vulnerability in the chakras, organs and muscles that need to be released. Accept and experience all these body sensations, along with the associated emotions that come into consciousness for clearing.

2. Chakra Breathing

In this meditation, prana is directed to any or all of the chakras. As you draw in each breath, visualize the prana filling that center. If you want to work with all the chakras, start with the first, the Survival center, and work up to the Crown chakra at the top of the head. As you exhale, visualize all the chakras emptying in reverse order.

3. Inner Sound / Throttling (Cleansing Breath only)

Use the inner sounds as the focus of meditation, feeling the vibrations as they resonate through the body. At the same time, be conscious of the throttling effect produced by the constriction of the throat.

4. Connected Breath / Ratio

Focusing on the connected aspect of the breath is an effective cleansing technique that can also bring on deeper states of meditation. If you are doing the Cleansing breath, stay aware of your counting as you maintain the 1:2 ratio. At the end of each exhale and inhale, take special care to transition smoothly and effortlessly into the next inhale or exhale, with absolutely no pause between them.

5. Orbiting

Orbiting is another energy exercise that serves to vitalize and balance all the chakras together, influencing the feelings. This is one of the best for steady, quiet, meditative breathwork.

Assume there is a path from the base of the spine up to the top of the head, right along the spine, in the back of the body.

Assume there is another path in the front of the body, from the top of the head down to the base of the spine. These two paths constitute the orbit.

Visualize energy traveling up the path at the back as you inhale, and down the path at the front of the body as you exhale. Both see and feel. When seeing, you can imagine a bright, luminescent, blue ball of energy.

6. Third Eye

Stay focused on the Third Eye point for the entire meditation, as when you entered Alpha. The activation of the Third Eye awakens the Witness.

III. SPECIFIC PROCESSING

The final phase of practice involves working on any specific problem that may be currently occupying you. This could be any emotional issue, for example. You might devote a period of a few weeks to working on recurring fear, anger, or loneliness.

Process the feelings or situation, as you have learned. Breathe into the corresponding chakra, enhancing the clearing and integrating effect. Use bodywork or Yoga poses whenever appropriate. Bring in healing energy and self-love by entering the Witness before, during, and after each session.

You may use any guided meditations that you find helpful, relive past unfinished situations, or just work with whatever is happening now.

Practice Summary

Practice has three main parts:

PART I: Activate Healing Energy. Perform this each time you sit for practice.

PART II: Meditative Breathwork. Use a different meditation for each day of the week, on a regular basis.

PART III: Specific Processing. Use chakra breathing as you work with any current issue.

You might start by devoting about an equal amount of time to each part, but as you become more comfortable with your routine, feel free to give more time to any part that seems to need it.

Describing our complete practice routine may have seemed involved. However, as you get into it, the various parts will help maintain your interest as well as give you a complete approach.

Don't think you have to learn it all at once. Feel free to go step by step.

It would be optimal to practice twice a day, from 20 minutes to one hour each time. Possibly one short session and one longer session would be most convenient for you. The above exercises are a synthesis derived from traditional Yoga, Buddhist, and other esoteric disciplines. Stay with it, and you will definitely get positive results.

I am conscious that I am engaged in

the work of healing. I maintain a

positive attitude as I welcome and

experience all parts of life, not only

the pleasant. I use affirmations not to

avoid my experience, but to enhance it,

and to help me with my self-acceptance.

I am conscious of my environment, and how

it may influence me. I no longer buy into

situations. I use my dreams as another

approach to working on myself.

12

Practical Inner Work

HEALING

Integration is concerned with healing. There may be emotional stress in your life that must be brought under control; blocks, addictions, and negative patterns may be keeping you in pain, and this pain must be healed; physical symptoms may be present that have resulted from inner imbalances; or you may just feel the need for an approach to activate growth and sensitivity to yourself. What you are concerned with is nothing less than *healing*.

There are several elements that come to my mind as central to healing: concern, understanding, patience, nurturing, and courage. You may have an item of your own to add.

Concern means caring enough about yourself to be interested in taking the time to explore, with an open mind, what might be done to implement healing.

Understanding is certainly required, but we have seen there is appropriate as well as inappropriate understanding. You must know the limits of understanding.

Patience is required for the necessary cleansing and rebalancing of the energy system. We have been abusing and suppressing ourselves for extensive periods. We cannot realistically expect overnight change.

Nurturing is an attitude applied toward yourself, and may be thought of as the first step in loving yourself. You nurture yourself by activating your Heart center.

Courage is required to face negativities instead of rejecting them. The warrior spirit will build as you experience the first results of working on yourself successfully.

Healing in regard to physical health is an area that we only have touched upon so far. The same principles that are used in integrating feelings or events can be used here. Awareness is the first step. So much negativity has been suppressed that it manifests in the physical body as illness. You should own your illness, instead of blaming external factors, such as a virus or accident. Such conditions are attracted and succumbed to because of the suppressed negative energies within.

The next step, acceptance of physical symptoms, does not mean that you are agreeing to continue having the unhealthy conditions in your body. It just means that you cease resisting the energy imbalance which is present now. As long as you resist the imbalance, healing cannot occur. The healing power of the Higher Self cannot enter.

Direct experience of the energy imbalance and the physical symptoms from the vantage point of the Witness allows the healing power to start working. Enter Alpha and bring in both Yang universal energy from above and Yin earth energy from below. Experience the feelings of the imbalance, do not deny them. Feel the healing power of the Higher Self as it enters the body and begins its work.

The healing transformation will come after you maintain direct experience for the necessary amount of time. You must trust in the process of the Higher Self, which may bring forth possibly even more suppressed negativity and physical symptoms as healing continues, in order to cleanse. Eventually, a healing crisis may be entered, and cleansing will have taken place.

POSITIVE ATTITUDE

Positive attitude is often spoken of as a requirement for healing. I agree, but I also feel that this is a subject which is sometimes misunderstood.

Many people think that having a positive attitude means never admitting that they have any problems, either psychological or physical. They think that denial of negative conditions is what is meant by positive attitude, and that if they hold an image of complete positivity in their minds, the image will materialize.

The problem with this approach is that it leads to suppression of negative conditions, instead of integration and release. If you are continually telling yourself how excellent you are, there is no room left for the perception of the negative side of life, which certainly will not go away just because you are trying to deny it. Your idea of the positive is just a concept, and is not related to the natural balancing of energies in the feeling body. Indeed, insistence on seeing only what is perceived to be the positive will reinforce the existence of the negative, since one depends on the other. In our work, we have learned that we must acknowledge the negative. Yet, maintaining the right kind of "positive attitude" can be of benefit.

For me, positive attitude results from the proper understanding of all we have been discussing. When we know that we are clearing long-held negativities; when we feel ourselves growing, positive attitude comes naturally. We become positive about accepting and experiencing the negative. We become positive about all of life, not just what is immediately pleasing. The finite mind surrenders to whatever the Higher Self brings forth, and we become the Witness. Such positive attitude can supply energy and enthusiasm to enable us to successfully confront our Karma.

AFFIRMATIONS

Affirmations are a type of positive attitude. They can be of benefit when used correctly, but can be detrimental when used incorrectly. Affirmations are used correctly when the intention is to recondition the unconscious mind to be accepting. As with positive attitude, they are used incorrectly when the intention is to avoid what is perceived as unpleasant experience or feelings.

My opinion is that affirming and visualizing have been overemphasized in the current New Age literature, and the need for real work on ourselves has become obscured. Affirmations have appeal because of the sensationalistic promise of getting whatever you think you need by merely affirming it. Even if affirmations were to work as easily as some would have us believe, there are limitations to their use.

*The mind tends to
maintain self-rejection*

When we try to bring something into our lives, we usually start with a concept of what we think we need – a concept of the mind. The mind, however, is the source of our problem of self-rejection. Consequently, the mind cannot be relied upon to provide solutions. What the mind generally comes up with are better ways to avoid experience, continue self-rejection, and maintain addictions. Granted, sometimes this must be done to maintain our toleration level, but we should be aware of how the mind works.

Any solution of the mind will be dualistic. Even if the solution is achieved, it will not provide the happiness that is expected. There may be apparent relief at first, but the new condition will change into or be accompanied by its complement. For example, if you try to affirm prosperity, you will also maintain your sense of survival anxiety. Prosperity that comes to you will be balanced by your increasing insecurity. The two are dualistically dependent, and cannot exist without each other.

In trying to satisfy addictions, we do not grow out of them. We experience horizontal activity; there is no upward growth of consciousness. This will always be the case when motivated by *lack*. When motivated by lack, we create solutions and bring things into our lives upon which we become dependent. We make no progress in transcending, in becoming free from problems.

What about using affirmations to attempt to satisfy what we think are genuine needs and not addictions? Unfortunately, it is difficult to maintain objectivity about this. We think we are satisfying real needs, but in reality, we are driven by compulsiveness. The use of affirmations to attempt to satisfy compulsive ego needs is what might be called "low-level" New Age activity. It is a mild form of magic, leading to a deepening of the isolation of the individual ego.

In contrast, when a situation is processed, the intelligence of the Higher Self works for us, providing a solution that the mind could never come up with. The solution will be genuinely creative, as well as leading to circumstances that result in the dropping of addictions.

Affirmations cannot change beliefs
nor clear suppressed feelings

When we use an affirmation to try to change our circumstances, we generally try to recondition a belief, since we know that beliefs are responsible for drawing events to us. Unfortunately, beliefs cannot be that easily changed.

Beliefs are supported and maintained by suppressed feelings. Feelings, in turn, are created by beliefs. A mutually dependent cycle exists. For example, you may experience fear when a certain belief about security is threatened, even if the belief is irrational. The fear is then suppressed, and maintains the belief.

Beliefs cannot be abandoned, changed or transformed until the underlying suppressed feelings have been cleared. This ties into what I said earlier about not trying to attack belief systems directly, but starting to work on ourselves with whatever belief systems we have, outgrowing them through integrating the related feelings.

Neither can affirmations affect suppressed feelings. Feelings will not evaporate simply because you try to affirm them away. Suppressed feelings are composed of energy, while affirmations are of the mind. They are different levels of being. The mind cannot dismiss feelings by the simple use of affirmations. Feelings must be cleared, and experienced as they are cleared.

Suppressed feelings are the source of power that attracts negative events into our lives. Feelings are where the power is, not beliefs. A belief, in itself, has relatively little power. It is unrealistic, therefore, to assume that substantial change can be made in our lives by trying to recondition a belief when the subconscious energy of the corresponding feeling remains to both support the belief and continue to attract events. Clearing of the feeling must occur.

Nevertheless, affirmations can be helpful to recondition certain negative *mind-sets* to be accepting. Let's explore how to use them productively. The use of affirmations falls into three classes: accepting feelings, accepting conditions, and changing conditions.

Accepting Feelings

The mind, our thinking center, is a different part of ourselves than the feeling center. Although there is often a correspondence between them, they are often in conflict. You may be feeling tired and in need of rest, but the ambitious mind may push the body into further activity to accomplish a goal of the mind. Such self-rejection is typical of the mind. The mind, not the feeling nature, is the home of self-rejection.

The mind can be reconditioned to be accepting with affirmations. In contrast, feelings cannot be influenced with affirmations, except to suppress the feelings. You should observe this distinction when formulating affirmations.

What happens in practice is that trying to use an affirmation to change a feeling serves to bring the undesired feeling more into consciousness. If you are unaware, you will then try to re-suppress the feeling, through one of the forms of self-rejection. If you are aware, however, you could use the opportunity to integrate the feeling.

For example, if you are angry, but try to reject your anger and yourself by affirming, "I am in a pleasant and joyous mood," your anger will become worse. If it seems to go away, which is unlikely, it has only been suppressed. The same will happen with any other negative feeling you try to eliminate through affirmation, like fear, anxiety, sexual or food hunger, resentment, or loneliness.

Affirmations should be used to help you accept feelings, not avoid them. If you wanted to use an affirmation to help you get past your self-rejection about anger, you might affirm, "It is O.K. to accept and experience my anger." You would avoid becoming angry about the anger, as well as possibly fearful and depressed.

You must be careful about how you apply affirmations. You need to distinguish clearly between thoughts and feelings, accepting the feelings, and using affirmations to change your mind-set regarding acceptance. The mind is the source of the *opinion* about the feeling. The opinion is what should be changed.

Accepting Conditions

When you recondition your mind-set to accept conditions, you are not resigning yourself to endure conditions that may need to be changed; acceptance means only that you have stopped resisting what your experience is *now*. In accepting present conditions, you allow growth to occur. When you resist, you perpetuate the very conditions you fight.

Suppose you believe that you are poor. This in itself is subjective, and certain people may consider themselves poor with a million dollars in the bank. You cannot recondition the belief about being poor directly because of the suppressed emotional energies – such as insecurity, fear, or anxiety – that maintain it.

If you affirm, "I am wealthy," you bring up the suppressed anxiety about being poor. Accepting and experiencing the anxiety would be beneficial, but usually it is re-suppressed. The affirmation may even work against you, bringing about undesirable conditions because of the suppressed negativity that is stirred up.

If you react to your feelings of poverty and the accompanying anxiety, thinking that it is bad to be poor and anxious, you reject yourself. Note that the original belief about being poor and the associated anxiety did not constitute self-rejection.

It is possible to recondition your opinion about being poor. You can accept your poverty along with the suppressed emotions concerning it, whether the belief of poverty is justified or not. Your opinion that it is bad to be poor is a mind-set. When you accept being poor, you can begin integrating emotions about being poor that have been suppressed and continue to bring about the conditions of poverty.

When you recondition yourself to accept being poor, you take the first step toward creatively dealing with the situation. You will be more relaxed about it. You still might prefer having more money, and that is fine, but you will have dropped the compulsive aspect of suppressed emotions.

Remember that you are affirming in the present. "It is O.K. to be poor" does not have a future reference; you are not conditioning yourself to be poor in the future. It simply means that it's all right, it's not a disaster, it's not so bad to be poor now. The intention is to become at ease with the present condition, not to reject it and therefore yourself.

You can try affirming conditions right now. Take any "negative" condition you have been fighting. Affirm "It is O.K. for me to be/have/feel_____." Say this mentally to yourself ten times. Do you feel the immediate relief from giving yourself permission to be/have/feel what you previously condemned? Do you feel the release in the body, in the feeling centers as suppressed emotions clear?

Suppose you have an addiction. Affirming that it is O.K. to have the addiction does not mean giving yourself permission to continue *to act on* the addiction. You are just affirming the present: that it's O.K., it's not a disaster, you are not worthless, you are not guilty because you have an addiction now. This has no bearing on the future. The future will be that you do not act on addictive impulses, but release the tension through process-ing techniques; you observe non-reactiveness. You accept, but do not react to or extend negativity into the universe.

What if you are sick, or in real physical or emotional pain? You have to trust that these extreme conditions result from the build-up of suppressed energies, and that the principles of acceptance and invoking the Higher Self will see you through. When you fight a condition, you impede the flow of energies as they try to balance themselves. Affirming the experience will help you accept it.

Changing Conditions

If you have reached the point of accepting and integrating current feelings and conditions, you may use affirmations to help shape future conditions.

Suppose you are still poor, according to your belief system, but have integrated the poverty. You have become at ease with "poverty," thinking it is not so bad after all. You may have used an affirmation to help change your mind-set regarding poverty. Or, you may still be insecure about poverty, but you have accepted the insecurity. You are not fearful about insecurity, you remain in the Witness with it. You do not self-reject.

Affirmations will work effectively now to change conditions because, in having integrated, you have released the subcon-scious feeling energies that create your poverty. Energy is no longer present to oppose the affirmation, as before.

In other words, we can change things only after we have accepted the present; when we are not motivated to seek change by the desire to escape. The present consists of the conditions and feelings we experience and the beliefs that create them.

When affirmations are used for change, you make the assumption that the conditions you desire already exist, such as "I am wealthy," or "I am becoming wealthier every day." The affirmation is repeated mentally or written.

I realize this is getting subtle and possibly confusing, but I do not want to give you a simplistic and unrealistic impression of what can be achieved with affirmations. You may have tried them without success. Possibly our discussion has given you an insight into why you were unsuccessful.

*Use affirmations to enhance your
experience, not to escape from it*

If you have accepted and are integrating conditions and feelings, would you need affirmations at all to bring about change? It is likely that you wouldn't. As you surrender to *what is* and invite the participation of the Higher Self, situations will change spontaneously. Still, there may be some fine tuning that is called for. Affirmations and visualizations can be helpful at this stage. They are not to be used out of desperation and lack, trying to counter suppressed energies, but simply to exercise discretion about how things are manifesting.

Is it possible to make really lasting and substantial changes by affirming? I would have to answer both yes and no.

No, because all the great religious philosophies I have studied, whether Buddhism, Yoga, Taoism, even the more reasonable side of Christianity, have basically taught acceptance of the negative. This viewpoint has been supported by psychologists. In working on ourselves, the focus is on release of suppressed energies. If affirmations could change these energies and the events they bring, I'm sure the use of them would not have been overlooked.

Moreover, although I have been active in spiritual, psychological, and New Age circles for years, I cannot say that I have ever met anyone who has actually had success with affirmations in bringing lasting material or psychological change into their lives. However, I have met people who have used affirmations to further suppress their unwanted qualities, and this has been plain in their personalities in that their suppressed negativities would jump out whenever possible. These people also have a sense of self-imposed concepts and hypocrisy about them. The real changes that I have seen have come through the more traditional approaches of acceptance, meditation, therapy, and spiritual practice.

On the other hand, yes, affirmations have a definite place if used correctly. Most of the people who misuse them are not aware of the basic principles we have just covered. Affirmations can be instrumental in bringing about self-acceptance, which is the beginning of self-love, as well as material change when used correctly. I would encourage you to include reasonable and intelligent use of them in your practice. Here are typical affirmations, in the three modes of 1. accepting feelings; 2. accepting conditions; and 3. changing conditions:

First center (Survival):
1. It's O.K. to be insecure.
2. It's O.K. to be poor.
3. I am getting wealthier every day.

Second center (Sensation):
1. It's O.K. to have sexual impulses.
2. I am comfortable with unsatisfied sexual desires.
3. My opportunities for sexual fulfillment are bountiful.

Third center (Power):
1. It's O.K. to be angry.
2. It's O.K. to be/have____. (Regarding self-image)
3. I am comfortable in limiting situations.
   My personal power increases daily.

Fourth center (Heart):
1. **It's O.K. to be lonely.**
2. **I accept my alienation.**
3. **I love myself for accepting my___.(Perceived weakness)**
I form loving relationships easily.

There is one more related point about affirmations that I would like to discuss. Perhaps you are wondering if holding negative feelings in awareness during processing might serve to further attract negative events. This is not the case.

The principle of affirmation is usually interpreted as meaning that thoughts held in the mind attract similar events. However, it is not primarily thoughts, but feelings that draw events to us. Feelings are where the power is. Subconscious negative feelings are already actively working to draw events to us, even though we are not conscious of them. Simply bringing these feelings into consciousness does not increase their tendency to do so. On the contrary, when we start to work with feelings, the attractive pull is lessened, for several reasons.

First, bringing feelings into consciousness makes us aware of the contents of the subconscious. Awareness itself lessens the attractive power.

Next, when we enter the direct experience of the Witness, we have stopped identifying with feelings. *Disidentification* breaks the power of the negative feelings to attract events. It is when we are identified with negative feelings that they have the power to attract events, and we can be identified whether conscious or unconscious of them. As integration proceeds, the negative energy becomes released, and the attractive power of the subconscious is completely dissolved.

ENVIRONMENT

The question of environment is a difficult one. There is no doubt that we are influenced by our environment. We are routinely exposed to negative stimuli, including noise, air pollution, crowding, work stress, as well as genuinely dangerous conditions and people. In urban areas, these factors are intensified. We absorb the negativity, and it affects us. In processing, we wonder whether we are working with our own energies or ones we have picked up from the outside.

An additional factor about large cities is the lack of prana; cities are prana-deficient. Living in a large city results in a condition of chronic prana deficiency. Most people are not aware of how significant this can be. Lack of adequate prana means lack of ample psychic energy. Basic addictive tendencies are developed to get the energy merely to function. We become dependent upon stimulants, ranging from coffee and sugar to T.V., drugs and sex.

When I am in the city, I immediately feel more stressed, and my lower centers start showing their negative sides. I become anxious, worrying about survival issues (money). I become sexually stimulated and at the same time frustrated. I become angry. This is caused by the combination of the basic negative factors mentioned above with the lack of fresh prana. Without prana, the chakras are literally starving.

In negative environments, it becomes easy to reach the point of *overload*. We are confronted with too much negativity and we go beyond our toleration point. We shut down. We start suppressing all the negativity around us, and end by also suppressing ourselves. However, the issue is not that simple.

To use an analogy, if you are caught out in the rain, and are cold, wet, and miserable, you could process the situation as a response to your condition. You could own, accept, experience, and transform being miserable out in the rain, possibly catching pneumonia as your toleration point is exceeded. Or, you could walk to the nearest shelter and get out of the rain. I would recommend walking to the shelter, and would also recommend this kind of solution to any problem whenever possible. Use processing when it is not possible to walk out of the rain.

We are all caught out in the rain in one way or another. What we don't realize is that we have the option of walking to the shelter, *but we don't.* The reality is that we choose to stay out in the rain.

This is because the negativity outside of us coincides with the negativity inside; we are attracted to it, unconsciously. We are drawn into the turmoil, it reflects us, we identify with it and it becomes our own. In the end, we have probably created it. The enlightened person simply steps out of the rain. The unenlightened stays in the rain, fighting it, perpetuating the conditions. The question of environment then takes on a different cast. If our environment reflects ourselves, this may be why it is so hard to walk away.

We attract and absorb energies
that are already within us

It is correct to accept negativity that appears to be coming from the outside, even in highly negative environments. Our reaction to an external condition corresponds to our Karma – it is part of the projection mechanism. If our environment makes us depressed or angry, it is only stirring up those feelings in our subconscious. The negativity should be accepted.

The problem with negative environments then becomes one of overload. Even though feelings that come up should be integrated, we become overwhelmed by the amount of negativity, we begin suppressing, and growth becomes stagnated. Therefore, we must control our environment to the extent that we do not exceed our toleration and reach overload. At the same time, it must be understood that if we shield ourselves from each and every piece of perceived negativity outside of us, we cut ourselves off from our projected subconscious.

You must also remember that it is important to open yourself to positive influences and energies, to receive the blessing that such sources can provide. You must, therefore, find the right balance in confronting life so that you are nurturing yourself as well as meeting your projections, but are not being overwhelmed by the negativity of the world. However, if you find that you cannot shield yourself from a particular negative person or circumstance, you can be sure that you are being presented with a Karmic lesson that must be integrated.

BUYING INTO

We "buy into" something when we identify with it, or when we choose not to walk out of the rain. We take situations seriously, not suspecting that we are largely the creator, through our projections. When situations come up, you might try the following to help get a perspective on what's happening.

Imagine that the other people who seem to be causing the problem for you are actually *cardboard cutouts*. See them as flat, one-dimensional, painted and pasted cartoon figures. Look behind them, and see the wooden sticks that hold up the figures. When you visualize a figure, see it doing whatever it is that sets you off. See it in a fixed pose that does not change. Understand that you have created the figure to test yourself. This need take no more than an instant of time; you don't want to hold the image so long that you drop out of the interaction. Visualizing this may even help you come up with a smile in the middle of a confrontation.

It might appear as if you are depersonalizing other people when you see them as cartoon figures, but this is not so. You are only dramatizing and deflating your tendency to buy into your projections. You depersonalize others when you buy into situations; then, you really do see them as cut-outs. You assign your projected roles to them. You do not see them as they are. I find this trick helps to get me out of reacting to my projections and enables me to relate to others more objectively.

PROBLEM SOLVING

Processing techniques can be used for problem solving in general, as well as for handling feelings and situations. The problem can be a practical matter, a question about a person or relationship, or whatever.

Hold the problem situation in mind, with no thought for the solution. Turn the problem over to the Higher Self intelligence. A solution will be presented to you that will be unique and creative. All creative people use a similar approach, even if they are not aware of it. The steps are:

AWARENESS: Clearly formulate the problem, but not the solution, in your mind. You might even write it out.

ACCEPTANCE: Accept that you don't know the solution. Enter the "don't know" state of Zen.

DIRECT EXPERIENCE: Keep the problem in your consciousness, by witnessing. Internally, assign the problem to your Higher Self, then forget about it. The first three steps might take minutes, or less.

TRANSFORMATION: Wait for the solution to appear, either directly coming into your mind, appearing in dream form, or in other symbolic representation. This might happen immediately, or after a period of time.

DREAMWORK

Dreams are a means for the subconscious to communicate its contents to the conscious mind. As you begin working on yourself, your dreamlife is likely to become more vivid and significant. Spontaneous clearing will occur during dreams.

The usual psychological, analytical approach to dreams is to try to understand what they represent. Although analysis may be appropriate at times, in our work, we approach dreams as we would any other event. The dream is seen to be the dramatic metaphor that triggers the accompanying feelings. Bringing feelings into consciousness is considered to be the purpose of the dream; intellectual content is considered secondary, and possibly misleading.

For example, you may dream of a particularly nasty interaction with your spouse, and that he or she hates you. If you take this at face value, you may think that your subconscious is trying to warn you about something concerning your spouse. You may become paranoid. You may get lost in analysis, ignoring the feeling. If you take a processing approach, you would consider that the dream is surfacing suppressed, complementary feelings about the relationship, or even about yourself which you are projecting onto the spouse. You do not allow the dream to undermine the relationship. You accept and experience the feelings, clearing them.

Dreams become significant when the feelings that accompany them are strong. Feelings are the essential part of the dream, which may be overlooked in the search for "meaning." If you don't realize that feelings are being cleared, you resist, and re-suppress.

Do not reject yourself by rejecting your dream feelings; do not look for intellectual meaning that is probably not there. Integrate the feelings either upon awakening or during your regular meditation. Working with dream feelings can become another powerful approach to working on yourself.

I understand that the conflict I undergo
is the result of being addicted to one side
of any dualistic experience while trying
to avoid the other side. I understand that no
amount of the "positive" will ever be fulfilling,
and that to heal myself, I must integrate
the "negative" side directly, through
accepting and experiencing it. In doing
so, I transcend the emotional roller coaster
I have been riding. I find true
fulfillment. I have grown.

13

Integrating

In working on ourselves, we integrate both sides of any dualistic experience. Our problem is that we reject one side and cling dependently to the other side, creating pain. Understanding this about any stressful situation is part of awareness, the first step in transforming it.

Our perception of the negative side of the duality is worsened because of our projections. We project suppressed emotions, thinking they are caused by the stressful experience. For example, we reject insecurity, and then project fear onto an insecure situation, thinking the situation is responsible for the fear. We self-reject, because we do not accept the fear. We become compulsive; the desire to satisfy the need is out of proportion to its real place in our lives.

What must be understood is that no matter what extremes we take in order to satisfy compulsive needs, we will never get enough, because of the dualistic nature of existence. Suppressed emotions cannot be satisfied through external means; this is the false promise of materialism. Suppressed emotions can only be satisfied through inner clearing and healing.

When emotions are suppressed, blocking results. Blocking

hides whatever feelings are being avoided, but also creates compulsive desires for the dualistic complement. For example, we suppress loneliness, and then become compulsive about being with people, but no amount of being with people is satisfying. The loneliness must be integrated directly.

Compulsive desire can be felt in any center of consciousness. What is needed is not the satisfaction of the desire, but the elimination of the compulsiveness, through integration of both sides of the duality. The energy flow in the center is normalized, and compulsiveness dissolved.

Of course, whatever situation we are confronting is something we have brought to ourselves with our suppressed energies, our Karma, to begin with. Accepting and experiencing the energies as they surface in the emotions will eliminate the subconscious cause for the conditions, and transformation will spontaneously take place. Remember that in working with feelings, you should first activate healing energy and enter the Witness. In doing so, you gain the power and perspective to confront strong emotions. After you become proficient, you will be able to enter the Witness in seconds, or less. Just remembering to do it will be enough. Witness consciousness can be entered into during activity as well as meditation – maintaining the Witness during activity becomes second nature.

Areas of personal challenge will usually fall into one or more of the first four chakras: Survival, Sensation, Power, Heart. This chapter will cover integration of each of these centers in more detail, but first, let's start with the general condition of depression.

INTEGRATING DEPRESSION

Depression is a condition of energy depletion. It can happen in one or more of the chakras. It is possible to lose perspective and project depression onto unrelated areas of life, thinking that you are depressed because of this or that condition, instead of understanding the real cause: energy depletion.

If you are used to seeking excessive stimulation or excitement, you will experience depression as its complement, when your reserves of energy are exhausted. You may seek to escape from the depression by means of more stimulation or even through substance abuse, falling into an addictive cycle.

Since we are active beings, a certain amount of depression is inevitable. It is the complement to activity. If you can accept and open to depression, you will recharge your energy reserves instead of suppressing the depression with self-rejection, such as becoming depressed about the depression.

Self-rejection can be a primary
cause of energy depletion

Constant self-rejection can lead to chronic depression. Self-rejection such as blameful thoughts, blameful expression, fantasizing about the future or past, judging, reacting to feelings, controlling, and especially being motivated by negativities all requires large amounts of energy. Energy is also required to block the chakras and shield ourselves from the part of ourselves that has been suppressed. When we are actually involved in the self-rejection, we feel a temporary high because of the rush of energy, but then the reaction sets in.

To integrate depression, you should understand that it is a sensation of energy depletion. Don't react by trying to escape or compensate through other activities. Don't blame circumstances, events, or other people for your depression. Instead, accept and experience the depression.

As you enter the feeling of depression, surrender entirely to the sensation. Enter the Witness, and allow the depression to just be. Doing only this can be a tremendous relief, because you are no longer trying to avoid. Ceasing resistance to the depression will change your entire energy flow.

When you start to work with the feelings of depression, you will begin to feel the recharging taking place. The Higher Self will draw energy to you automatically to replenish your exhausted reserves. You can assist by activating healing energy, entering

Alpha and using the energizing and grounding meditations, and especially by breathing into the feelings of depression.

When depression is integrated, it becomes the natural complement to using your energies. Depression becomes the time to recharge, to heal. It can be joyous and restful, once surrendered to. Physical imbalances that may correspond to the energy depletion will also come into line.

Depression can be suppressed and stored in the energy body – the depletion becomes larger, not being able to recharge. If you have a pattern of avoiding depression, you probably have a good deal of suppressed depression. You may have to work with it, in a reasonable manner, not exceeding your toleration point. Do not react to your depression; do not become motivated by it. Acceptance will eventually bring you to the point where depression is experienced in a balanced way as the natural recharging of energies.

INTEGRATING FEAR

Fear is of the first chakra, the Survival center. Fear comes into awareness as anxiety, insecurity, apprehensiveness, nervousness, or paranoia. We become fixated on issues of work, money, health, physical protection, life itself.

A certain amount of fear is necessary to survive in the world. Fear protects us. When fear is integrated, cautiousness and groundedness result, balanced with the impulses to provide for basic survival needs. Our impulses are tempered, we become sensible.

Unintegrated, we fear fear itself. We don't allow for fear as part of our groundedness; we reject and resist fear. We perceive fear as undesirable, something that should be eliminated instead of having a balanced place in our lives. In being motivated to eliminate fear, we suppress it.

In suppressing fear, we enter a cycle of self-rejection. Fear builds in our subconscious until we become obsessed. We start projecting onto inappropriate situations. We become paranoid, imagining threatening circumstances when there are none. We seek to arrange our personal reality to fight fear.

Fear cannot be defeated
by manipulating reality

It may take many years to learn that no matter what we do to fight fear, it will never be enough. Fear will always remain, because it is within. Some people never learn this. They spend their entire lives being motivated by fear, never eliminating it from their lives. Fear does not go away just because we make changes. It's true that we may find apparent temporary relief in a certain area, but fear will emerge in another area. We just change the object onto which it is projected.

For example, you may have urgent financial needs, but you project onto the situation, and feel stress out of proportion. You experience suppressed anxieties as they are projected. You become further confused and anxious when you find that it is not possible to satisfy your "needs," no matter how much money you acquire. Your income may increase, but on the psychic level, your suppressed fears keep bringing you more expenses. You never get ahead. It is not the current situation that is causing the stress, but the suppressed feelings. If the feelings are cleared, you enable yourself to work with the real situation in a more rational and effective manner.

Moreover, when we allow ourselves to be motivated by fear, we become dependent upon whatever we acquire. We become dependent upon the job, the bank balance, the stock market, the economy, which leads to more insecurity and unrest.

Using other people as a means to eliminate fear results in unhealthy dependent relationships. We become resentful of our dependence, and it becomes impossible to maintain love. Unfortunately, fear is one of the main reasons for relationships today. We turn to relationships to try to eliminate fears regarding security, finances, loneliness, self-esteem, or sexual lack. We must learn that we can never escape from fear by means of buffers. Our fears are compulsive, and must be integrated, not fought.

Are you being motivated
by fear or love?

We need to be aware – it is all too easy to be unconsciously motivated by fear. To check your motivation, simply ask yourself whether you are being motivated by fear or by love. These are the two major types of motivation. When fear is the motivation, our interest is in the results of the activity; we don't really enjoy the activity itself. When love is the motivation, we do whatever we do because of the joy in the actual doing. We express our love in the doing. Any kind of reward is secondary.

It is possible to live a life based on the motivation of love, but not many of us achieve this. We are almost entirely motivated by fear. Fear on the Survival level usually comes into consciousness as anxiety about money and security, leading to greed and selfishness. Of course, we need money to survive, but if we were motivated by love, the money would follow.

You may want to look closely at whether fear or love is ruling you. If you can add just a little each day to being motivated by love, your life can transform. Note that this doesn't mean being motivated by the fear of not having or losing a "loving" relationship.

The problem is that we can't be motivated by love when we hold suppressed fear. To be motivated by love, you must first clear the fear, otherwise, fear will always creep into your motivation. Facing and integrating the fear will result in its eventual release.

Accept and experience your fear

Fear is integrated like any other emotion. When you feel anxious or insecure, or are about to make a decision or be motivated in order to eliminate fear, stop and process first. Accept the fear, enter the Witness and the direct experience of it. Do not be afraid of the fear. Feel the fear, without resistance. Open to it, in a controlled way, until you sense a change in the energy. If you have a chronic fear problem, you will have to do this over a period of time. Work with all emotions related to the Survival center, such as anxiety about loss of property or possessions, abandonment by others on whom you depend, or insecurity in general. Do not blame anyone, including yourself, for your situation.

Always remember to breathe into the emotion. Breathe directly into the Survival center. Use bodywork to free up the energy congestion in the chakra. Bring light into the area, and clear negativity by grounding. Emphasize working in the Survival center in your practice if fear is a particular problem for you. You will bring about the condition of being motivated by love.

INTEGRATING SEX

When we have suppressed and blocked our second chakra, the Sensation center, we feel compulsive and distorted cravings for sex, food, alcohol, smoking, drugs, or other physical sensations.

I have found that cravings can be handled effectively by working with them on the energy level, accepting and experiencing the craving without acting on it. Processing techniques will give you the power to do this. Do not condemn, try to fight, eliminate or avoid cravings. They are very strong, and you will only fall into additional suppression.

Free up the energy
in the second chakra

In working on yourself, the goal is to free up blocked energy in the second chakra. Start with basic, semi-regular physical exercise. Follow with a regular practice of bodywork and Yoga, emphasizing the second center. Use contractions of the perineum and lower abdomen to stimulate release; they can be especially helpful. Use meditation and breathwork to bring in light and prana to the second chakra, and grounding to remove negativity. The second chakra can be difficult to work with, so entrenched is our sexual repression, which I feel is the main reason for problems in this area.

As you work with the center, desires will be stimulated, and all kinds of feelings will surface. None of the desires or feelings should be condemned; that is what caused them to be suppressed in the first place. They must be accepted and experienced but not acted on, because at this stage, they are still compulsive. Accepting but not acting on is a fine distinction, but a critical one.

Accept, but don't act on
compulsive sexual impulses

We have become conditioned to think that sexual impulses must be satisfied immediately. The reality, however, is that life, even under the best of conditions, does not allow for immediate expression of sexual impulses. We then feel cheated. We feel as if we are missing out on what is our normal right. We develop a judgmental attitude about sexual impulses, unconsciously condemning them because they seem to bring more frustration than joy. We start suppressing sexual impulses as they come up, along with the sense of sexual frustration. Suppression builds, and we become blocked and compulsive.

There may be other ways that suppression of sexual impulses begins, relating to our personal history. What is important is not why we do this, but the recognition that this is what happens. Intellectually understanding the cause of the suppression will do little to change the pattern of suppression. The pattern has become established on an unconscious level, and is maintained by the suppressed energy. It has reached the point of repression, where we suppress unknowingly. Working with the feelings of frustration that are conscious will bring eventual integration.

What needs to be acknowledged is the reality that sexual fulfillment is created and balanced by sexual tension. We reject and suppress the tension, creating the blocking. Part of our rejection is due to the intense nature of the sexual impulse, especially in men. As we reject sexual tension, we try to escape from it. We pursue sex for its own sake instead of as the means to share and bond energies with a loved one.

If you begin accepting and experiencing sexual tension without acting on it, you can make major changes in your energy and growth patterns. This may sound like much to ask for, and it is. Only seekers who are committed to their growth and practice would want to extend such an approach to its logical conclusion, which would involve periods of sexual abstinence.

The esoteric physiology of celibacy is well understood by the masters of the East. They teach that as the sexual impulse is accepted but not acted upon, the energy builds to the point where it rises to the other chakras and serves to stimulate them into awakening. The sexual center becomes integrated, and serves as the main energy source for personal transformation. Transmutation of sexual energy is the basis of all advanced Yoga, but should not be attempted until one is ready, when the paths in the body are opened so the energy actually can rise instead of building in the second chakra.

In practical terms, accepting but not acting on means allowing the sexual impulse to exist, even possibly taking part in love making, but without orgasm. Relinquishing orgasm is not the problem that it may first appear to be, because the build-up of sexual force is released upward, into the other chakras, instead of outward as in conventional orgasm. In the branch of Yoga known as Tantra, the focus is on controlling and transmuting the sexual force, relating it to the Kundalini energy. Transmutation is facilitated by the right kind of practice, involving Yoga postures, breathing, and locks. Contraction of the perineum is the main lock used to diffuse and disperse sexual energy out of the second center and into the other centers. Mantak Chia, in his illuminating books, has done much to make information about this subject available. From his popularity, it appears that more people are interested than one might have expected.

What is important, is to accept before not acting upon. I feel many spiritual seekers make the mistake of suppressing their sexual impulses in the name of celibacy, even though they may not think they are doing so. The impulses must be consciously and deliberately accepted, even celebrated, but not acted on. Compulsive sexual impulses dissolve, like any other integrated feeling. After a while, the energy is likely to rise up higher into the body, without having to be forced. If the impulses are not accepted, the energy does not rise up to the other chakras. It becomes suppressed and held in the second chakra.

I realize that transmuting sexual energy may not be something you are ready for yet, but knowing about it may help influence your attitude about needing immediate release from sexual impulses. I might add that once sex is integrated and celibacy established, sexual frustration evaporates. There is no sense of continuing frustration, or even the need for ordinary sexual release. Instead, there is a joyful sense of liberation from being a slave to sexual tension. On the other hand, sexual activity without conventional orgasm can still be entered into, without compulsiveness. It is like having the best of both worlds.

In my own experiments in this area, I found that it took a few weeks to get past the initial frustration of not having the energy exit in the usual path when it built up. The energy would then rise to the top of my head, where I could feel the pressure building, and would release back down into my body. After a few months, I felt a tremendous release of sexual tension in the lower abdomen, the area of the second chakra.

It occurred only after I had reached the point of fully accepting the sexual impulses I was feeling. Before that, I thought I had accepted, but had not; I was unconsciously resisting. The release happened one day when I was doing Yoga postures and witnessing the sexual impulse at the same time. I fell into the complete acceptance and experience of my sexual impulse, and almost simultaneously felt a release of suppressed sexual tension. Included was suppressed tension of which I had not even been aware. The relaxation in the chakra was tremendous.

In this one experience, I cleared a good amount of the suppressed material that I had been carrying in the second chakra. A major healing was beginning for me, as the sexual energy activated centers above it. I went into a period of cleansing the Solar Plexus, and started to go through the suppressed negativity of that center as it came up.

Most of us are suppressed in the second center. It is therefore difficult to go without normal sexual release. The very suppression blocks the energy from rising up and out of the chakra into higher chakras, and release through orgasm is the sole alternative. If you begin working on this center, your experience of sex will gradually transform. Your capacity for non-compulsive enjoyment of sex will increase, as well as in other related areas, like food, alcohol, or drugs. If you are dealing with one of these related substances, you can treat it exactly like sex.

INTEGRATING ANGER

Anger is the manifestation of the unintegrated third chakra, the Power center. It is probably the single most projected emotion. We constantly avoid responsibility for anger, thinking that others are the cause of it. We constantly blame, rejecting ourselves.

*Do not try to think
away your anger*

There is no rational basis for anger. It cannot be controlled by intellectually identifying what is making you angry and trying to change your reaction through reprogramming yourself or others. "Rational" types of therapy, in which you try to reprogram the context of your reaction as well as the stimulus, can be positively dangerous. If you use a rational approach and appear to be successful, you have merely re-suppressed your anger, and it will come forth another time.

Unusual amounts of anger always represent suppressed energy. It must be released on the energy level. Reprogramming is not the answer. Reprogramming starts with the assumption that anger must be avoided; this is doomed from the start. Anger must be accepted in order to be cleared.

You may also experience what could be called "ordinary" amounts of anger, which does not involve suppressed energy, and is not as strong as suppressed anger. Processing is the best approach I know for handling either ordinary or suppressed anger.

We have already discussed the ineffectiveness and self-destructiveness of venting anger upon those who appear to have caused the anger. Processing, breath, and bodywork will release anger effectively, without alienating others.

I have used anger as a working example throughout this book because it is such a common problem. Let's summarize the steps of integration with regard to anger:

1. **AWARENESS.** Own your anger. Understand that whatever is "making" you angry is just bringing up your own suppressed anger. There is no rational reason why you should choose to be angry, but your subconscious is taking the opportunity to project and clear itself.

2. **ACCEPTANCE.** End inner resistance to your anger. Do not think you have to avoid it. Accept it, but do not act on it, or blamefully extend it into the universe. If you blame or attack others who appear to make you angry, you reject yourself and re-suppress the anger.

3. **DIRECT EXPERIENCE.** Surrender to the experience of the anger. Feel it in the body, as the energy moves. If possible, use bodywork and Yoga postures that work on the Solar Plexus. Feel the anger, in the moment, with no thought of changing it. KEEP BREATHING.

4. **TRANSFORMATION.** Activate the Witness through concentration on the Third Eye. Allow the energy of the anger to find its own equilibrium. Allow the outcome to be directed by the Higher Self. Allow change to happen on the inner psychic planes, without your conscious knowledge or intention. The anger will be dissolved, not suppressed, and creative change will occur spontaneously.

If anger is a problem for you, you have to accept that it will take time to bring yourself into balance. Learn to work with anger during meditation; you will gain the ability to do so in confrontation.

At one period of my life, I felt tremendous waves of anger when I sat to meditate. Things would happen that would disturb my meditation, and I would become angry. I decided that my subconscious was cleansing, and that once I sat down, I would not get up to change anything in my environment until my meditation was over.

I would sit. The phone would ring and the answering machine would not be on. Neighbors would start to play music and my windows were open. My cat was locked out and would start scratching on the door. Carpenters next door started hammering, etc. This was when I had moved to the seashore to find quiet from the city.

I would release large amounts of anger during these meditations. Many times, my body started trembling and shaking, but I would not break from the experience of the anger. The crisis would last up to ten minutes at a time, happening over a period of several months. I realized that I was drawing these events to me and reacting to them in order to cleanse. I didn't need the stress of the city to provoke me; I provided my own provocation. Anger was cleansing because I wasn't in a stressful environment, but in a healing environment. Gradually, my meditation started to calm down. You may also go through a similar period, when anger or another emotion may start to cleanse. If you work with what is cleansing, you can make lasting change.

Anger is of the Power center. We feel angry because we have not integrated the complementary sides of the Power duality: our capacity to control versus our helplessness. We reject helplessness, and feel anger when our power, really our infantile desire for omnipotence, is threatened. We must accept that we have this desire for omnipotence, and that we are also helpless and powerless much of the time; helplessness is actually the basis for our sense of power. Therefore, we are angry – we cannot avoid it at our present stage of growth.

When the Power center is integrated, you will still have flashes of anger as you exercise your will. The anger will dissolve and pass away quickly if it is not resisted, but accepted. When integration in the center matures, you will experience personal power balanced with surrender to the Higher Self, because when the conscious ego is not capable of acting, it means the Higher Self is taking control. Recognizing this, you integrate the expression of personal and higher will. But do not try to reach this realization intellectually. Process your anger, and you will become clear.

Other areas related to the Power center are issues of self-image, self-esteem, the need for control in general, and the need for significance in your life. If you feel pressures in these areas, do not be compulsively motivated by the feeling. Process the impulse, bring it to a reasonable level, and make your decisions with your real – not your compulsive – needs in mind. Then, don't question if your present perception of your needs is as "real" as it could be. Your needs will change throughout your life. There are many things we are supposed to do that expose us to opportunities for learning. We do them, and we outgrow them. Find your true goals, and don't be afraid to follow them.

INTEGRATING RELATIONSHIPS

Relationships come under the Heart center. We have a genuine need for relationships of all types: to be part of a community, to work with others, to be intimate. Relationships are also important because others serve as mirrors, reflecting our suppressed qualities and stimulating growth.

In our society, we have developed a special compulsiveness about one specific kind of relationship: romantic love. We search for a partner; we hunger for intimate relationship, but satisfaction often remains elusive. Can this need ever be realistically fulfilled?

I believe that it can, but only with the proper approach. There is a real need to be with someone, as well as a need to be alone. However, when we are compulsive in seeking relationships, we prevent a relationship with integrity from developing.

When our sense of relationship is unintegrated, we try to avoid being alone. We find being alone depressing, fearful, and so on. We look for a relationship, thinking that it will be the solution to our unhappiness. We become dependent upon the relationship, even when it is not living up to what we expected from it. If our need for relationship is integrated, autonomy becomes balanced with relatedness. There is no compulsiveness; we value our time alone as well as with others.

It is probably safe to assume, because we are not fully enlightened yet, that most of our intimate relationships will be of a dependent nature, in spite of our best intentions. There is no problem in this, if we can accept the pain that dependency brings.

Pain is felt whenever what you are addicted to in the relationship is threatened or absent; this is the simplest method of identifying addictions. You may respond to the pain by arguing that your needs are legitimate, or that your partner is being unfair. You may rationalize your needs endlessly, but in the end, it comes down to being addicted and dependent. Moreover, you attract to yourself the kind of person who acts exactly to trigger your insecurities. Such is the precision of Karma. You will be with someone who will make you conscious of your addictions; that is why you chose them.

Whenever you feel pain in a relationship, whether insecurity, sexual frustration, anger, or loneliness, you must remember that *you* are responsible for the pain because it is your suppressed energies that are surfacing. They surface when you are denied those qualities or behavior in your partner to which you are addicted and which enable you to continue to suppress your pain. If you can remember this, you make it possible to maintain the relationship; you will not blame the other.

Use your relationship as a vehicle for growth

If a relationship is used to help identify what you are addicted to, it becomes a most powerful vehicle for growth. However, if you blame the other, growth does not occur, and the relationship collapses.

It helps to be a little philosophical here, and realize that life is, indeed, for learning. It also helps if you happen to know there is more to life than just this one time around in your current body.

Actually, I have noticed that usually most of the time spent in relationship is harmonious, except for a small percentage, varying from 10% to 30%, let's say. If your relationship fits this description, you may assume that you have a perfect relationship. You will be happy most of the time, and when those terrible times come up you can dig in and make leaps in your self-work. The relationship becomes win-win.

This is how to make a relationship work. There is no "perfect" relationship, because *we* are not perfect. The relationship serves as a mirror for our imperfections. When disharmony surfaces, you must begin to process. You must begin by being aware of and taking responsibility for your reaction – it is your addictions that are being threatened. You must accept your pain without resistance or *blame*. You must experience the pain, understanding that it is your suppressed material that you are clearing. The transformation will come. The other will sense, without fail, that you have changed, and will change in return. There is no need to fight, discuss, explain, argue, or persuade. These are all self-defeating because even if you win, you lose: your addiction continues.

However, it is hard to maintain perfect acceptance in the face of continual relationship stress. Even when we take responsibility and are processing, there comes a point when we say, "enough." You must strike a reasonable balance between processing and confronting. Do not use processing as an excuse for tolerating a bad situation or as justification for unassertiveness. If processing has not brought a transformation and your toleration is reached, you may have to discuss your feelings in a non-blaming way if you haven't already, saying something like, "When you do such and such, it brings up my feelings of____. Could you do something different?" If you partner cannot respond and if your toleration is truly reached, or if your partner keeps blaming you when you have taken responsibility, the relationship may have to be abandoned.

Relationship addiction can tie into any level of being, such as Security, where we depend on the other for material support; Sexual, where we are compulsive and using; Power, where we control the other because we gain energy from them; Heart, where we seek to escape from loneliness. Of all of these, the escape from loneliness may appear to be the most justified. It may be hard to understand why wanting a relationship to ease loneliness would be called an addiction, because isn't this what relationships are for?

The question of loneliness is one that we all must confront. We must understand that because we are compulsive, no amount of being with others, even a special loved one, will eliminate loneliness. What happens is that the newness and the excitement of a relationship, especially if it is sexual, will cover loneliness temporarily. After a while, it no longer has the same effect, and loneliness returns. We may then look for another relationship, but we continue to suppress our loneliness, becoming superficial and using others. Eventually, our Karma will create a situation which is designed to teach us once and for all that we cannot escape from loneliness.

If you have not developed your capacity for loving yourself, you will be lonely regardless of who you are with. You will not be able to accept love from others, even if they are genuinely loving. You may have experienced this in reverse – possibly you have been with someone who could not accept your love because they could not touch the love within themselves.

Integrating loneliness is the only way I know to work with it. Integrating the pain, the isolation, the separateness that you feel will result in its eventual transformation, and it will no longer be felt as painful. It is painful now because you have developed the habit of suppressing it. When integrated, you will gain a sense of personal empowerment. You will feel complete unto yourself, and will choose to be with others to share yourself and your joy, not in the hope of finding happiness because you are with them. Relying on myself is a lesson that I have to relearn from time to time. Whenever I feel sad and turn to a friend for support or to find happiness, it never works. I am reminded that I must go within, and welcome whatever feelings are there.

There is much suppressed sadness in the Heart center. It drives us into compulsive relationships of all types, not only sexual. You must take time to go into sadness, experiencing it without avoidance. Sadness can become the focus of the Witness. You can experience an emotional peak in its transformation; you enter the ecstasy of emotional pain. Sadness can be approached much like depression, as an opportunity for healing and bringing in energy. As you surrender to healing, you invoke ecstasy.

We may perhaps gain additional understanding into the nature of loneliness by becoming aware of the dynamics of *sexual completion.* We ordinarily feel incomplete without a link to someone of the opposite sex. When we have such a link, we gain a sense of pseudo-wholeness. The real sense of wholeness is exactly what can be found within, by ourselves, through the growth that eventually comes from spiritual practices such as we have been discussing. I know it is possible because of my own personal growth. I am not as compulsive about relationships as I used to be. I have a greater ability to be complete and content alone.

We reach inner sexual completion by integrating the opposite sexual polarity within. We all have both male and female within. Our conditioning has brought us to deny the opposite within ourselves, however, and we seek to find him or her in the world outside. We become attracted to others who will carry our projection of the female or male within. Jung called this the question of the *anima and animus*. I feel it is one of the main areas for advanced self-work.

Integrating the sexual other within is essential, because the projection upon the lover never works completely. The other never lives up to the ideal, and our growth would become limited if they did. When the break occurs between what we are projecting and what is real, we fall out of love. We have created our love object, we react to that creation, and we suffer pain when the collapse occurs, as it must. If you accept the pain, you burn away the tendency to project onto the other. You become in touch with the sexual other inside yourself. You find wholeness and self-love. The soul-mate is within.

*As I open to myself, I look deeper than
I ever have before. I take responsibility
for and accept feelings that I have
always rejected because they were
too painful. In going so deeply into
myself, I surrender to the Higher Self,
and I begin deep and lasting
transformation.*

14

Opening to Yourself

In learning any skill, there are times when a personal teacher may be helpful. Although I have tried to present the fundamentals of processing in such a way as to enable you to apply them as a self-therapy, it could prove useful if you found a counselor who was sympathetic with the principles we have been discussing to help you get started. This would especially be the case if you have no previous exposure to inner work. If you have previous experience, then possibly no further outside assistance is required.

I would like to relate some examples of my work with clients to give you a further insight into how I approach the counseling relationship, and a deeper view of the actual process. I think this will be instructive as you begin to enter into your issues.

In working with a client, my approach is somewhat different from the usual therapist's. I try to function more as a consultant, and less as a therapist; I try to minimize the emotional dependence of the client. I am not there primarily to receive the client's projections, even though I understand the power of this approach, and that it will be unavoidable to a certain extent. Minimizing the emotional dependence of the client also helps me to minimize counter-transference and becoming attached to and dependent upon the results of therapy, a pitfall quite common among therapists, I feel.

Instead, right from the beginning, I teach the client to find the therapist, the guru, the acceptance within. My energy goes toward supporting the inward focus, not being the focus. I feel the means is the end, and that encouraging emotional dependence leads to mainly emotional dependence and a slow course of therapy. It's not that I feel there is no place for emotionally dependent therapy – it is an essential step for many. It's just that my work, as I see it, is to teach self-therapy, self-healing, and self-support, not to primarily be the support.

In the following stories, I have briefly summarized the astrological factors that helped me identify each client's patterns for readers who are interested and have some knowledge of astrology. If you are not one of these, you may safely skip over this material.

SANDY

Sandy is a 32 year old, very attractive woman with a charming and engaging personality, and a gift for making friends easily. She has been unable to settle into any specific career since college, and has supported herself by doing office work. She was prompted to seek counseling by a series of crises in her romantic relationships. I met with her once a week for three months, and then once a month for eight months, and still see her occasionally. I also met once with Richard, the man with whom she was involved in her longest relationship, which covered a 6 year period.

Sandy was emotionally suppressed, and addictive. She consumed large quantities of alcohol and drugs, and had a tendency for sexual straying. She had no concept that this behavior constituted self-rejection, and that she indulged in it to shield herself from her painful feelings. A large part of our time was spent in overcoming her resistance to the idea that there was something wrong with this behavior. She viewed it as recreation.

Sandy's astrological chart showed the following stressful elements: Saturn conjunct Moon (very close) in the twelfth house. This represents a depressive and emotionally blocked nature, resulting in a fear of intimacy. Saturn, the planet of fear and limitation, is blocking the planet of feelings, the Moon. Being in the twelfth house further exaggerates the unconscious nature of her feelings, implying a highly repressed condition. Fear of feelings, as well as the feelings themselves, such as depression, need to be integrated. Next, Venus square Mars adds to her sexual magnetism, but also represents a lack of integration between her loving and sexual sides. Then, South Node in the fifth house suggests that whenever she fell back into self-defeating behavior and avoidance of feelings, she would seek escape in love affairs, entertainment, or acting like a child.

In her relationship with Richard, she unconsciously chose a man who was not emotionally expressive, so that she would not feel threatened. An emotionally demonstrative person in intimate relationship would have been stressful for her, pointing out her own lack of emotional contact with herself.

At one point in her relationship, she experienced the sudden need to escape, and did so by flinging herself into a week-long sexual affair with someone she had just met. She soon rejected this person, who had become attached to her, causing him pain and disappointment. As we examined this incident and I met with Richard, the details that triggered her behavior came to light.

It seems she had always wanted a commitment in her relationship with Richard. For 6 years, this had been an issue, which included the discussion of children. Richard was unable to commit, and remained emotionally distant. She did not realize that she was dependent upon the aloofness. When Richard, who had been working on himself, finally began to open emotionally to Sandy, telling her that he really deeply cared for her, she panicked. She could not handle the expression of real emotion because of her inner blocking and fear of intimacy, and she escaped into the week-long fling, not the first of her affairs outside the relationship. After learning about the affair, Richard decided to call it quits for good, greatly hurt that Sandy had reacted to his finally opening to her in what he felt was an enormous step for him by throwing herself into the arms of a stranger. At this point, Sandy and I began meeting.

Although not actively working on herself, Sandy was familiar with meditation, and seemed motivated to make changes in her life. Exactly why she was motivated, I don't know, but she seemed to have finally realized that her life was misdirected, and that something important was missing.

We spent time discussing the concepts of emotional self-acceptance, and how critical it was for her to accept and experience her feelings instead of trying to escape from them through alcohol, drugs, or wild sex. Once she understood and agreed with this concept, we were able to start work.

Our work together consisted of bringing up her feelings in a controlled way so she could integrate them. Her primary problem was an irrational fear of feeling itself. We had to go into this basic fear, and then the actual feelings she was blocking.

I would lead her into awareness of fear in general. She became able to feel the fear that had been unconscious. I instructed her to bring up the fear by thinking of Richard. Such was her projection, that doing this would bring up tremendous fear. I kept pointing out the fear, making sure she felt it was safe to feel it, telling her that it would not hurt her, and that she should not fear the fear, but just be with it. I had her enter her body, and continuously breathe into the root chakra with the Integrating breath, sometimes breathing gently and quietly, sometimes more forcefully, bringing up the fear. Occasionally, I had her hold Yoga poses: Forward Bend, Hero, Bridge, Hip Rotation. Together, we activated the Witness and brought in healing energy to the fear.

As she witnessed, I had her access the feelings of self-love that resulted from her facing the fear. I would assist her by resonating with her as I brought up my own feelings of self-acceptance and self-love. After about four sessions, Sandy reported that she thought she was "beginning to get it."

Then, gradually, as the fear emerged, so did one of the primary feelings she was suppressing: her resentment and anger toward Richard for his lack of commitment and support. I reasoned with her that she attracted this kind of partner, and was heavily projecting her own inability to commit onto him. Gradually, I was able to start getting her past the blame that was keeping her in self-rejection, and making release of the anger impossible. She was able to understand that she was reacting to her own fear of intimacy, not to her partner.

I had her feel the anger, instructing her to keep shifting from the blame to the experience of the anger. I told her to use her thoughts of Richard as a stimulus for the anger, but to intellectually understand that the blame was a mistake, and to set it aside. During our second month, she reached the point of being able to access her fear and anger in a non-blaming way, and began to cleanse significantly.

The next major emotion to emerge as cleansing continued was her depression, which was a large part of her motivation for escapist activities. Depression became the focus of our work for the third month; she had a large amount of suppressed depression. I emphasized accepting and experiencing it in a controlled and reasonable manner. She started attending Yoga classes, and became involved with a women's group, shifting from her usual habits of diversion in the form of second chakra substances. At the same time, we worked more with this chakra, breathing into it and bringing in healing energy. She learned to sit with and witness her depression instead of reacting to it. During this period, Sandy did become dependent on our meetings. I did not discourage this, but kept re-directing her focus inwardly.

As we further examined her relationship with Richard, another aspect emerged. When I met with Richard, he mentioned that he felt Sandy wanted to be too dependent upon him in terms of material support, almost as if she wanted him to be her father. This was reinforced by a gap in their ages (he was older), and more financially established. Richard said he was not comfortable with this role, feeling he was being used. As I discussed this with Sandy, she started to see the possibility of her projecting a fathering role onto Richard, although at first she was annoyed and rejected the idea, which was also how she reacted whenever Richard tried to discuss it with her.

Her own father was an alcoholic, and was functionally and emotionally absent. Sandy had been attracted to an emotionally distant man as her biological father, and now had repeated the choice in selecting Richard as a partner, in an unconscious attempt to bring up those feelings for clearing that the relationship triggered.

We examined those feelings. She wanted to be supported and protected in her relationship, but felt like she had to acquiesce when Richard pointed out that he felt her demands were unreasonable, or were just not what he wanted in a relationship; nevertheless, she remained resentful. She created the structure to support her resentment: her partner would not support her. Traditional psychologists might say she transferred her resentment about her father not supporting her to her partner, but we have discussed that a more basic cause may lie in previous life Karma.

I asked her to try to accept these feelings of resentment about not being supported by her father. I had her bring up her feelings of utter dependency as a child by regressing her to an early age after entering Alpha and the meditative state. She re-lived the dependency and the experience of complete fear of being left alone, of turning to him when he was drunk and being slapped by him. Constantly, as she relived these events, I would bring her out of blame, and into the experience by reminding her to drop blameful thoughts and enter the feeling; to bring her self-love and healing energy to the pain of being alone, of being hurt.

We worked on the regression for three sessions. In the third session, I had her go back to a fantasy about herself as a child, to a time not of the earth, a dream-time. She saw herself as a very young girl in a light blue dress, in a place of blue-gray clouds. She saw herself as innocent, tender, open, and loving. I asked her to bring her father to her, so she could speak to him. What immediately appeared was an image that she could not physically identify, but she could feel as Richard, her present partner. She was struck by the realization that he had been her father in a previous life. He was unable to speak to her because he was bound by his own chains, but she could sense that he loved her, and wanted to express his love even though he was unable. I told her to reach out to him.

At this point, Sandy entered what I could only describe as a major catharsis. Tears and release of emotion flooded her for at least 20 minutes. She was physically shaking and convulsing. I held her, and let her go on with the release until she was finished.

The release of emotion convinced me that the fantasy was true – her partner had indeed been her father in some previous life. They had come together again in order to heal their relationship. Richard was the first to have taken those steps, but Sandy was not yet ready, and reacted by trying to escape.

Sandy later told me that she discussed this session with Richard. This in itself was a giant step of growth for her, because she was never able to talk meaningfully about her feelings before. Today, she and Richard are no longer lovers, but remain supportive friends for each other.

As Sandy and I ceased our work together, I had the impression that she had gone through a turning point in her life. She understood herself much better. She no longer reacted to her fears or her projections unconsciously and compulsively, and her use of drugs and alcohol was coming under control. She had an approach to working on herself, and trust that she was going forward in her growth. She had cleared a large amount of the subconscious negativity that had been driving her. We still meet professionally whenever she needs some help in clarifying events or feelings.

JIM

Jim is 43 years old. He has always been interested in the quest for higher consciousness and the pursuit of spiritual goals, and has at times practiced meditation. He has had a fair amount of therapy, is conversant about the basics of psychology, and has the capacity for self-objectivity.

His current crisis takes the form of a conflict within his marriage of four years. He finds himself at an irreconcilable position with his partner, and is experiencing great pain at the possibility of losing contact with his two children of the marriage. This prospect is even more painful because this is exactly what happened with his two children from a previous marriage, when he was in his twenties.

In spite of his spiritual idealism, and his desire to be a loving person, he experiences tremendous anger when dealing with his partner, feeling he is being manipulated and treated unfairly. On several occasions, he went over the edge and became physically abusive. This violence further alienates his partner, who feels she must protect herself and the children from him, and he becomes further enraged at being separated from the children. This cycle has built up over the past year.

Although there is enough emotion on the surface to begin work, looking at Jim's chart provided some interesting insights. Knowing that the issue centered around children, I looked at the fifth house. The only significator here is the North Node. The North Node represents the area of life where we are to focus if we are to move ahead in our personal growth; the South Node represents going backwards. Jim was correct in focusing on children as a means to his own growth, but the afflictions to the North Node indicate that he has a tremendous amount of negative Karma to contend with as he does. The Node is opposite Sun, square Moon, and square Venus, indicating basic conflict with the individuality, the emotional nature, and the love nature. Children will bring up pain in the form of conflicts that must be integrated.

Even more telling are the parallels to the Node. I have found that parallels of declination act as strongly as conjunctions. The Node is parallel or contra-parallel within 20 minutes, which is strong, to Pluto and Mars as well as the aforementioned Sun and Venus. Having Pluto, Mars, and the Sun conjunct (through parallel) is a powerful and potentially violent energy, indicating difficult Karma. The patterns that need integrating: Sun conjunct Pluto – manipulation, power struggles. Jim attracted someone who would in fact behave this way, but then projects on top of that, perceiving her as heartless and controlling; Sun conjunct Mars, Mars opposite Ascendant – large amounts of suppressed anger, manifesting also as conflicts with authority; Mars conjunct Pluto – the potential for violence, either as victim or perpetrator.

In spite of these afflictions, Jim was highly idealistic, actively trying to be loving and spiritual, as indicated by the positive side of his chart: Sun conjunct Venus; Venus sextile Jupiter; Neptune trine Asc., sextile Mercury, sextile Pluto, trine Uranus. However, with South Node in the eleventh house of ideals, being idealistic represented going backwards, avoidance of issues, and self-rejection.

In our first month of meeting once a week, we discussed and implemented all aspects of processing, but focused mostly on awareness. I felt that Jim would not be able to really begin working with his negative energy until he had clearly recognized and then owned his feelings. But it was also important for him to look at his idealism.

Jim heavily entertained idealistic goals, thinking that things would resolve if these goals could be achieved. Living in a spiritual community was one. Entering into a helping profession was another. I tried to point out that these might be the result of an integrated personality, but that they would not lead to integration, and that dwelling on them only served to suppress his real feelings. The idealism was Jim's self-rejection, taking him out of the moment, and the experience of himself as he was. It took time for him to understand that he had to drop the focus on ideals as a means to accept the feelings. We often came back to this issue.

Tied to the idealism was the guilt that he felt in not being able to live up to the ideals. Jim had to see that the guilt was misplaced and was another form of self-rejection – his defense against really having to feel his feelings. We discussed this as well.

We went into the issue of anger. I pointed out to Jim that his anger was suppressed from previous times, and was only being brought up by present circumstances, not being caused by them, no matter how painful the anger was. We discussed this until he grasped the idea of emotional responsibility, and could intellectually own his anger.

As we explored the concept of owning the anger, it came out that Jim felt he had the right to be angry with and to express his anger to his wife, that he was being honest in doing so, and he further resented that she would not "accept it." This kind of expectation for unconditional emotional acceptance from the partner seems to be typical of men in our culture. Just as Sandy was projecting her unfulfilled needs for a father on her partner in her expectation that he support her financially, and then resenting him when he refused, Jim was projecting his quest for mother fulfillment. His expectation was that his wife receive him unconditionally, at any time, on any emotional/sexual basis, and he became resentful when she wouldn't.

I explained to Jim that once he had established his own emotional self-acceptance, he would no longer be dependent on a woman's acceptance. Furthermore, Jim's sexual needs were strong and compulsive. I thought that he was unconsciously trying to get rid of tension from the suppressed anger through sexual release, another common behavior trait, although more common in men than women. There was no way to deal with this directly, but to expect that sexual compulsion would decrease as the anger was cleansed. As I ventured these ideas, Jim perceived the truth of them with the clarity and courage that was to typify his work on himself.

We worked on clearing the anger. Our primary tool was the Integrating breath. I had Jim lie down, activate healing energy and enter the Witness, and then start to breathe full and fast. Jim's anger would usually be the first feeling to come up. I encouraged him to drop blame and shift to the energy experience. I had him report to me constantly about his feelings. By reporting that he was experiencing the anger and not the blame, I could monitor where he was, and that clearing was proceeding. We worked on accessing self-love as he was feeling the anger, all the while continuing with the breath. Jim took to this kind of breathwork easily, and altogether we did nine hour-long breathwork sessions. Jim said that he always felt better after the sessions, and he experienced dramatic catharsis in about half of them. I felt he was getting tremendous benefit in releasing his feelings.

Jim reported being able to activate the Witness and feel the healing of self-love at home, in his own practice. At home, he worked with both the Cleansing and Integrating breaths, finding them useful at different times.

In counseling Jim about how to deal with his wife, I stressed non-reactance – not reacting to or expressing the anger that came up in the encounters with his wife, but containing the anger for later release through processing. This was difficult, and Jim was not able to immediately succeed. It was only after a period of time, after we had been working together, that he began to develop the skills of non-reactance.

Behind the anger were the feelings of being used, manipulated, and controlled. My impression was that Jim was correct in feeling this, that his wife really was behaving this way. But, I had to point out that Jim had drawn this situation to himself because of the exact same energy blocked in his subconscious, in order to become conscious of the energy. He had to intellectually accept this possibility before he could work on clearing the power issue. If he fought back and got involved in a power struggle for his children, the energy would only be suppressed again because of his non-acceptance. He had to accept, at least emotionally, that his children were being torn from him, and he had to accept the pain that he felt. I pointed out that this pain was present in him before the situation developed, that the purpose of the situation was only to bring it to the surface.

This insight proved to be a turning point. Jim had never before taken responsibility for the pain of losing his children. I further tried to point out that he was addicted to his children, that he had idealistic plans for them, that he was trying to find his own fulfillment through them, that they were to bring meaning to his life. What had happened was life's way of showing him that he was looking for fulfillment in the wrong place – outside of himself. The very expectation and heavy hope upon his children had already created the pain of loss – the two went together. He now had to face and integrate the pain of the loss to go beyond being blocked at this level.

His craving for significance that was to be fulfilled through his children was another result of his unintegrated power center, the home of his anger. He had to stop looking for the satisfaction of this craving through his children. The compulsive craving for significance was another feeling that he had to integrate and stop being motivated by.

We worked with the concept of acceptance and surrendering the outcome of the acceptance to the Higher Self. Jim was familiar with this concept from his previous spiritual work, but he had never before brought it to such a personal level. Gradually, he developed a reverent attitude toward his pain. Surrender became a working force in his life.

In his personal practice, Jim continued applying the principles we have discussed. His work was mainly with his rage, his helplessness and pain about losing his children, and his sense of insignificance. He learned to activate the Witness, and to bring healing to these painful feelings. He would use thoughts of his wife and children to bring up the feelings, and then consciously drop blame and settle into experiencing the feelings. Sometimes he would just work with the breath, and be with whatever came up. He worked with simple affirmations to implement his self-acceptance: "It is O.K. for me to be angry; I accept the pain of losing my children." These affirmations also served to bring up painful feelings, which he then witnessed.

About two months after we first met, Jim reported that he

was able to confront his wife and maintain non-reactiveness to his feelings of anger. This was both because the anger had subsided due to his regular practice, and because he had developed the skill of non-reactiveness in sitting with his feelings. Nothing had really changed in the actual situation, but Jim realized that the possibility of maintaining contact with his children was real and feasible, and could not be blocked by his wife once he had released the extreme feelings that compelled him to see the situation in a distorted way, and to act irresponsibly.

At this writing, about 10 months have elapsed from our first meeting. Jim has been able to clear much of his suppressed feelings with success, and reports that he is more stable in regard to communication with his wife. In not having fought her, he realizes that to a certain extent he has not played into her game, and given her more justification for possession of the children. In being non-reactive, he has forced her to become more reasonable, both in response to the change in him, and because she would be acting irrationally if she didn't. The relationship with this woman is obviously karmic; they probably have a history that goes back into many lives.

As Jim maintains non-reactiveness to her, and integrates the pain that she appears to be causing, he frees himself from the negative aspects of the bond between them. Because of Jim's courage and aptitude for intense inner work, and his comprehension of the power of acceptance, I feel he will continue to grow. I feel his present circumstances will prove to be the springboard to a valuable life of inner transformation.

ELLEN

Ellen is 38 years old. She has been operating a retail clothing store for the past two years with her partner, 37, with whom she has been romantically involved for three years. They are experiencing marginal success with the store, and are considering whether to continue the business or to drop it as well as their relationship. The factors Ellen related that prompted her to seek counseling: continual and unresolved anxiety about financial concerns, and the problems in her relationship. The fact that Ellen is conscious of her anxiety is already a sign that she will be able to work productively with it. Many people remain unaware of feelings like these, but continue to be unconsciously driven by them into self-destructive situations and relationships.

Ellen's chart showed the following relevant stressful aspects: Sun in the second house of money square Saturn; Saturn, the planet of fear and survival, is in disharmonious aspect to the Sun, which represents her will and individuality. She experiences great fear when she tries to satisfy material needs. Next, South Node in Taurus indicates that a primary life orientation of seeking material security signifies going backwards for her in her personal growth; in order to go forward she has to focus on the North Node in Scorpio, spiritual regeneration. If she did so, her material needs would be provided automatically.

It appeared that she was being driven by irrational survival fears. Not being integrated, the fear was continuing to attract conditions of failure and insecurity. She was experiencing projection-manifestation; she then reacted to the condition she had created/attracted, experiencing even more fear, entering an expanding cycle.

As we spoke along these lines, Ellen said she had previously been a painter, and felt she was expressing her spiritual self in her art, but had decided she needed more of a financial base. The opportunity for the clothing business arose only because of her relationship; she felt she would be unable to run it alone. Her partner did the business, and she did the selling. As they began to run the business, their relationship got worse. Ellen thought this was because they had more contact and were bound to experience stress.

My first step in working with Ellen was to advise her about the depth of her fear, and that it was irrational – not that there was no reasonable cause for it in the past, but that she was projecting the suppressed fear onto inappropriate events in her current life. Her capacity to understand the nature of suppression, projection, and clearing would determine if she could make progress with inner work. She was able to grasp these concepts, and to take responsibility for her fear.

Next was the actual acceptance of the fear. I explained that by allowing herself to be motivated by the fear into the mechanics of the business, she was rejecting herself. She was reacting blindly to the fear. She feared fear itself. She rejected herself by expecting that the future attainment of a stable business would resolve her fears – she hungered after the idea of future attainment. She was blocking her feelings of fear with the fantasy of success in the future.

We worked on acceptance and direct experience for about six sessions. As her acceptance increased, her experience of her fear became possible. We worked on separating her fear from the object of her fear. Using the object (the business) to bring up the fear, I told her to drop thoughts of the business, but stay with the fear. She developed the capacity to be with only the fear, not her projections. She went deeper into the experience of pure fear. She noticed that after most of these sessions she would feel better, even though she mentioned once that she found the actual experience of the fear "like going to the dentist."

I responded that I admired her bravery, but also noted that this was a cue that we needed to work more on self-love. We spent more time on activating the Witness together, bringing up the non-identification and healing power of the Higher Self. I would enter meditation with her, and we would build the energy together.

We developed a personal program for her practice at home. I taught her the breathwork meditations that I detail in Chapter 11, along with a personal prescription: Since her energy block was between her first (Saturn) and third (Sun) chakras, she was to alternate breathing into these two centers, along with emphasizing them both in Yoga postures. Ellen used mainly the Cleansing breath, because she felt more comfortable with its gentleness than the intensity of the Integrating breath, but she also used a gentle Integrating breath with Yoga as well as at other times.

As our work continued, it emerged that as a child, Ellen had broken her coccyx – the tailbone at the base of the spine – and had had a difficult healing. The coccyx relates to the first chakra. My interpretation was that this "accident" was the result of the fear she carried in the first chakra – the energy had built to the point of releasing through injury. I urged her to go back to the incident, and work with all the feelings related to it. She reported experiencing more fear, vulnerability, and helplessness, but there was no particular cause in her childhood to which she could trace the feelings, except for the injury. She worked with clearing the feelings related to this traumatic injury for about a month, going back and re-experiencing the injury, opening to all the feelings surrounding it. She always reported that she felt better after her sessions, and that she was aware that suppressed feelings were, indeed, being cleared.

I felt satisfied that Ellen was progressing in her work. After about two months, however, Ellen reported that her fear and anxiety had become worse, along with some problems in the business. She had even started smoking some marijuana, something she did not do regularly. Looking at her chart again, I noticed that transiting Saturn was conjuncting her natal Sun. This signified a period of about three weeks when her fear issues would be intensified. I told her that this was a critical time, that the worsening represented a healing crisis and the opportunity for emotional clearing, that it would be over in a few weeks, but that she could realize great benefits if she stayed with her inner work now, and not reject what was happening.

We met twice a week for three weeks. I tried to encourage her to work on her own, but she felt she needed support now. Our work was more of the same, with Ellen sitting with her anxiety, bringing in healing energy and self-love, and doing breathwork. I did some contact bodywork on her, and some polarity between the first and third chakras. She really showed admirable bravery, faith, and aptitude in opening to the shadow side of herself.

This period proved to be a turning point. After it had passed, Ellen reported feeling better than she had in the last few years, and that things had cleared somewhat in the business. After a few more weeks, we decided to meet once a month. Ellen was obviously committed to her personal practice at home, and I felt she had the capacity to carry on by herself. We had been working together for about four months.

Throughout all of our sessions, Ellen never experienced any peaks of emotional catharsis, any crying or relating her fear to an incident in her childhood or past lives; nevertheless, she appeared to be experiencing genuine cleansing of suppressed and abnormal fear. In one of our next meetings, she related an incident that occurred during her practice at home.

She had been reading a book on co-dependency, and started thinking about whether her relationship was co-dependent. She was sitting with her fear during her meditation, when she suddenly realized that she feared her partner. Immediately, she came into contact with her anger – her anger against her partner, on whom she depended and feared. This realization triggered a catharsis of the anger. She went into deeply emotional weeping, seeing how her unconscious resentment of her partner had been a major cause of the emotional and sexual problems they were having. She connected her present relationship to her father – how she had basically the same feelings about him. She knew enough to allow the catharsis to continue, and kept crying for about two hours.

Of course, I had immediately spotted when we first met that Ellen's relationship was strongly co-dependent. I chose not to bring this up because I felt that her fear issue was primary and was enough for her to handle. I was pleased that she had come to the dependency issue by herself.

Now, about eight months since we met, Ellen continues to work on herself. She reports that her fear and anxiety have subsided drastically, but that it is an issue she still works with. I have told her that it may be the work of a lifetime, and she has accepted that the fear may never clear entirely. However, she is no longer motivated by it; she allows it to exist as a sub-personality. She is no longer afraid of it, and takes loving care of it. These are the conditions that will allow it to continue to clear and normalize.

Nothing has changed much with her business, but she thinks that the situation may not be so bad; after all, she and her partner are making a living. She feels eager and ready to work on her next phase of growth – her relationship, and what she brings to it. We continue to meet monthly, but she does most of her inner work on her own.

GROUP WORK

Since I have been discussing my work with individuals, it seems appropriate to also mention my approach to group work. I have found that sometimes integration can be more easily accomplished in a group than any other format. The group becomes the source of energy that each individual can take in and use to support his or her work. The collective energy of the group can build to a very significant level, and can be a major aid in transformation.

In the workshops that I direct, I like to include some inter-personal contact work in partnering and small groups, but my primary intention is that the group energy be used to facilitate individual work. This is useful in two ways:

If a person is new to processing and inner work, the group energy provides a strong training benefit; the steps can be learned more easily by tuning into the group-mind. If the person already has an established practice, the group energy can provide a powerful stimulus to bring issues into integration that may have been resistant.

I usually start group work with some physical loosening up and a few Yoga postures. Then, as a group, we enter the Witness, accessing healing energy and self-love. This step alone is very powerful, when everyone performs the same visualizations simultaneously.

Next, we begin deep work. I remind people that emotions and issues that come up can usually be related to one of the lower four chakras, and that by breathing into that center, they can further enhance integration:

1. **SURVIVAL:** Fear, insecurity, nervousness, and anxiety about health, money, possessions, or work.

2. **SENSATION:** Cravings for sex, food, smoking, alcohol, drugs, or entertainment.

3. **POWER:** Anger, helplessness, insignificance, or lack of meaning in one's life.

4. **HEART:** Loneliness, jealousy, disappointment in love, heartache, relationship dependency.

ALL CHAKRAS: Depression, stress.

Breathwork is a primary tool we use in our session. Breath gives us a non-intellectual means to clear the subconscious emotions that form the basis of the problems we experience. Breathwork sessions become very powerful and emotional as inner release is facilitated.

I ask people to sit or lie down, whichever is more comfortable, and instruct them to begin the Integrating breath, starting with a full and fast pattern. They are to regulate the intensity of the physiological and emotional aspects they experience by slowing down or speeding up the rate of breath, breathing into the body or appropriate chakra, and sensing the feelings in the chakra or anywhere else in the body. As we proceed, I talk the group through the steps of processing. While we are working, we continually activate feelings of self-love and the healing power of the Higher Self to cleanse the negativity that is surfacing.

This is very intense work. Given permission to have feelings, and the technique to draw feelings out, people experience meaningful catharsis. It must be noted, therefore, that this type of work must be approached cautiously and reverently. Persons who are completely new to inner work will have to use their judgment about whether such an experience would be an appropriate way for them to begin. Persons who have experienced major trauma are advised to participate only under the permission of a qualified psychologist.

• • • • •

I hope discussing personal work has been inspiring for you. It is sometimes difficult to see the depth to which we must open to ourselves. Perhaps this has been somewhat clarified. Your everyday feelings, problems, and circumstances are the very ones with which you must work. If they are ever to be transformed, you are the only person who can make it happen.

Often we assume that there is no question that our situation is being caused by forces outside ourselves; we react blindly and with no real awareness. If this book is to have any value for you, you must realize that you are creating your experience, as it is manifesting right now. You must take responsibility, and begin working on yourself.

If you do, you will no longer be dependent on whether other people change or don't change; but they will. You will feel your individuality as you never have; and with this individuality will come strength, peace, and inner communion. You will surrender your conscious will to the Higher Self; but you will be fulfilled as never before.

Do not allow this tremendous opportunity for personal growth to go unused. I wish you the best of everything.

John Ruskan

appendix
Astrology and Integrative Processing

I have found that astrology works very naturally with *Integrative Processing*. Before I had a working knowledge of the principles of processing, I approached astrology as a system to warn me about what was troublesome about my or another person's character that had to be minimized or avoided; I had no concept of acceptance. The result was suppression of feelings and experience. In approaching inner work with the attitude of acceptance, astrology greatly aids in identifying the energies that need to be integrated, and provides insights into motivation and basic psychological makeup. Transits and progressions may be used as indications of when issues that need attention will come up - these are the times to work with those issues.

I have developed a certain correspondence between the planets and the chakras that has proven useful in relating emotional/psychological issues to the body. Aspects between planets represent either blocks or harmonious paths of energy between chakras, depending on the nature of the aspect. Chakras that are affected can then be worked with directly, by breathing into them, Yoga, massage, polarity, and contractions of that part of the body (for lower chakras). In assigning planets to chakras, I use the Taoist chakra system, which goes into more detail about the energy centers than the classical Hindu model. I have found these additional points to be of practical use.

PLANET	CHAKRA
Jupiter	Crown
Neptune	Third Eye
Mercury/Uranus	Throat
Venus	Heart
Sun	Solar Plexus
Moon	Navel
Mars	Lower Abdomen
Pluto	Perineum
Saturn	Root

INDEX

THE INSTITUTE
FOR INTEGRATIVE PROCESSING
PROFESSIONAL CERTIFICATION

INTEGRATIVE PROCESSING is a system of holistic therapy developed by John Ruskan out of personal consciousness work and the study of existing therapies. It is a synthesis of Eastern and Western psychological philosophies and techniques. *IP* is a spiritual, feeling-oriented psychotherapy. With the emphasis on feelings as they are happening right now, this approach can provide important complementary tools for the therapist who might be primarily analytical in orientation, or who wishes to become more familiar with Eastern and spiritual principles and their application to therapy. Therapists already familiar with such principles will find a formalized system that will enable them to effectively work with clients. *IP* can then become one of several modalities the therapist can offer to clients, or it can be the main one. Although the basic principles of *IP* are presented in detail in John's book, *Emotional Clearing*, the application of the principles to client work is modified and expanded, since the book describes an approach to self-therapy. The training for therapists falls into several areas:

Theory: A strong understanding of the principles behind *IP* is basic to the therapist. Working within the principles allows the process to unfold without efforting.

Dialoguing: How to offer unconditional support through conscious listening, validating the client's experience as well as defenses.

Energetics: Includes training in the use of breath to facilitate integration of feelings; how feelings emerge through the body; how to invoke Witness consciousness in the client through resonance.

AlphaTrance: *AlphaTrance* is the unique, distinguishing feature of *Integrative Processing Therapy*. It is derived from the basic healing induction explained in the book - similiar to hypnotherapy, but with no intent to recondition; similiar to meditation, but with a facilitator. The therapist's energy enables the client to go deep into alpha, where suppressed material can be easily integrated. Learning to guide a client through *AlphaTrance* is a major focus of the training.

Certification takes place over a long weekend in New York City, San Francisco, and other locations. Contact John for information.

EMOTIONAL CLEARING WORKSHOPS

Three-Day Training / Clearing

This workshop covers the basics of using *Integrative Processing* as a spiritual self-therapy. The participant learns how to work with troublesome feelings on the path to higher consciousness and is empowered to achieve deep emotional integration, clearing, and growth. The program includes both training in techniques that will become a permanent, life-enhancing resource and powerful experiential group work to facilitate emotional breakthoughs. Workshops are held at various places around the country on Friday evening, Saturday, and Sunday.

Six-Day Clearing Intensive

This residential intensive is designed to go deeply into feeling work and to effect a permanent change in consciousness and life experience. Self-limiting patterns that result from holding suppressed feelings are brought fully into the light to be released as feelings are deeply cleared. This workshop is now held primarily in the San Francisco Bay area.

What you can expect from the workshops:

• **An approach to understanding and validating your real feelings and how to use them for emotional and spiritual growth.**

• **How to prevent negative feelings from contaminating your life and relationships.**

• **A highly pragmatic self-therapy system that will enable you to release trapped, negative feelings on your own.**

• **Esoteric methods for enhancing emotional release, including unique breathwork, witnessing, alphatrance, and body-release techniques.**

• **Powerful experiential sessions to show you how to apply these principles and to initiate deep transformational releases.**

The experience gained in these workshops can be vital in any healing program that recognizes the connection between physical and emotional illness. Typical emotional issues include depression, anxiety, anger, love/hate, loneliness, sexual blocks, control tendencies, food and other addictive compulsions, relationship dynamics, etc. **Contact John for info on upcoming locations. Consider sponsoring a workshop in your area! Sponsors share in workshop revenue.**

Recordings from John:

John is a dedicated musical artist. Here, his intent is to communicate directly on the right brain, emotional level, in order to complement the largely left brain, intellectual mode of writing. You will find the messages moving and effective for enhancing inner process work, as well as showing another side of John.

Desert Dawn

This is music that John has composed specifically to induce the deep relaxation, alpha healing state. It can be used for meditation, emotional clearing sessions, bodywork or yoga, or simply for setting a soothing and striking mood. John has carefully researched and designed the sound to produce its psycho-acoustic effect by using slow moving, repetitive, beautiful musical textures - quite unlike anything else on the market. As you sink into the sound, you easily enter altered states of consciousness. This is the music that John plays at his workshops to create a healing mood. Workshop participants always respond strongly to the music and ask where they can get it, even before they know it's John's. There is no talking on this selection. John composes and performs all music on synthesizer and acoustic instruments, multi-tracking for a thick, lush sound.

This is a double album, with a total of two hours, 15 minutes on two CD's or cassettes. The long running time is required to faithfully present this unique musical/meditative concept. There are two short pieces of 7 1/2 minutes each, and four 30 minute pieces. Each of the pieces is designed to invoke a slightly different consciousness. The music can be listened to sequentially, but it is also intended that one piece only be played for a particular 30 minute meditation, processing, or bodywork session. A session could even be extended by putting one selection on repeat. In his workshop, for example, John plays the title piece, *Desert Dawn*, for one hour to create the energetic ambiance for an intense "soul communing" session, a workshop peak.

John Ruskan   Desert Dawn

disk 1:
Zen Garden (7 1/2 min.)
Listening (30) Grounding.
Opening (30) Opening the heart.

disk 2:
Entering The Circle (7 1/2 min.)
Red Sands (30) Deep dreamscape.
Desert Dawn (30) Spirit merging.

Double Cassette: $ 14.90

Double CD: $19.90

EMOTIONAL CLEARING GUIDED MEDITATION

RELEASING NEGATIVE FEELINGS
AND AWAKENING
UNCONDITIONAL HAPPINESS

JOHN RUSKAN

Emotional Clearing
Guided Meditation

John has recorded guided meditations in which he speaks and leads you step by step in clearing feelings. These meditations are the same that he uses in workshops and in private sessions. There are two meditations on this cassette-only release:

1. Grounding and AlphaTrance Healing Induction (20 min.)

2. *Emotional Clearing* Guided Meditation (20 min.)

Cassette: $10.90

Recordings and additional copies of *Emotional Clearing* are available in New Age bookstores, or may be ordered by calling **1-800-247-6553** for credit card sales (Visa, Mastercard, American Express, Discover). Retail stores may order from New Leaf or BookPeople Distributors.

Visit the *Emotional Clearing* world-wide English speaking website at:

http://www.emclear.com

The website contains articles, talks, interviews, and other information from John that complement the book.

Most important, there is an **interactive dialogue** section where readers may post their own stories and receive as well as give support to others about their emotional journey and their experience applying the principles of *Emotional Clearing* to their real lives. John occasionally also gives feedback, but he hopes that this forum will become a widely used, self-supporting place for opening the heart through sharing, being heard, and helping each other.

John Ruskan is a graduate of Cornell University. He has had an eclectic career in the arts, business, and counseling fields. A life-long spiritual traveler and expert in yoga and esoteric healing, he is now sharing his knowledge in a desire to help others in their quest for inner fulfillment. John lives in California. *Emotional*

 *Clearing* is his first book. John is the founder of *Integrative Processing Therapy*, in which professional certification is offered. Please contact him to learn this powerful, innovative adjunct to psychotherapy. John has led his three-day workshop all across the country and in England. The workshops are always an extraordinary event, deeply touching all who attend. Contact him for information on workshops scheduled in your area, or consider acting as a workshop sponsor, especially if you have access to a group that might be interested.

John reserves a portion of his time for individual clients at reasonable rates. At this point, all of John's client work is by telephone. John has found telephone counseling to be equally effective to in-person work, and that the energy of a therapist can serve to catalyze and deepen the experience of emotional integration. If his schedule does not allow for additional clients, you will be referred to another certified *I.P.* therapist, in your area if possible. Please drop a note to him with your address and phone specifying your interest in certification, workshops, or individual work:

John Ruskan
c/o R. Wyler & Co.
220 West 19th St., Suite 2A
New York, N.Y. 10011

or call anytime to leave a message:

1-800-988-6560

Visit the *Emotional Clearing* website at
http://www.emclear.com for on-line sharing.